ⓒ Martin Leonard 1988
First published 1988
Reprinted 1988 (twice), 1989

Published by Basil Blackwell Ltd
108 Cowley Road
Oxford OX4 1JF
England

British Library Cataloguing in Publication Data
Leonard, Martin, 1937 -
The 1988 Education Act : a tactical guide
for schools.
1. England. Education. Law. Education Act
1988
I. Title
344.204'7

ISBN 0-631-16455-3
ISBN 0-631-16456-1 Pbk

Typeset in 10.5 pt Palatino
Printed in Great Britain by Dotesios (Printers) Ltd, Bradford-on-Avon

Contents

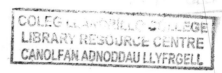

Foreword

The Education Act of 1988 is the basis of a sequence of changes which will affect quite radically the public education service in England and Wales. To this extent it is comparable in importance with that of 1944. But the two Acts differ fundamentally, in two distinct ways. Each of these differences, considered on its own, would bring the 1988 Act into a different order of importance from its predecessors; taken together, the total effect can only be described as revolutionary.

The first of these special characteristics is that the Act is not the product of a lengthy, thorough and sensitive series of consultations and negotiations, as was the case in 1943-44. This is not the place to comment on the consultation processes of 1987-88, or on the extent of professional concerns over most of the key features of the Act. But the net result - a series of major and inter-related measures, devised and voted through largely by amateurs against strong professional advice - makes the 1988 Act into something quite different from 1944, and indeed from the two other major Education Acts, those of 1870 and 1902.

The second radical difference between 1988 and earlier Acts is that it creates a wholly new role for the Secretary of State. The rules governing the 'national education service, locally administered' have long been felt by successive Secretaries of State to have restricted unduly their ability to bring about change. The Secretary of State had (indeed, still has, since the 1944 Act has not been repealed) a duty 'to secure the effective execution by local authorities, under his control and direction, of the national policy...'. But LEAs had their own powers of direction and control, as did head teachers and governors of individual schools. In consequence, the Secretary of State was often left fuming on the touchline. For over 40 years, governments did little to alter this imbalance, if imbalance it was; the 1988 Act has done so, radically. Further, the Secretary of State's new powers are in many cases set down in very general terms, with no well-defined boundaries: this is most obviously the case in respect of the national curriculum.

If the Act is indeed revolutionary, the response at school level needs to be thorough, measured and above all far-sighted. Revolutions tend to be untidy, affecting the peasant in the field and the carpenter at his bench as much as the generals and civic leaders - and this one shows every sign of being decidedly messy. The aim of this book is to offer a guide to those in schools who want some help in thinking through the implications of the Act, as it applies to their own situations. As the sub-title indicates, the tactics of a school's response are all-important, and a watch-but-do-nothing approach is not to be recommended.

I am not, incidentally, defining closely who 'those in schools' might be: I use terms such as 'school managers' to include anyone whose primary concern is the quality of education in a particular school, be he head teacher, governor or whatever.

I have attempted to cover the significant features of the Act, as far as they affect schools in England and Wales. A few sections receive only a brief mention because they cover contingencies (such as the mechanism for winding up a grant-maintained school) which are not likely to affect the great majority of schools. I have not touched on the implications for further and higher education, or on the sections related to education in Inner London.

I write as an educationalist, not as a lawyer or an accountant. This is not said in order to disclaim responsibility for accuracy in legal and financial matters, but to make clear that the thought processes which I am endeavouring to share with you, the reader, are set primarily in an educational context. At certain decision points - most obviously that of applying for grant-maintained status - it will be clear that legal and financial advice, as well as educational guidance, should be sought.

An Act of Parliament has to be a statement of the highest precision, which makes it wordy, repetitive and difficult to read - not the best qualities for a book. I have therefore relied on a commonsense interpretation of terms and concepts where appropriate. No satisfactory balance is in fact possible between readability and total precision, since some common terms ('school', for example) would need a full legal definition in order to meet the latter requirement. Needless to say, anyone making a decision based on the terms of the Act should refer to the original, and not rely solely on a description written mainly for clarity and readability.

For some purposes, reference may need to be made to the text of other Acts, particularly those of 1944, 1980, 1981 and 1986. In order to allow easy reference both to the new Act and to others, the index covers not only the contents of this book, in the normal manner, but also the parts of the Act itself which refer to schools, and key sections of other Acts.

In looking at the application of the Act to different situations, the various types of school need to be understood carefully. In general, a school includes everything within the direct management responsibility of its head teacher, as far as relates to school-age pupils. But this definition does not meet all situations, particularly that of a community school under local management. Subject to that, I have mainly used the following terms:

a   *County schools*: all LEA primary and secondary schools, other than voluntary schools.

b   *Voluntary schools*: voluntary-aided and voluntary-controlled schools.

c   *Aided schools*: voluntary-aided schools, usually including special agreement schools. (Managers of the few special agreement schools will be aware of where the rules differ.)

d   *Non-aided schools*: LEA county and controlled schools. (For many purposes the Act treats these identically.) Note that this excludes special schools.

e   *Maintained schools*: all LEA schools, (including special schools), together with grant-maintained schools, but not city technology colleges.

f   *Secondary schools*: to include middle schools deemed to be secondary, and sixth form colleges.

g   *Primary schools*: to include middle schools deemed to be primary, but excluding (unless stated otherwise) separate nursery schools.

h   *Special schools*: to include special units if under a separate head teacher, and hospital schools unless stated otherwise.

It will be evident that I am among those in the profession who believe the Act to be misconceived, in every major respect other than the local management scheme. I think also that it is flawed, in every one of its significant provisions. In particular, the intended arrangements for the national curriculum seem to lack any general educational merit; to be expensive in staffing, in equipment and in the assessment arrangements; to require, for their implementation, teachers who are not available; and to rely on a scheme for aggregating test results which is theoretically unsound.

I would much have preferred to stay with the 1944 system, in whose merits I firmly believe - though I do not, of course, deny that the freedom which it allows has in some places been misused. Under this system, the very best results have been achieved when well-qualified teachers, working effectively as a team, have been given the facility and the resources to use their expertise, judgement and commitment for the benefit of the pupils in their care. By contrast, experience of working with the Department of Education and Science in various ways has convinced me that taking away this freedom, and replacing it with the heavy hand of bureaucracy, will not be of benefit to the education service.

But my belief that so much is at risk is not important in the present context. Like it or not, the Act is with us. We have not only to live with it but also to adapt our professional approach so as to maintain the very highest standards under the new rules. It may even be that the Act's principal and laudable aim, to improve the quality of education, will become a reality in spite of the fears expressed by myself and others. I hope my personal doubts will not be too intrusive, though at some points they certainly will be obvious: no-one with a professional concern for the public education service could, for example, write in neutral terms about the city technology colleges. I have allowed one little item, to which I take particular exception, to affect the text as a whole, by omitting one tendentious word from the full title: The Education Reform Act.

The Act itself is divided into distinct parts, in an order which the book follows. But those who have the job of running schools under the new rules will find that the practical effects cannot so easily be divided into separate sections. As a result, a book such as this has to contain either many cross-references or frequent minor repetitions. I have tried to keep a balance between the two, in the hope that the reader will not find too much of either.

An Act of Parliament is by convention written in such a way that terms indicating gender are male only, with a general rule that both male and female are implied unless the context otherwise requires (which in this Act it never does). I have used this convention both as a reason and an excuse to follow the same practice; no gender bias is implied either in this or when the terminology is gender-related, as for example with 'chairman'.

If there is a single theme in the book, it is this: that education is a partnership, under the Act as it always was of old. As with any partnership between independently-willed humans, the result has often been imperfect in the past, and no doubt the new-style partnership which includes a powerful Secretary of State will continue to be so. But the right professional approach is, as ever, to keep on trying to make it work, and work better.

Martin Leonard,
Lichfield, Staffordshire
July 1988

Footnote on reprinting

In the few months which have passed since the first printing, quite a lot has happened to the detail of the Act's effects on schools. Some changes result from decisions made outside the education service: the Training Commission, for example, barely had time to take on the role of the MSC before it was itself abolished. A few points have become the focus of dispute because they were not fully thought through when the Act was drafted: the main one is Section 118.4, where implications for the charges allowed for school trips are still far from clear.

But the main developments have arisen from various sets of regulations issued by the Secretary of State, and from other official documents, particularly those relating to the national curriculum. The torrent began soon after the Royal Assent was given, and shows no signs of easing off. There is no way in which these changes can all be taken into account at each reprint, and so the book remains (except for a few minor corrections) as it was when first published. The possibility of a new edition will no doubt be considered, if and when the pace of change slows sufficiently to make it practicable.

JML
March 1989

Chapter 1 The requirements of the National Curriculum

A new direction for the school curriculum

Nothing is closer to the centre of the whole public education service than the curriculum. The term is a wide one, covering everything taught and learnt in school, whether laid down in the rules or not, whether deliberate or accidental, and whether it is learnt from the work of the teacher in the classroom, from the incidental contacts between him and his pupils, or from the example he sets outside the classroom - or indeed whether it is picked up from the actions and words of his fellow pupils. Only some of what we mean by 'curriculum' can thus be codified and written down; the rest, sometimes called the hidden curriculum, cannot. Of the part which can be written down, some will come to realisation in the form intended and some will not.

But however tightly prescribed it may be, the curriculum still relies for its successful realisation on the teacher - and on the fact that he is just that, and not a lecturer who communicates mainly in one direction. His success depends on the breadth of his background knowledge; on his ability as a communicator who can adapt his approach to the needs of the situation; on his skill in tackling the difficult through the easier, and approaching the unfamiliar by way of the well known; on his ability to start where the pupil is, and not where someone else has assumed him to be; on his ability to vary the manner in which he presents and illustrates his material according to need; on his sensitivity to the differing levels of understanding among his pupils; on the way he involves them in the learning process; and on the way he uses to advantage any chance events or unexpected responses.

The curriculum is not, in short, something that can be set down on paper, and given to the whole body of teachers with an instruction to put it into effect, in the expectation that schools will become as a result both more uniform in what they teach and more effective in teaching it.

Of course, it helps if the teachers are well trained, and if the schools are well managed and resourced. But it helps even more if the great majority of teachers are highly motivated. The factors which determine this elusive quality include the level of public esteem in which teachers as a whole are held, the environment in which they work, the level of resourcing, the quality of management, the general background influences on the pupils themselves, and of course the current salary scales and promotion prospects. At the time the Act was passed, many of these factors were by no means favourable, and this will make more difficult the task of everyone involved in the change to the new curriculum. It is therefore critically important that the management of this change should be carried out in a manner which encourages such a positive response. The opposite could easily happen and, if it does, the effects will be deep and long-lasting.

The aim of the first section of the Act, which lays the foundations for the introduction of the national curriculum, is a greater degree of uniformity across the schools of England and Wales, together with higher standards all round. As an aim, it is worthy enough. Indeed, it is so self-evidently good, in the judgement both of politicians, of many teachers and of the general public, that the problems of its realisation may not, perhaps, have been given enough attention.

However, before looking at the possible outcomes, the actual provisions of the Act need to be examined. Some features are obvious enough, most of all the very wide powers of the Secretary of State. Others, particularly where apparently simple words like 'subject', 'knowledge', 'technology', and 'assessment' are used, imply concepts and impose technical problems of considerable difficulty. Hidden complexities of this kind are likely to generate major problems of interpretation, both legally and in the classroom.

To return to the point made at the start, the concept of the curriculum is itself so complex as to defy precise description in the legal terminology of an Act of Parliament. But the attempt is made all the same, and it is to play a major part in the development of the education system of England and Wales well into the next century. Its implications, both the obvious and the hidden, thus need to be thought through very carefully.

The key section is worth quoting substantially in full.

It shall be the duty of the Secretary of State, of every LEA, and of every governing body or head teacher of a maintained school, to exercise their functions (including, in particular, the functions conferred on them with respect to religious education, religious worship and the National Curriculum) with a view to securing that the curriculum satisfies these requirements: that it should be a balanced and broadly based curriculum, which promotes the spiritual, moral, cultural, mental and physical development of pupils at the school and of society, and prepares such pupils for the opportunities, responsibilities and experiences of adult life.

As a general statement this is itself broadly based, and no doubt commands wide assent. Two phrases only require comment at this stage. First, RE and religious worship are given particular mention, and are not part of the national curriculum as such. This is on account of the special conditions which have applied to them since the 1944 Act and which, in a modified form, still apply now (they are the subject of a separate section below). Second, the phrase 'and of society' is included, almost as a throwaway line. Just what it means in the context is by no means clear: what is 'the spiritual' (and the rest) 'development of society', and how can the curriculum of a school promote it? As a subject for discussion it has possibilities; as a phrase which the courts may have to interpret, its value is open to question.

The national curriculum is to be part of the whole curriculum, for all registered pupils of compulsory school age at every maintained school, including special schools. Together with RE, the national curriculum forms a basic curriculum, which may not be specified as a particular proportion of the whole, but leaves an undefined part to the discretion of the governing body of the school. The national curriculum is defined in terms of foundation subjects, three of which (four in Welsh-medium schools) are described as core subjects.

The curriculum for the four key stages

The school years are divided into four sections, known as key stages. The first corresponds to the part of the infant age range which starts at the age of compulsory schooling; the second to the junior age range; the third to the first three years of the secondary school; and the fourth to the last two years of the secondary school, or until the pupil is eligible to leave school. The national curriculum does not apply to a nursery school or to a nursery class in a primary school; it applies to a grant-maintained school, but not to a city technology college.

For each foundation subject, the national curriculum is to set down:

a *Attainment targets,* which are defined as the knowledge, skills and understanding which pupils of different abilities and maturities are expected to have by the end of each key stage;

b *Programmes of study,* which are defined as the matters, skills and processes which are required to be taught to pupils of different ages and maturities during each key stage;

c *Assessment arrangements,* which are defined as the arrangements for assessing pupils at or near the end of each key stage, for the purpose of ascertaining what they have achieved in relation to the attainment targets for that stage. The word 'assessment' is to include examinations and tests.

The core subjects are mathematics, English, science and (in Welsh-medium schools) Welsh. The other foundation subjects are history, geography, technology, music, art and physical education, plus Welsh in English-medium schools in Wales, and in the third and fourth key stages a modern foreign language specified by the Secretary of State. A school in Wales is defined for this purpose as a Welsh-medium (or Welsh-speaking, to use the term in the Act) school if more than half of the foundation subjects (other than English and Welsh, but including for this purpose RE) are taught, wholly or partly, in Welsh. This means five out of nine subjects in a primary school, and six out of ten in a secondary school.

The Secretary of State has extensive powers to modify these rules and definitions. But the consent of Parliament through a resolution in both Houses is required before he can change the core or other foundation subjects, or vary two of the three dividing points between key stages. Without such a resolution, he may vary the division between the first and second key stages. In addition he (meaning in this context the Secretary of State for Wales) may without such a resolution remove the obligation for Welsh to be a foundation subject in specified English-medium schools in Wales.

Where a pupil is taught, either generally or for particular subjects, in a class with pupils of whom a majority are of a different age group, the head teacher of a school may treat him, for purposes related to the work prescribed for the relevant key stage and the assessment at the end of the key stage, as if he were of the same school year as the rest.

The task of the Secretary of State

The Act requires the Secretary of State to establish the national curriculum as soon as practicable, taking first the core subjects and then the other foundation subjects. He is to do so by specifying, for each foundation subject, the attainment targets, the programmes of study and the assessment arrangements which he considers appropriate. For art, music and PE the specifications are to be less detailed than for the remainder. He may revise these specifications whenever he considers it necessary or expedient to do so. In making any order in this respect, he may give full details or may refer instead to any HMSO publications. In respect of assessment arrangements, he may also specify how they are to be carried out, by causing the details to be published by HMSO. But he has no powers to specify the proportion of time, or the timetable periods, for any subject.

The Secretary of State also has powers in relation to courses leading to a qualification which is authenticated by any person or body outside the school. Such courses may only be provided, at or on behalf of a maintained school and for pupils of compulsory school age, if the qualification is approved by the Secretary of State or by a body (meaning in most cases an examination board or organisation of similar standing) approved by him. Further, a syllabus must be provided by the person or body authenticating the qualification, and must be approved by the examination board or other body; or, alternatively, criteria similarly approved may be provided for the purpose of determining the syllabus. The Secretary of State may extend these rules to cover school pupils (or further education students) up to the age of 19, but only after a resolution has been passed in both Houses of Parliament.

Since the national curriculum will come into operation only in stages, the duties imposed on the LEA, and on the governing body and head teacher of each school, relate to that curriculum only as far as orders have been made to implement it. Decisions by schools on these matters have to be made only once a year, at the start of each school year, and it is reasonable to expect that orders by the Secretary of State will be made so as to allow adequate time for planning.

There is a slight difference between the definitions of the various duties in respect of the national curriculum. Those of the LEA and the governing body are 'to exercise their functions with a view to securing...'; that of the head teacher is 'to secure' that the national curriculum is implemented. The same applies in relation to observance of the rules about RE, religious worship and externally authenticated courses. The Act frequently places major responsibilities on governors, where some doubts may be felt as to who will really do the job; but in this instance at least it is clear whose position is the most exposed when things go wrong.

But there is also a sting in the tail of the requirement to implement the national curriculum. It is that, at any time before the full national curriculum is in operation, the duties mentioned above still apply, but in a modified form. With effect from a date to be determined by the Secretary of State, each foundation subject which is specified for a particular key stage must be taught 'for a reasonable time' during that stage. This will have an impact in several ways, most obviously in requiring primary schools to include science and technology, and secondary schools to include a foreign language, for all pupils.

The Curriculum and Assessment Councils

Three new bodies, one of which is for Wales, are set up by the Act to fulfil the task of advising the Secretary of State on matters concerned with the national curriculum. The National Curriculum Council advises on the curriculum itself, in England; the Curriculum Council for Wales has the same function in Wales; and the School Examinations and Assessment Council (SEAC) advises on the matters implied by its title in both England and Wales. In this section, the term Curriculum Council refers to whichever of the first two is appropriate, and the words Council or Councils refer to any or all of the three.

Each Council is to consist of not less than ten and not more than 15 members, who are appointed by the Secretary of State, under terms determined by him. A member may be dismissed similarly, either if he has been absent without the Council's permission from meetings for six months or if, in the opinion of the Secretary of State, he is unable or unfit to discharge the functions of a member. One member of each Council is to be chairman, and another may be deputy chairman. Members may receive salaries, fees or expenses, as decided by the Secretary of State. No restrictions are placed on the persons who may be appointed, except that the members 'shall include persons having relevant knowledge or experience in education'. The functions of the Curriculum Councils are:

a   to keep all aspects of the curriculum for maintained schools under review;

b   to advise the Secretary of State on relevant matters, either at his request or otherwise;

c   to advise him on, and at his request assist him to carry out, research and development work;

d   to publish and disseminate information about the curriculum;

e   to carry out such other activities related to these tasks as the Secretary of State may direct.

The functions of SEAC are similar, and relate both to the public examination system and to all aspects of the assessment programme for the national curriculum. It has:

a   to keep all these matters under review;

b   to advise the Secretary of State on matters of his choice or of the Council's own;

c   to advise on and assist with research;

d   to publish and disseminate information;

e   to set up the moderation arrangements related to the assessment aspect of the national curriculum (no mean task, as mentioned later);

f   to advise on the authentication of qualifications;

g   to carry out other related activities.

All the Councils must have regard to the provisions of the Act relating to the national curriculum and RE, and to the general requirements of the curriculum as quoted above. Each Council has also to make such reports to the Secretary of State as he may require, and must comply with any directions given by him and with any plans approved by him. None of the three has an obligation to take account of the actions or the advice of the other two, though doubtless commonsense will prevail sufficiently for each to do so. The first appointments to the Councils included some common membership, which will ease such matters.

Each Council is a corporate body, able to appoint staff and generally to manage its affairs within the rules outlined above. Each must have a Chief Officer, who may also (at the discretion of the Secretary of State) be its Chairman; if he is, the Secretary of State also appoints him, or if not he is appointed by the Council with the Secretary of State's consent. The Councils are funded by the Secretary of State, up to an amount fixed by him with the consent of the Treasury. Other details are set down in the Act, relating to committees, accounts and so on, and are of little interest to those not directly involved. But the requirement that an action must have the consent of the Secretary of State appears frequently, particularly in respect of staff appointments.

The Councils replace the School Curriculum Development Committee and the Secondary Examinations Council, and in doing so take over the rights and obligations of these bodies, particularly those relating to the employment of staff. The details are the responsibility of the Secretary of State.

The Secretary of State is required to refer certain matters to the National Curriculum Council. He must do so before making any orders or regulations (or before presenting them to Parliament where required), where these change the list of foundation subjects, or alter the timing of any key stages, or vary any attainment targets or programmes of study. He must also do so before making regulations modifying the national curriculum in particular cases (a provision of the Act which is discussed later). When anything is referred to a Council in this way, it has to make recommendations to the Secretary of State within a time set by him.

The Curriculum Council must in turn refer the matter to associations representing local authorities, teachers, and school governors, and to other persons or bodies as it thinks fit; it must allow time for a written response from each. Having considered these responses, the Council must make recommendations to the Secretary of State, accompanied by a summary of the views expressed by those consulted, and must also arrange for the recommendations to be published.

When the Council has reported, the Secretary of State must publish (and send to the Council) a draft of the proposed order or regulations, together with a statement explaining why he has not followed the Council's recommendations, if such has been the case. He must allow one month for the submission of comments, objections and further evidence, and may then make (or place before Parliament where so required) the order or regulations, with modifications if he so decides.

The procedure in Wales is slightly different, in that the Secretary of State for Wales may consult directly, both with the Curriculum Council and with any others he wishes. The collation and publication of the views expressed is then carried out by him, and not by the Council. If in this instance the Secretary of State decides to ignore all or part of the Council's recommendations, he does not have to give any justification for his decision. The Secretary of State for Wales has further powers, not matched in respect of England, to commission research and development work related to the introduction of the national curriculum in Wales; he does however have to obtain the consent of Parliament through a resolution in both Houses first.

The Secretary of State is not required to consult the third council, the School Examinations and Assessment Council, at all. In particular he may, without reference to the Council, determine assessment arrangements and approve qualifications. This Council (like the others) may offer advice on any relevant matter without being asked, but the Secretary of State may ignore it without giving reasons. The Council may, however, publish information about assessment without restriction, and its responsibility for moderation arrangements may be exercised without reference to the Secretary of State (unless the latter uses his general power to give directions that it must make such reference).

In summary, the Secretary of State appoints all members of the Councils, and only two of them in each case need have any expertise in the relevant area of responsibility; he may dismiss the members without too much difficulty; he may direct their work as he chooses; he determines their fees and expenses; on many matters he does not have to consult them at all, and when he does he may ignore their advice, sometimes without having to give a reason; many of their routine actions, such as those involving the appointment of staff, require his consent; finally, their budgets are controlled by him.

No doubt the Councils will, in normal conditions, consist of some of the most able specialists in the field of the curriculum and its assessment, will be consulted routinely, and will have their advice treated with respect, if not always with full agreement. But, with rules like these, and even in the normal state of educational politics, when it happens that some advice given by a particular Council does not command full agreement, the temptation to refer to it as the Secretary of State's poodle may be too great to resist. The School Examinations and Assessment Council is probably in the strongest position to show that it is a force to be reckoned with, because of the technical complexity of its work; of the others, the Curriculum Council for Wales is clearly the weaker of the two, and not just because of the smaller size of the Principality.

Modifications to the national curriculum

The national curriculum, as specified by the Secretary of State, is to be part of the whole curriculum for every pupil in every maintained school, unless modifications or exceptions are authorised. The programmes of study may themselves make provision for some variations, either explicitly or simply by being phrased in terms which permit differences of interpretation. In addition to variations of these kinds, the Act allows for four instances in which changes may be made and which require such authorisation.

1 The Secretary of State may direct that, for a specific school or group of schools, and for a stated period, the national curriculum shall not apply, either as a whole or in defined areas, for the purpose of enabling curriculum development work (or experiments, as they are rather oddly described) to be carried out. A direction of this kind may only be given on request: in a non-aided LEA school this may come either from the governing body or from the LEA, in each case with the agreement of the other party, and in an aided or grant-maintained school it may be submitted by the governing body. Alternatively, a request may be made by the National Curriculum Council (or that for Wales), with the agreement of each governing body and of the LEA if appropriate. The Secretary of State may require reports on the development work being undertaken, and may vary or revoke any direction given.

2 The Secretary of State may by regulations specify that certain parts, or all, of the national curriculum shall not apply, or shall apply with stated modifications, in cases or circumstances defined in the regulations. This power is very widely drawn, and may well have been included in order to allow for things going wrong. For example, the new requirements for a modern foreign language will create a demand for specialist teachers which there is no likelihood of meeting for a decade or more, and many governing bodies charged with implementing this section of the national curriculum will therefore be unable to do so. A regulation made under this section could, after a fashion, resolve the issue.

3 A statement about the special educational needs of a particular pupil, made under the 1981 Act, may direct that part or all of the national curriculum shall not apply, or shall apply in a modified form. This is clearly a necessary provision, and the phrasing of it is probably unavoidable in the circumstances. But it is much to be regretted, in that it implies that the curriculum for the special needs pupil should be the standard curriculum with the parts thought to be inappropriate cut out. It would be preferable by far that the curriculum for each such pupil should be designed positively, in order to provide the very best for him. This is not the only time in the Act that special needs pupils are left to be fitted into the whole picture after the perceived needs of the main body have been provided for.

There is a further practical difficulty, again unavoidable in the circumstances, in that the work of drafting individual statements and carrying out the consultation processes required, already an onerous and time-consuming task, will be made more so by this provision of the Act.

4 The Secretary of State may (after consulting those whom he considers appropriate) make regulations by which head teachers may modify the requirements of the national curriculum for individual pupils. The regulations are to specify a maximum period for such variations, which may not exceed six months, and this provision cannot therefore be used to exempt a pupil permanently from a subject thought to be inappropriate for him. Renewal for a further period, up to the same limit, is allowed. Any head teacher giving or renewing such a direction must inform the pupil's parent, the

governing body, and (in the case of a county, controlled or maintained special school) the LEA.

The information supplied must include the reasons for and the probable effect of the direction, the alternative to be provided, and the long term implications. The last of these aspects may either give an indication of the time and manner in which the direction will cease to be needed, or state an opinion that the pupil has special educational needs of a kind requiring the LEA to make extra provision, through the statement process defined in the 1981 Act. The head of a grant-maintained school must, in the latter case, also inform the LEA, because of its statutory responsibility in this respect which extends to pupils in these schools. When the LEA is told of such needs, it must consider whether the statement procedure is required. If it so decides, the parent muct be consulted as laid down in the 1981 Act; if the LEA later wishes to amend the curricular provisions of the statement, it must under the new Act again consult the parent.

A parent who receives information from the head teacher about the curricular provision to be made for his child, under the six-month rule, may ask the head teacher to vary or revoke the direction given. Alternatively, a parent may at any time request the head teacher to give a direction of this kind in respect of his child. If the head teacher does not respond in a manner which the parent considers acceptable, the parent may appeal to the governing body; the governing body may in turn reject the parent's request, or may uphold it, in which case it may give directions to the head teacher with which he must comply. The governing body must inform both parties in writing of its decision. An appeal is possible, as indicated in the next section.

Documentation and other procedural requirements

The introduction of the national curriculum means that a great deal of information will have to be circulated in written form. The Act specifies in general terms what is required, and permits the Secretary of State to make regulations filling out the detail. The regulations will cover both specific documents and also information of a more general kind. The documents include: the statement of LEA curricular policy as required by the 1986 Act; any formal statement made by the governing body of the school, as allowed under the same Act, which specifies a modification to that policy; any other policy statements by the governing body; copies of governors' annual reports.

The other information will need to describe the whole curriculum, the provision made for giving effect to it (including syllabuses to be followed), and the educational achievements of pupils.

This last category includes the results of any assessments of the pupils' achievements which have been made, whether in the context of the national curriculum or otherwise. But the regulations may not require any such information about individual pupils to be made available, other than to the parents concerned, and to the governing body or the LEA as far as their respective functions require. Where copies of documents have to be made available on request, a charge not exceeding the direct cost may be levied. Both LEAs and governing bodies have to ensure that head teachers comply with these regulations.

There are also provisions allowing for complaints and appeals, made on or after 1st September 1989, which relate to the national curriculum. These are the responsibility of each LEA, subject to the agreement of the Secretary of State, and after the LEA has consulted with the governing bodies of aided and special agreement schools. An appeal under these arrangements may only refer to a school maintained by the LEA (other than a special school in a hospital) and must concern one of three kinds of complaint:

a That the LEA or governing body has acted, or is proposing to act, unreasonably, or has failed to act adequately, in respect of its duties to implement the national curriculum as at that time established, or its duties in advance of this to ensure that the subjects to be included in the national curriculum for that key stage are taught for a reasonable time during the key stage;

b That the LEA or governing body has fallen short similarly, in respect of its duty to make full information available in the manner described above;

c That the governing body has acted, or is proposing to act, unreasonably in respect of an appeal following a disagreement between a parent and the head teacher about modifications to the national curriculum, as applying to the pupil concerned in the manner described above.

In a grant-maintained school, the arrangements are different, and are laid down in its articles of government. If an appeal on any of these matters is made directly to the Secretary of State, under the provisions of the 1944 Act, he may not deal with it until the procedures outlined above have been followed.

The implementation of the national curriculum

The main provisions came into force on the passing of the Act. Much of the background work was already under way by this time, though much more remained to be done even in relation to the core subjects which are to be tackled first. Most of the future members of the three national Councils had been appointed, with the intention that the groups should operate in 'shadow' form until the Councils were formally set up. Only one of the really difficult areas, that of establishing the general principles of the assessment programme, had been tackled, and this is discussed in Chapter 2.

The main part of the development work for the curriculum itself will involve drawing up the attainment targets, programmes of study and assessment arrangements for each subject. But this work will take time (far more time, in fact, than was envisaged in mid-1988), and the first point at which the change will affect schools directly is the start of the requirement that all foundation subjects must be taught for 'a reasonable time' pending the introduction of the full curriculum. This is at the discretion of the Secretary of State, but the expected date is September 1989.

For the rest, little more than hints are available for those who want to plan ahead, and this has been unavoidable. The reason is the very real difficulty which faces the decision-makers, in that the rate of introduction ought in principle to be very slow. The five-year-olds of 1989-90, who are the first group to be in at the start, do not reach school leaving age until the year 2001; the school leavers of earlier years will not have experienced the new approach from the start of their school careers, and the assessment programme should ideally (though to a decreasing extent over the ten years) take this into account. Clearly this is unrealistic.

The first indications are that a start will be made, in the school year 1989-90, at the beginning of the third key stage as well as the first, and this is a reasonable compromise. The first subjects will be mathematics and science, with more year groups and further subjects added each subsequent year, and with English (and Welsh where it is a core subject) as the priorities. But one consequence of this is that the first few secondary school year groups, which will be tested in the first half of the 1990s, will not provide a baseline for fair comparisons with those that follow, even to the extent that such comparisons are technically feasible. Not until well into the next century can the system reach a stable state; most probably it never will, for many reasons of which some are mentioned below. Some of these are explored in more detail in the next chapter.

The basic curriculum (national plus RE) as a whole

The whole curriculum for the age range of compulsory schooling is not, as noted at the start of the chapter, something which can be set down on paper as a sort of rule book for teachers and schools. Yet the attempt has been made, and the rule book is included in an Act of Parliament, just one step below the status of a tablet of stone.

It is possible to question the wisdom of those who decided to create such a rule book, and even easier to question whether all those who voted for it understood the implications of what they were doing. But it has to be recognised that the essence of the new approach has wide support, both in the main political parties and beyond. Those working in and for the education service cannot expect to be able to ignore it and carry on as before. However, it is fair for them to point out to the clients of the service the practical implications of the change, and the next chapter looks at these implications. Some of them appear again in the final chapter, whose purpose is to consider some aspects of the Act as a whole.

To bring to a close this section of the chapter, which has been so much concerned with the language of the Act, a comment on some of the terminology it employs seems appropriate. This may usefully start with the familiar concept of a 'subject' - familiar, that is, to those whose standpoint is an interest in the secondary curriculum. In a junior context, some distinct subjects are recognisable in most schools, but what of topic work or environmental studies? What, in the junior context again, is history? What, most confusingly of all, is technology? The Act makes no attempt to define it, and many who have been involved in its growth during the 1980s would be cautious about using the term at all, on the grounds that no agreed and understood definition exists. Above all, what of the various aspects of language work, and where is the dividing line between the 'English' part of the curriculum and the rest? This last question indicates quite starkly the problems facing the DES in drafting the new laws, and in writing the regulations which will provide the detail.

In the infant school, the idea of a subject would be perceived in various ways, from a feeling at one extreme that it was acceptable if mildly inappropriate, to its rejection at the other as totally irrelevant and unacceptable. Of course a good infant teacher, being a resourceful and adaptable person, as anyone in that job has to be, could match what the pupils were doing against what was set down, in any manner which satisfied the requirements - for example, defining sand tray work as mathematics, science, language development or physical education according to need. But the exercise would hardly impress on anyone the value of the new curriculum.

The problems in the secondary curriculum are different, but no less fundamental. Subjects are there all right, but the definitions (particularly 'English' and 'technology') are just as difficult. 'Art' is a term well understood, but the areas of work it covers can differ across a vast range. But the central problem here is that the division of the secondary curriculum into discrete sections is a change which reverses the clear trend of curriculum development during the 1980s. The DES booklet *Better schools* put it this way in 1985:

> Subject boundaries are not rigid and need to be approached flexibly... some elements or aspects of a subject arise naturally in the course of teaching another subject... timetables need not be, though particularly in secondary schools they often are in practice, structured by reference to subjects.

Since this was the document which declared that 'the Government does not propose to introduce legislation affecting the powers of the Secretaries of State in relation to the curriculum', perhaps it should be treated with caution - but at least in relation to the status of the term 'subject' it was right. All through what is written down about the national curriculum, the word needs to be interpreted with care.

The other terms which merit the closest scrutiny are the three phrases which together define the extent of the requirements in respect of each foundation subject: attainment targets, programmes of study, and assessment arrangements. At the root of the thinking behind these terms seems to be a picture of the educational process which goes something like this. First take a part of the full attainment target, for example that pupils should know the dates of the kings and queens of England since 1660. The required programme of study is that there should be a planned sequence of lessons which approach the topic in different ways. The assessment arrangements are that an untimed written test should be set, requiring a date response to each named monarch, and with the aim of attaining 18 out of 20.

No doubt this will be dismissed by some as a travesty, or with more justification as an unfair example. It is unarguably simplistic: it uses as an illustration something which is unrealistically simple, when the reality is quite complex. But that is just the problem which these terms, as they are defined and used in the Act, actually pose. Even the word 'study' is inappropriate to describe the method of learning of the younger pupils. The terms describe a simplistic picture of the process of teaching, which runs like this: decide what you want the pupil to know/understand/be able to do (the attainment target); work out a sequence of steps through which you can teach it (the programme of study); and finally assess what has been learnt, in such a way that you can either try again using a modified approach, or go on to teach whatever comes next (the assessment arrangements). This is not how teaching is done or, in almost any real situation, how it could be done.

Thus there are problems ahead, and the aspects described here are only the start.

Religious Education and the national curriculum

The special place of RE in the curriculum is preserved in the new arrangements. It is not a foundation subject, and so is not at risk of being taken out of the compulsory curriculum as those subjects are (at least in principle); nor does it, for the same reason, come within the provisions for assessment. Its special place is based still on the 1944 Act: '...religious education shall be given in every county school and in every voluntary school'. The time to be allocated each week is not specified in either Act. The full legal background is quite complex, but needs to be understood to some extent in order to see the effects of the new Act, and a summary may be helpful. It will also serve as an introduction to the provisions for RE in a grant-maintained school, which are outlined in Chapter 8.

All county primary and secondary schools have to follow the

LEA's 'agreed syllabus'. A procedure is laid down in a schedule to the 1944 Act (and slightly modified by the new Act) for an LEA to change this syllabus. Controlled schools follow broadly the same syllabus and arrangements, with some variations to allow for a denominational interest. Aided schools follow a syllabus in line with the requirements of their trust deed or articles of government, or in the absence of such provision the governors follow a policy of their choice.

The term 'denomination' has in recent years been interpreted quite widely, so as to include the various religious groups represented in a particular area, and in the Act this is now made explicit. Sometimes groups following a non-religious philosophy of life have also been included, though this was more questionable and is now clearly outside the provisions of the Act. The opportunity has been taken to amend earlier Acts in order to use 'denomination' consistently, and also to replace 'religious instruction' by 'religious education'.

The requirements of the 1944 Act also cover the daily act of worship, and these are altered by the new Act in a manner described in a separate section below.

The provisions for RE, as now modified by the new Act, cover all pupils at maintained schools, other than those in special schools. They thus affect those under or over the statutory age range, as they always have done, while the national curriculum does not; they also cover pupils with special needs in ordinary schools and in special units attached to ordinary schools.

The exemption relating to special schools is not new. The 1944 Act, long superseded in most of its provision for special needs, still contains the only valid rules about RE in special schools: they consist merely of a vague injunction to teach RE where practicable. It must be acknowledged that this is not an easy matter on which to legislate, but it is unfortunate that an opportunity to make the attempt has been missed.

The provision for a parent to withdraw his child from RE on request is not altered by the Act. Nor is there any significant change in the arrangements for RE in aided and special agreement schools. There is no change either to the various rules for enabling arrangements to be made, on request, for RE of a form different from that generally applying within a school to be given in or outside the school; these rules have never been widely used.

Revision of the agreed syllabus

Since RE is not part of the national curriculum as such, none of the permitted variations, modifications or exemptions for development purposes which were described earlier may be utilised. The only agency which can vary the agreed syllabus remains the conference set up under the 1944 Act.

In the 1944 Act no particular requirements were laid down about the agreed syllabus itself. The new Act does so, by specifying that any syllabus adopted through the procedure specified 'shall reflect the fact that the religious traditions in Great Britain are in the main Christian, whilst taking account of the teaching and practices of the other principal religions represented in Great Britain'. This is sufficiently broad and general both to command respect and to allow for variations which suit local needs.

There is one other significant change, which relates to the procedure for altering a syllabus. It may pass almost unnoticed if the agreed syllabus is a recent revision, allowing, as most have done since 1975, considerable flexibility around a simple and broad framework. The change will most affect those LEAs which have evaded their responsibilities in this field, and have retained a syllabus long overdue for replacement. (At least one dating from 1944 was still a legally recognised LEA syllabus in 1988.)

The 1944 Act gave to each LEA the power to set up a Standing Advisory Council on religious matters, including RE and the agreed syllabus. But the LEA was not required to do so, and by not doing so some LEAs have been able to defer indefinitely making any change to their syllabuses. The new Act rectifies this anomaly.

The title remains that of Standing Advisory Council, but the constitution is now more closely defined, and so also are its functions, particularly in respect of the agreed syllabus. The constitution matches quite closely that of the conference which has to be set up under the 1944 Act to change the syllabus. It is made up of four groups (three in Wales), each consisting of persons appointed by the LEA to represent respectively:

a Such Christian and other religious denominations as will in the LEA's opinion appropriately reflect the principal religious traditions in the area, with the exception in England of the Church of England;

b In England only, the Church of England;

c   Such associations representing teachers as ought in the LEA's opinion to be represented;

d   The LEA itself.

The denominations and associations to be represented, the size of the groups, and the terms of office of each member, are all determined by the LEA, and no procedural rules are specified, with the single exception of the method of voting. But there is a detailed requirement about consultations relating to the actual persons to be appointed. The whole exercise is clearly a matter calling for both diplomacy and sensitivity, and so an LEA would be well advised to consult very fully about all aspects of it.

The actual requirement about the appointment of members of the Council is that the LEA has to ensure that every person appointed must be representative of the denomination or association in question (or of the LEA, in that group), and that he remains so during the term of office laid down; the LEA may terminate his membership if the latter ceases to be the case. In practice such action will no doubt be rare, and would be taken only at the request of the local leadership of the group concerned, other than in the case of the LEA group where the criteria are clear enough.

One further member may be appointed to the Advisory Council by any governing body (or bodies if more than one, acting jointly) of a grant-maintained school in the area which uses one of the LEA's syllabuses. Such a member may be removed from office by those who appointed him. Additional members may be co-opted, by vote of (and on terms decided by) those members of the Advisory Council who are not themselves co-opted. However, the voting method specified for the Council explicitly excludes both the GM representative and the co-opted members.

The Advisory Council may act at the request of the LEA or otherwise, and may at any time require (not just request) the LEA to put into action the review procedure for the syllabus. That word 'require' is the key factor in the new arrangements.

The procedure operates as follows. The representative groups on the Standing Advisory Council, other than the one representing the LEA, have to consider the matter separately (in formal terms, that is, though in practice some detailed liaison work will be needed). If two of the three (or both of the two in Wales) resolve to require the LEA to act, the Council must inform the LEA in writing. The LEA must then set up the conference as specified in the 1944 Act. Though the LEA group does not on this occasion have a vote, it would clearly not be tactful for its members (or indeed the GM and co-opted members) to be excluded from the discussions.

Alternatively, the LEA may initiate the procedure directly, and by resolution set up the conference. Since the Standing Advisory Council is now mandatory, however, this method is less likely to be used.

At this point the reason for the close match between the provisions of the two Acts becomes clear. Though the LEA has formally to set up the conference, all it has to do in practice is to declare that the members of the four (or three) representative groups on the Council are also to constitute the conference. (Some details may need changing, if terms of office are nearing their ends or if additional groups are thought to merit representation.) The only significant difference is that any co-opted members or a grant-maintained representative are not included; in practice, however, some informal arrangement would no doubt allow them to continue, albeit still without voting rights. Thus the Advisory Council, in initiating the review procedure, is in practice asking the LEA to instruct the Advisory Council itself (with this one change) to do the job.

If the existing agreed syllabus is used by any grant-maintained schools in the LEA area, the conference must consult the governing bodies of those schools before making any recommendation.

The only other significant difference between the Standing Advisory Council and the review conference lies in the voting procedure. As in the Council, the conference divides into its four (or three) separate groups in order to vote, but this time the vote within every group must be in favour of the draft syllabus. This is formally described as a unanimous recommendation of the conference.

It is important to note that the requirement for unanimity does not mean that the vote within each group has to be unanimous - the procedure is left to each group to decide for itself. The best approach would clearly be to seek a consensus, but otherwise the procedure will probably follow the normal rules by which each member has one vote and the chairman a casting vote.

The LEA, on receiving the recommendation of the conference, may give effect to it. If it fails to do so (or if a conference fails to make a unanimous recommendation), the Secretary of State may himself set up a 'body of persons' to do the job instead. When it has done so, in accordance with the rules laid down, the Secretary of State may direct that the resulting syllabus shall become the agreed syllabus on the terms stated. The mere threat of this possibility has always been sufficient in the past to ensure that it does not arise, and no doubt this will continue.

The new status and power of the Standing Advisory Council is a minor but valuable innovation, which has every prospect of being well suited to the needs of each local situation in which a change to the agreed syllabus becomes desirable.

Other functions of the Standing Advisory Council

The Council may advise the LEA on the implementation of the agreed syllabus, on resource materials, on methods of teaching, on in-service training needs, and on the arrangements for the daily act of collective worship. On the last point, the Council must, in certain circumstances, be consulted by individual schools, as mentioned below. The Council must publish an annual report, outlining in particular any matters on which it has given advice to the LEA and, when the advice was given other than at the LEA's request, why it has done so. The mode of publication is not specified.

The act of collective worship

A daily act of collective worship has been a requirement for all county and voluntary schools since the passing of the 1944 Act. There is a provision allowing a parent to withdraw his child from attendance, and this remains. In an aided or special agreement school, the act of worship may on special occasions be held other than at the school, but otherwise it must take place at the school; this last provision is extended in the Act to grant-maintained schools. Otherwise, the new Act modifies the requirements in four respects, and also extends them generally to include grant-maintained schools.

First, the act of worship no longer has to be at the beginning of the school day. This is a welcome change, which allows schools to choose the time in a flexible manner while not affecting the central principle, and needs no comment.

Second, the responsibilities for determining the arrangements for the act of worship are now laid down. In a county school the decision is to be made by the head teacher in consultation with the governors, and in a voluntary school by the governors in consultation with the head. The difference reflects the special responsibility for religious education, in its widest sense, which is held by the governing body of a voluntary school. Again, it is a simple and welcome change, and no further comment is required.

The third change alters the rules for county schools in relation to Christian and other faiths. In general, the worship must be wholly or mainly of a broadly Christian character. 'Mainly' means that most acts of worship during a school term are to be as specified, and 'broadly' means that the worship is to reflect the broad traditions of Christian belief without being distinctive of any particular Christian denomination.

However, the Standing Advisory Council may direct that the requirement about the broadly Christian character of the worship may be modified or removed in relation to a particular school. It may do so at the request of a head teacher, who must first consult the governing body. The Council must give its decision in writing to the head teacher. It must review the decision, either at the request of the head teacher, or at intervals of not more than five years. The head teacher may make representations to the Council about both the decision and any review. If a decision is not confirmed by a review, it lapses at the end of the five-year period.

In making its decision, the Council must take into account the family backgrounds of the pupils concerned. Where there is a majority or significant minority of pupils from backgrounds other than Christian. these provisions allow for the rules governing the act of worship in a county school to be operated with considerable flexibility. The facility to withdraw by parental request remains, and one test of the value of the new arrangements will be how few parents make use of it.

The fourth change seems quite simple and straightforward, and appears to do little more than add a useful degree of flexibility to a previously rigid requirement, that the daily act of worship should involve the whole school together. As stated in the Act, the change is distinct from that just mentioned in relation to assemblies for different faiths, but in practice the consequences will interact whenever the question of non-Christian worship arises. Under the new rules, and when only Christian worship is involved, there may still be a single act of worship for all pupils; but, alternatively, there may be separate acts of worship, either for pupils in different age groups, or for different groupings of a kind used elsewhere in the school, such as those of a house system.

The groups may not, however, be arranged solely for the purpose of the act of worship, again when only Christian worship is being considered. When one or more other faiths are involved, this restriction will probably not have any effect.

The problem created by this change arises, paradoxically, from the flexibility it allows. There is in the 1944 Act what is in effect a let-out clause, allowing schools to modify (and in many cases to avoid altogether) their obligation to have a daily act of worship. The provision which allows such avoidance is that, if the school buildings do not allow the whole of the school to meet together (which, of course, is so for most secondary schools and some primaries), the act of worship need not take place. Whether the clause has been invoked as a reason or an excuse is perhaps debatable, but there is no doubt that it has been used very extensively. Further, this widepread practice has been implicitly accepted by HM Inspectorate. The major change which results from this section of the Act is that the let-out is no longer there. Even a school without a hall of any kind could meet the requirement as it is now, by holding separate acts of worship in the classrooms.

Bearing in mind the changes in the ethnic and religious composition of the school population since 1944, including the reduced extent of formal Christianity, this change will require some thought, both in itself and when linked with the rules for non-Christian assemblies. Further, there have been developments in theological awareness over the same period, which could add to the complexity of the situation. At that time, perhaps, it was not thought odd for a few hundred pupils, covering a seven-year age range and from a variety of backgrounds, to meet together to sing (after a fashion) some words that few of them understood, and to mumble what was called a prayer but for most of them did not merit the description.

Even in 1988 this still does happen, though more rarely. To a thoughtful observer such a performance bears almost no resemblance to a true act of worship. It seems, in fact, very odd indeed. To those who voted this change into the new Act, presumably it did not seem odd at all, if indeed they did actually think about it in this way. But in many schools such things will be happening, not just by unthinking tradition but for the first time. If its implementation is strictly enforced, the change will cause no end of problems.

Chapter 2   The National Curriculum: a tactical response

The practical implications of the new curriculum

Not even the most forceful proponents of the national curriculum have claimed that its introduction would be easy. For each key stage in each foundation subject, both the programme (or programmes) of study and the assessment arrangements have to be devised and approved, first in outline and then in full detail. Assessment arrangements have to follow the general principles of the assessment process, which were worked out during the second half of 1987, and approved in outline before the Act was passed; these principles and their implications are the subject of a separate section below.

For each subject, a working group has been, or will be, formed, to propose a general approach for the approval of the Secretary of State, and then to specify for each key stage the attainment targets and programmes of study. There are no rules indicating how much detail these will contain, though the balance needed is clear enough. Too little detail will allow the teachers to go on doing their own thing, and will increase the difficulties of specifying the assessment arrangements; too much will restrict the ability of teachers to match their approach to different situations, and will also cause the amount of paper involved to grow to unmanageable proportions. When completed, these documents will have to be passed to the Curriculum Council for the consultation process to take place, and will then be formally approved.

During this period, each set of documents will become the basis for the assessment arrangements for that part of the new curriculum. This task will be done mainly by the working groups, but there will be some consultation with the School Examinations and Assessment Council (SEAC). The form of consultation is not specified in the Act, and much will depend on how SEAC sees its own role. The formal requirement is merely that the Secretary of State may specify by order the assessment arrangements for each foundation subject and key stage.

All of this has to be done at a pace dictated by strong political pressures. But, at many points in the sequence, the pace may be affected by things going wrong. It may be that a working group will decline to accept the terms of reference given to it, or will fail to agree; perhaps its recommendations will fail to gain the Secretary of State's approval. The resulting delays could cause the whole complex programme to slip back. Also, wherever these various plans impinge on each other, as they often do, consultation will have to take place between the groups involved, and the schedule allows little time for this. Some of the boundary lines, particularly that between science and technology, will cause great difficulty in this respect.

The formal part of the process will also take time, while the Secretary of State arranges for the necessary order to be placed before Parliament while it is sitting, and then waits for the prescribed period before (in the absence of a resolution in either House to reject it) the order may be formally made.

The next stage ought not to start until this happens, but in practice will no doubt begin as soon as the outline has been approved by the Secretary of State. After details of the programmes of study have been published and sent to schools, the training stage will get under way, starting with the selection and intensive training of those who are to train others. For head teachers the training will concern general principles, and then there will have to be thorough training for class and subject teachers.

All this will need some well-qualified and able people to work full time as trainers, much as happened for GCSE but on a larger scale, and many others to pass on to the rest what they have learnt. It will also require the services of many supply teachers for cover purposes. The total cost will thus be considerable, and will clearly involve (if only because in many areas there will continue to be a shortage of supply teachers) a diversion of effort from the existing in-service programme.

These preparations will impinge directly on the work of schools, of course, not least because of the disruption caused to their normal programme. But there will be a breathing space before the major changes are implemented, and, in view of both the magnitude and the nature of these changes, it would benefit all concerned to do some preparatory reading, thinking and planning.

Preparing the way for the new curriculum

The document which began the process leading to the introduction of the national curriculum was the consultation paper of July 1987. This set out the principles which govern the whole, and which, with two exceptions, have not significantly changed. The first of these exceptions relates to RE, which was initially not to be given any greater emphasis than it already had through the 1944 Act, and this was mentioned in Chapter 1.

The other exception concerns the time allocation to the foundation subjects, which the consultation paper specified in detail, by way of illustration, for the fourth and fifth years of the secondary school - 10% English, 10% mathematics, and so on. This came under extensive criticism, and (for whatever reason, as many other proposals were criticised just as fiercely but to no effect) was eventually withdrawn. A new clause was at this point inserted into the Bill, as a result of which no order of the Secretary of State may require that any particular period of time should be allocated to the teaching of all or any part of a programme of study.

However, the damage was in some respects done, well before the limits were dropped. The idea of a 10% slot in the timetable - and not only for the GCSE years - became firmly established in the minds of many, not least those whose areas of special interest were omitted from the list of foundation subjects. The proposed time allocations have been used for projections of extra manpower requirements, and by the Training Commission (the former Manpower Services Commission) for its own questionable purposes. The percentages have also been used by head teachers to justify a change in timetable allocations, particularly when there has been a pragmatic justification for the change on account of a shortfall in the teacher-periods available. It is important, therefore, to reject as invalid any arguments for changes in timetable allocations which are based solely on what purport to be the requirements of the Act.

The consultation paper also contained some clear commitments which are worth keeping in mind, and perhaps also worth quoting when the right moment arises.

The Secretaries of State believe it to be important that schools should have flexibility about how they organise their teaching... The Government intends that legislation should leave full scope for professional judgement and for schools to organise how the curriculum is delivered in the way best suited to the ages, circumstances, needs and abilities of the children in each classroom... There must be space to accommodate the enterprise of teachers, offering them sufficient flexibility in the choice of content to adapt what they teach to the needs of the individual pupil, to try out and develop new approaches, and to develop in pupils those personal qualities which cannot be written into a programme of study or an attainment target.

Using the available planning time

In the planning period before the national curriculum begins in earnest, the thinking of everyone concerned needs to maintain a balance, between on the one hand the clear and specific requirements of the Act, and on the other some less explicit principles which derive from different sources but are just as important. The paragraph above illustrates this very effectively. There are perhaps three such principles involved, in addition to the fundamental one that the provisions of the Act itself are, as part of the law of the land, not open to rejection.

First, the reasons which were used initially to justify the introduction of the national curriculum are sound enough, and merit the agreement of every teacher involved. There may be different interpretations of what is meant by raising standards, but, if teachers are allowed a little flexibility as to which meaning to choose, they can give full support to the idea. Continuity through the years of compulsory schooling is equally unexceptionable, and many would admit that schools have not always been very good at ensuring it, particularly across the primary-secondary divide; this should likewise cause no difficulty. Also, a way of easing the problems facing children who move to a school in a different area would be of benefit to those involved, and as a general idea is therefore welcome. Lastly, there can be no objection of substance to the principle of increased accountability. Whether the methods used to encourage these changes are equally sound is another matter, but teachers are bound to give support to their general thrust.

Second, teachers must continue to discharge their professional duties in the same responsible manner as they have always done (despite some wavering during and after the sanctions period of the mid-1980s). A teacher is not, and can never be made into, someone who simply uses a standard rule book in order to transmit knowledge and skills by word and by demonstration. He remains a professional, as the above extracts from the consultation paper confirm. He must therefore question, firmly if necessary, anything he is asked to do under the guise of the national curriculum which is not demonstrably within either the Act or orders made under the Act, if he considers it is right to do so and if he has the support of his senior colleagues. He has a dual responsibility in these matters, to observe the law and to provide the very best education for his pupils. If this creates a conflict, the law must take precedence - but only if it really is the law, and not a wrong application or interpretation of part of it.

Third, there is a general principle that no-one in public service work can reasonably be required by law to follow a duty laid down as part of his job, unless he is provided with, or given the opportunity to acquire, the necessary means of doing so. The person who is most at risk here is clearly, as so often, the head teacher. He has the duty first of all, in the period before a particular section of the national curriculum is established, to secure that each foundation subject in the stage concerned is taught 'for a reasonable time' during that stage. This requirement is unusually strongly worded, as noted in Chapter 1; the corresponding duties of the LEA and of the governing body are merely `to exercise their functions with a view to securing...' the same end. Head teachers will need to keep this obligation firmly in the minds of all those responsible for resource allocation, both at LEA and governing body level and within the school itself. The implications of this are far-reaching, and are mentioned in more detail in the section below on resources for the new curriculum.

The process of changing to the national curriculum will not divide neatly into a planning stage and an implementation stage. After the initial breathing space, which ends at the point when the requirement to teach each relevant subject 'for a reasonable time' comes into force, implementation and planning will continue together, within each subject as well as overall. Management of the exercise will thus become highly complex, both when considered on its own and even more in the light of other pressures relating to open admission and local management. This makes more critical than ever the need to make the best use of the lead-in period.

The approach used will vary according to the type of school, and will also be affected by the ability range and the nature of the background of the pupils. Whatever the context, however, the exercise may best start with a thorough look at the whole curriculum of the school, including its documentation and the resources currently available for its implementation. The matter of documentation is important: when at any later stage questions arise about the curriculum, most of the answers will be given in terms of what is written down about it, not what actually happens in the classroom.

Matters affecting special schools

For special schools and units, and in relation to special needs pupils in ordinary schools, a curricular review presents particular difficulties; the whole matter of the national curriculum in this context is the subject of a later section of this chapter. In relation to pupils with statements (or where one is pending), the statement or draft statement will provide the documentation necessary; for the greater number, for whom a statement is not required, much will depend on the regulations issued, and there is little that can be added here. But many of the points made below still apply.

Matters affecting primary schools

One of the first changes will concern the documentation for the curriculum. This has always served a dual purpose, first of providing guidelines for class teachers (covering content, methods of teaching, assessment, and record-keeping), and second of informing parents, governors and inspectors, whenever the need arises, of what the school is doing. In primary schools, and particularly in relation to infant pupils, the problems relating to documentation may well be extensive. Because of the whole nature and ethos of primary education, it will not be easy to link the requirements of the national curriculum, as it is at a given stage of implementation, to the curriculum (whether written down or otherwise) currently being followed within the school. The actual arrangements concerning school organisation, class management, and the content and methods of teaching, cannot be described in their entirety in such formal terms - indeed, this could only be attempted at all if the curriculum was very narrow and prescriptive.

Much will depend in practice on the form in which the programmes of study and so on are set down. When this is known, head teachers and class teachers will have to match 'required' against 'actual', not necessarily in the most obvious manner, but rather in the way which produces the closest fit - by what might be called, using an illustration suggested in Chapter 1, the 'sand tray method'. If a first attempt at a match makes the actual curriculum a little short on science, then sand tray work counts as science. If the shortfall is on RE, the sand tray itself may not be much help, but the general idea remains the same. For every 'subject' required to be taught in a primary school, there are various ways in which the boundaries can be drawn, and a little movement one way or another will bring about a closer match.

It may be thought that the sand tray method smacks too much of pragmatism or worse, and that an analytical and unbiased approach should be used instead. But a fair case can be made for the former. The sand tray does not, after all, fit neatly into a curricular category, and one aspect of it (that it provides a useful distractor allowing the teacher to give time to other pupils) does not fit into any. Nor would teachers all agree as to a way of sharing it between language, science and so on. So a pragmatic approach to the classification of the sand tray is inevitable, and the same is true of most activities at primary level.

The method also makes sense if approached from the other direction. Teachers (and particularly head teachers) will need to be ready for criticisms of their curriculum; if they can show that, using the resources available to them, they have got as close to the requirements of the national curriculum as they are able, they will have an answer ready to meet such criticisms. Further, if a head teacher's own estimates show that the school falls short of requirements in this way, he can then make a strong case for extra resources.

In a primary school, the most difficult boundaries to define include those of the two areas most likely to require an increased share of the curriculum, science and technology. Both would be accepted by many teachers as areas which merit greater emphasis, perhaps, in the case of technology, with some doubts as to which aspects of it would suit different ages, and in both cases with some apprehension about how far into it teachers without a scientific or technical background could go. Both, also, require greater material resources than most schools have, and so may well be suitable areas for which to request more.

Matters affecting secondary schools

In a secondary school, the problems are easier to measure but are likely to prove more difficult to resolve. The labelling of subjects is standard practice, with little local variation about the actual labels used, and the teaching week is normally divided into timed sections in a manner which is the focus of much discussion among those involved. Further, a rapid change of emphasis has implications for the teachers themselves, to a greater extent than in the primary sector. This applies particularly when fewer teachers are needed in total as pupil numbers fall. Specialist teachers cannot easily be retrained (if at all),even though this would enable schools both to keep their services and to meet the demands of growth subjects. Problems in some schools will be made worse by the need to take out some of the best teachers on short-term secondments, in order to lead the in-service training programme for the introduction of the new curriculum.

The balance of subjects in the national curriculum for secondary schools will clearly create a demand for more teachers of modern languages, and likewise of science and technology - with some doubts about what kind of technology, and about the place of information technology. Which of the other subjects will as a result come under pressure to give up a share of curricular time will depend too much on local conditions to forecast with equal confidence. Clearly, minority subjects in the GCSE years (particularly home economics and the school's second foreign language) will become even more at risk than has been the case in the past.

Other pressures will also be having an effect. In many schools the pattern of interaction may become very confused; this in turn will have effects both on problems at management level and on staff morale. The nature and extent of these factors should become clearer during the implementation of the whole Act, as open admissions start to affect pupil numbers, and in turn, through a formula which calculates each school's income by reference to the number on roll, affect also the school's balance sheet. Salary costs will still have to be paid, even if the teachers concerned are no longer needed to cover the curriculum in its new form. There are some very real problems here, familiar enough in themselves but likely to appear in greater numbers and under a new and untried set of rules.

How all this will be resolved is by no means clear. Schools will in any event be greatly influenced by local factors. But two things are clear: the quality of management will be vitally important, and the ability to plan ahead will become even more necessary for managers than has been the case in the past. To those who do plan ahead sufficiently, the rewards will be considerable - not least because the planning will probably have included an early and successful claim for extra resources, so as to meet the new requirements in science and technology. For those who, by ill luck or through having more limited management skills, do not meet these demands, the penalties may be harsh.

The practicalities of the assessment arrangements

The requirements of the Act for the assessment of the foundation subjects present difficulties of a far more extensive and fundamental nature than most of those involved in drafting them were aware of. (In the case of those who did know, there were more difficulties than they found it practicable to bring into the debate.) As a result, it may well come about within two or three years that the Act's definition of 'assessment arrangements' will be seen to be simplistic, and the arrangements themselves unworkable in the form laid down. The technical aspects of any large-scale assessment process are complex, but well understood by those with a specialist interest; as a result, some quite simple rules can be stated, observance of which is essential if success is to follow. When the rules are ignored, as some have been in this instance, such success simply cannot come about, however strong the political will.

For those in schools who are attempting to come to terms with the new requirements, the technical aspects of these matters need be of little concern, and the occasional references to them below may be skipped over. But the practical aspects are of real importance, and these will be covered in more detail. Before this, a summary of the main features of the intended system seems appropriate.

The assessment arrangements are to come into effect, near the end of each key stage, for the purpose (as the Act puts it) of ascertaining what the pupils have achieved in relation to the attainment targets for each subject and key stage. The arrangements are to be specified by the Secretary of State.

The School Examinations and Assessment Council (SEAC) has responsibility for moderation of the arrangements. This term is not defined in the Act, but there is a definition in the TGAT report (mentioned below) which will serve well: moderation is the process of checking the comparability of different assessors' judgements of different groups of pupils. The term may also be used to describe various statistical procedures which have the same purpose. SEAC may be, but need not be, consulted on the assessment arrangements themselves, or on the resources needed to bring them about. Where the Act allows for modifications or variations to the national curriculum, it must be assumed that the assessment arrangements are altered accordingly, though this is not stated in the Act: it should therefore be made clear in other formal statements, whether by the head teacher or in regulations by the Secretary of State.

The Secretary of State may by regulations specify how the results of the assessment process are to be made available to others. The form and extent of publication has been the subject of much argument, and the clear intention is to aggregate and publish (by class and year group within each school, by school, and by LEA) full information about test results at ages 11, 14 and 16. But results can only be aggregated if they have been derived from similar tests taken in similar conditions, and the degree of similarity has in both cases to be very close. This condition will not normally be met in practice, and the resulting impossibility of true aggregation is the main reason why failure is inevitable.

The detailed plans for the assessment programme have been drawn up mainly on the basis of work done by a group set up by the Secretary of State for the purpose, the Task Group on Assessment and Testing (TGAT). Working to a difficult brief and within the very short period of four months, the group produced a comprehensive and highly praised report. Though some doubts were expressed by those who had naively declared in advance what was going to be done, these could not in the circumstances be sustained. The report has gaps, of course, and in particular the detailed resourcing of the whole exercise was outside the group's brief. The form of assessment programme outlined below follows directly from the proposals in the TGAT report.

Assessment of seven-year-olds

For pupils in the year in which they reach age 7, teachers will be asked to play a major part in the assessment process through the course of the year. First, on a continuous assessment basis, allied to programmes of study and attainment targets, they will have to arrive at judgements of their pupils across a number of profile components and using three levels of performance. Next, they will have to select from national item banks three standard tasks out of those within the range of work covered, at least one of them to be chosen in common with other local schools. These tasks are to be incorporated into the teaching programme so that each pupil is assessed, over the three tasks, in the required profile components.

A detailed moderation process then follows, involving a group of schools, through which it is intended that differences among teachers in the standards of marking will be resolved. The class teacher has in addition three other duties: to compile a confidential report for the head teacher and governors, which must cover 'the overall performance set against local and national distributions'; to write a report for each parent on the level of performance of his child; and to enter the result in the school records. No rank orders, results obtained by adding or combining marks, or whole class or school reports have to be prepared for this age group.

The levels of performance mentioned above are part of a wider scheme, which is to cover the full age range from 7 to 16 in ten levels, levels 1 to 3 being appropriate for age 7. Each level relates to a particular profile component, so that the information given to the parent of 7-year-old would consist of a list of these components, each accompanied by a figure from 1 to 3, and presumably also by a brief interpretation of what each level implies. No allowance is to be made for the pupil's age within the twelve-month range, though of course this is in practice highly significant. The ten levels are not linked to particular ages, so that the 14-year-olds for example could be at any level from 4 to 7, while the brightest 11-year-olds will have reached level 5.

It is not necessary to be a specialist either in the assessment field or in infant teaching for the list above (and the idea of reporting results to parents on a three-point scale) to raise some questions of a very practical nature. Most obviously, where is the time to come from, and how much will the process affect the normal work of the class? Also, what happens when the class teacher changes, or when a child transfers schools or has a lengthy absence? What if the pupil has a home language other than English, and only limited command of English itself? How are parents to be informed of the results in a form that makes sense, particularly if they are of limited ability or have themselves litle knowledge of English? Which parents or quasi-parents have the right to be told? None of these questions is considered in the TGAT report, and most are not even mentioned, since the practical arangements were mostly outside their brief.

But there are other questions also, which lack answers in the same way. What, for a 7-year-old or for his teacher, is a 'programme of study'? What is a 'standard task' which is defined on paper by someone else, or a 'level of performance' that is defined in such a way as to be comparable to those of pupils in other schools? What is a 'profile component'? - a familiar term in the secondary context, though even there its technical implications in terms of the size of standard errors of measurement are not well understood. What will be the effects on a child (and on his parents) when the clear implication of the results is that he has failed? What will be the effects on a school in a deprived area, when the implication likewise is that almost all its pupils have failed?

Answers will be needed, and as noted earlier can only be provided (to the extent that they are feasible at all) through an in-service training programme of considerable length and complexity. The matter of moderation alone, which is a reasonably well understood procedure in theoretical terms, and as a result known to be fraught with difficulty, will need more than just a brief explanation in order to make it practicable for primary teachers unfamiliar with it. Probably a series of supervised dummy runs will be needed to do the job properly.

Some attempts have been made to answer the last two questions above - how to avoid a sense of failure, first in pupils and then in schools where the level of achievement has to be related to a low starting point, but the answers have not so far proved convincing. It seems clear that these questions were not priority concerns of those who created the system.

Since the assessment programme for the top infant year will not come into full operation until the fourth year of the working of the new curriculum, there is a reasonable time in which the in-service programme could be set up. Meanwhile, those teachers in schools which encourage the movement of teachers between years might be well advised to press quietly for the top infants to be left to someone else for the next few years.

Assessment of older pupils

For the assessment of 11-year-olds, the general principles remain the same, but the details become rather more complex. The aggregation and reporting procedures come into full operation, leading to reports on the overall performance of the year group, and on the comparable performance of classes or part-classes (if more than one) within the year group. The reports have to be published by the school, but accompanied by a general report for the area, prepared by the LEA, which is to indicate the nature of the socio-economic and other influences which have affected each school's work.

The head teacher, of course, takes overall responsibility for these matters. Further, the modifications relating to individual pupils are the head's concern, as are any complaints by parents about aspects of the process. Head teachers will also be centrally involved in the reporting and publishing arrangements, and will need to look very carefully at the draft of any LEA report on the social background of the schools in the area, so as to ensure that the school's particular situation is stated fairly.

From the head's point of view, a major concern is the public relations aspect of the process, both for the school as a whole and for individual parents. It is not a mere by-product of the Act, but a clear purpose, that parents should be able to use the published data, first to inform their choice of school and, once it is chosen, to follow the progress of their child through it, in much more detail than has previously been possible. Thus, given the concerns expressed above about the value of some of the measures to be used, the head's task is likely to prove both complex and time-consuming, particularly in those areas where each child's progress through the first reading books has been the subject of a competitive interest among parents.

The whole process repeats at ages 14 and 16, in the latter case with the further complication that an assessment system is already in place. Space is not sufficient here even to summarise the details given in the TGAT report, and those who are interested should obtain a copy, together with a further volume containing three supplementary reports, which are available free from the DES information department at Elizabeth House.

But, as noted earlier, these reports do not tell the whole story, and schools will need to exercise vigilance for many years to come, as the tensions and anomalies of the scheme begin to show themselves. The possibility of a curriculum which is partially controlled by a national assessment system has for many years worried teachers of the upper parts of the secondary age range, and with reason; but even this trend had checks and balances built into it. The assessment arrangements for the national curriculum, being determined by a powerful Secretary of State, do not have any such checks. The price of even a measure of curricular liberty, to the extent stated quite fairly by the Secretary of State in his consultation paper of July 1987, may thus be vigilance of a very high order.

The special needs pupil and the national curriculum

The provisions of the Act for modifying the curricular requirements of individual pupils were outlined in Chapter 1, but the manner in which they are likely to operate is by no means clear. Much will depend on how specific the regulations are, but the main practical problem is likely to be how to relate the brief and general statements which will be set down on paper to the complex needs of individuals. This is made more difficult by the underlying method employed, which starts with the full curricular specification and then cuts out any parts which are thought inappropriate.

Three groups of pupils have to be considered: those with statements under the 1981 Act, those awaiting such statements, and those with special needs but not likely to require a statement. The first are easy enough to allow for, in principle at least: the statement must be written or amended in order to state how far the requirements of the national curriculum apply. How much detail is required is not clear, but the right approach tactically must be to use as broad a description as possible. This will preserve flexibility, which is clearly desirable; it will also reduce to a minimum the additional administrative and procedural burden, which is already heavy enough, as all who have had this responsibility under 1981 Act arrangements will know.

Where a statement is pending (a period which often lasts for a year or more, to the pupil's disadvantage in several respects), the head teacher may use the provision in the Act for a six-month (renewable) modification to the curriculum. This was mentioned in Chapter 1, and was designed with this need in mind (though the Act does not say so). The administrative work involved is considerable, and if objections are raised by parents the whole process could get completely out of hand. There are practical difficulties also, if the permitted variations lapse, because it may then be difficult to return the pupil to the activity which, six months or a year earlier, he stopped because it was thought unsuitable. The common sense approach is to work within the general requirements of the national curriculum where possible, making use of all the options built into it in order to meet the needs of each pupil, rather than go through a cumbersome procedure which will benefit no-one.

Much the same applies for the pupil with moderate learning difficulties, whether in a special school or unit or in an ordinary school. Eventually there will no doubt be regulations which make the whole process workable; until then, it may be sufficient to employ a commonsense approach, together with the occasional use of the tactic of not asking certain questions because, if they were asked, the answers would then have to be acted on.

Other than for pupils with statements, this is likely to be for some time a grey area. But in one respect a specific decision will be required for each pupil, as to whether (and if so to what extent) he is to be subject to the assessment process. The Act contains no details as to how these decisions are to be made, though the effects are far-reaching. The ten-level scheme makes no allowance for pupils who have an exemption of some kind, and both the reporting and the aggregation of results are made more complex by partial exemptions. The TGAT report offers some general and helpful suggestions, and draws particular attention to the need to avoid a feeling of failure, either by pupils who do not take the national tests, or by those who take them without, in their own estimation, achieving success.

For the school anxious to ensure that its results will look well in the local league table, there will be a strong reason for exempting as many slow-learning pupils as possible from as many tests as possible; if this happens the effects on individual pupils will be most regrettable.

For many of those in the education service who are concerned with the special needs pupil, the provisions of the 1981 Act were a major step forward, restricted only by the very small additional resources made available to bring them into effect. It is difficult to see the introduction of the national curriculum, as it affects special needs pupils, in the same light, and much more likely that it will prove to be a step backwards.

Management and the national curriculum

The effects of the introduction of the national curriculum on the management of schools will be far-reaching, and in some respects more complex than a book of this kind can cover. In particular, the effects on certain subjects in the secondary curriculum will develop over a period of some years, in a manner impossible to forecast at a time when many of the basic principles are quite new, and when some aspects (particularly teacher supply) are unexplored. But a few problem areas can be set down with some confidence.

First, of course, there is the fundamental change that the direction of the major part of the curriculum is now the responsibility not just of an outside body, but of one which has no personal link with the school. No LEA has ever directed the curriculum as the Secretary of State now can. But, to the extent that the LEA did have an influence, the head teacher always had the opportunity to telephone an LEA officer, or arrange a meeting with one, who could resolve any points of difficulty. Where these points were of general relevance, routine meetings between head teachers, union officials and LEA officers could usually sort the problem out. Dealing with a distant DES, or deciding that it is far enough distant to be safely ignored, is a game with very different rules.

Next, pressures from teaching staff, always a major factor in school management, may grow considerably. One of the saddest features of the sanctions period of the mid-1980s was that head teachers, who had had no control over the matters of national dispute which had caused the problem, caught the full effects of teacher unrest and lack of co-operation. It may be that, when changes in the balance of the curriculum leave teachers unhappy, as in some cases they clearly will, the head teacher will again be the focus of blame even when this is known to be unfair. Problems of this nature should be visible in advance and, when they are foreseen, the best course of action will probably take the form of a damage limitation exercise.

Further, the balance of the work of teachers (particularly in the final year of each key stage) will change, to an extent which was not thought out in advance as it clearly should have been. Teachers will find that the assessment process creates pressures, both on the time available for teaching and on their workload outside the classroom, which in some cases will prove too heavy to bear. How this will be resolved remains unclear. It will no doubt be the subject of strong representations from the teacher unions, but head teachers will as usual have to respond at the local level before an acceptable balance is reached through national negotiations.

A further pressure, and one which has barely been noticed or allowed for, is that the amount of administrative work and documentation is set to grow, to an extent presenting major problems of cost and time. The documentation for the curriculum itself will be considerable; the assessment arrangements and the modifications for special needs pupils will generate more, and any complaints made will add more still. Much of this information will have to be made available to class teachers and governors, and in some cases to parents also. When the paperwork generated by other parts of the Act is added as well, the task of the typical part-time secretary in a primary school (never much of a sinecure, even in less paper-dominated days) ceases to look possible at all.

Finally, there is the resources issue. This is so important that it merits a section to itself.

Resources and the national curriculum

As noted at several points in these two chapters, the decision to introduce the national curriculum was taken with little regard for some of the practical consequences. The resulting problems - the extra workload, the mountains of paper, the changes in the level of demand for particular specialist skills - will impinge on the work of teachers and head teachers, but not in a manner allowing much scope for argument or complaint. However, some of the changes can only come about if extra resources are provided, and when such changes become operative there will be scope for a more effective response.

An example may help to indicate what the possibilities are. The national curriculum requires technology to be taught to all pupils from ages 5 to 16, initially for a reasonable period in each key stage, and later in a manner to be specified in terms of programmes of study and so on. Most teachers are happy with this as a general idea - recent developments in various aspects of technology are so far-reaching that schools ought to become further involved than they already are. But technology (however defined) requires resources - equipment such as computers, electronics kits and modelling materials, expendable materials particularly for younger pupils, staff time in order to keep the size of teaching groups low, and in-service training perhaps of a far-reaching nature. Its introduction or expansion cannot be imposed by fiat, within existing limits of running expenses and staffing.

Hence the school's response to an instruction that technology should be done has to stress the resource requirements. Some care is needed: it is not legitimate to spend the bulk of the school's disposable income without reference to the requirements for technology, and then claim extra in order to purchase technology equipment and to train teachers in its classroom use. Head teachers (and LEAs and governing bodies) have to use the resources available to them in such a way as to give priority to the requirements of the national curriculum, and only if this fails to create conditions in which the whole requirements can be met does it become feasible to claim more. But with good planning a great deal ought to be possible and, since the level of resourcing overall is not likely to rise significantly, a claim for more should be submitted at an early stage. A further factor in this is that the LEA will be able to respond more easily to such requests before the local management scheme is fully implemented.

The main arguments are likely to concern the appointment of teachers to cover subject specialisms for which the demand will grow. The three main areas concerned are modern languages, science, and technology. Teachers of all of these were (with others) in short supply well before 1988, and the actions taken at national level to correct the imbalances were few in number and insignificant in total effect. It is clear that such shortages, having already lasted for many years, and now being made worse by executive action which increases the need without increasing the supply, will last well into the next century.

For those concerned with school management, two kinds of response to this unsatisfactory situation are required. First, it will be even more important to make a vacancy attractive when it arises, and sometimes to avoid vacancies in key areas through the tactical use of incentive allowances. Second, when a vacancy cannot be filled and as a result some part of the national curriculum cannot be taught as it should, it will be necessary to report the facts in some detail, to governors and to the LEA. The resulting arguments may prove to be quite lively.

Chapter 3 Open Enrolment to Schools

The intentions behind the change

Ever since the passing of the growth years of the 1960s, school managers have been acutely aware of the effects of falling pupil numbers. The number on roll has always been the major factor in the LEA's allocation of staffing and funds to the school, and under the local management provisions of the Act this is an explicit requirement. But governors and head teachers cannot respond quickly and flexibly when the number falls: staff contracts cannot simply be terminated, and some expenses such as heating costs, telephone bills and the running costs of the school office are not likely to be reduced in proportion as numbers fall. When the number rises, there are fewer problems, but they may still be significant if the rise is big or if it only becomes known at a late stage.

So any major change in the number of pupils admitted each year will have corresponding implications for the management of the institution. The open enrolment provisions of the Act are designed to allow - indeed, to encourage - such changes in admission levels. Some schools will of course gain and others will lose, and penalties for the losers may be severe.

The new system applies to all county and voluntary schools, primary and secondary. In respect of county and controlled schools, the power of the LEA to limit admissions is curtailed, and that of parents to send their children to schools of their choice is increased;

in aided schools, it is the power of the governors which is reduced. In recent years most public debate about admissions has been about transfers to secondary schools, and it is probable that this will continue to be the case. Disputes about entry at primary level have more usually been confined to individuals and small groups, though in future these may well become more public.

Whether in public or private argument, the LEA has been, up to the present time, in a strong tactical position on questions of admission to non-aided schools. It has been, for practical purposes, the highest level of authority involved. It has been able to set admission limits, both directly and through the establishment of catchment areas, which have been difficult to challenge even when their justification in law has been highly dubious. Now all this is changed, and the ability of the LEA to plan ahead has been curtailed.

Though the small print of the Act is important, the really fundamental change is in the balance of power. It calls for an equally fundamental review of management strategy.

The requirements of the Act

From the date when this section of the Act comes into force, the power to set admission limits for all county and voluntary schools is held by the Secretary of State. This date is itself to be decided by the Secretary of State: it is likely to be early enough to affect admissions to secondary schools in September 1990. However, admissions in September 1989 will be affected to some extent, since many parents will know of their new powers and because in the circumstances LEAs will be reluctant to employ all of their normal tactics. The new rules are not to come into force for primary schools until a year or two later.

The new admission limit

The details of the new rules are covered below. As they appear in the Act, they are not easy to read - indeed, they are written in some of the most tortuous prose of the entire Act. For most purposes, the detail is of little importance to school managers; what may be vitally important is the figure which represents the new admission limit. Each LEA ought, by the time the Act was passed, to have carried out the calculations for its own purposes, and to have made known the results to schools.

For a school which opened in or before September 1979, the new admission limit (called the standard number) is the number admitted in that year, or in September 1989 if that is larger. For a school not open in 1979, the standard number is the admission number in the school's first year, or again the 1989 entry if larger. Children of nursery age are counted as admitted for this purpose only on their transfer to a reception class.

The admission authority for non-aided schools remains the LEA. For aided schools it is still the governing body. For both types of school, the admission authority has to allow pupils to be registered at the school if their parents so choose, provided that the admission is within the general policy set down in the school's instrument of government, until the number in the year group reaches the limit set by the standard number (or such higher number as may be determined through a procedure described below). The instrument will specify the nature of the school in terms of the sex of the pupils, and whether the ability range is selective or not; it may also for a voluntary school refer to a religious affiliation.

There a special provision for aided and special agreement schools, designed to preserve the established character of the school. It takes the form of a change to the 1980 Act, and allows the governors to ask the LEA to agree arrangements with them about the admissions procedure. If an agreement cannot be reached, the Secretary of State must determine the arrangements. In view of the LEA's very limited powers in the matter, the main effect is to strengthen slightly the position of the governors. The relevant clause of the 1980 Act, as now amended, should make it easier for governors to refuse admission for reasons related to the character of the school.

For all schools, casual admissions, in years above the normal admission year, must be allowed up to the same number as for that year. The question of admissions at sixth form level, for long a minor but significant matter of contention, is not separately mentioned; clearly the year group numbers (for most schools with a sixth form) will drop between years five and six, so a limit which stays the same is rather unrealistic. In the absence of clear rules, it must be hoped that commonsense will prevail.

When this part of the Act comes into force, any existing arrangements which specify an admission limit under the provisions of the 1980 Act are automatically altered by inserting the newly defined standard number in place of the former limit. Also, a further provision in the 1980 Act no longer applies, by which admissions could be limited using arguments based on the efficient provision of education and the avoidance of unreasonable public expenditure.

Where the admission authority is the governing body, the LEA has certain rights, and it is referred to as 'the other authority' in what follows; where the LEA is the admission authority, the 'other authority' is the governing body, which has similar rights. Even if no change is proposed, the admission authority must still consult with the other authority once in each year, in accordance with the provisions of the 1986 Act.

Changing the admission number

The Secretary of State may vary the rules which determine the standard number, either for all schools or for a specified type or group of schools. He may likewise vary the number for a particular school, after receiving a written request in a prescribed form to do so. The rules depend on which authority takes the initiative, and on whether the request is for an increase or a decrease. The procedures outlined below cover the principal points, but the full text should be consulted before any actual proposal is made.

The admission authority may increase the admission number above the standard number, for any year or age groups, having first consulted the other authority as above; it may not, however, decrease an admission number in this way to a level below the standard number. Any observations made by the other authority must be given due consideration, but there is no right of veto or appeal. Any number fixed under this procedure is valid only for the period stated, and the standard number is unaffected.

The other authority may likewise propose an increase, either for one year or for longer, which may relate to one or more age groups. The proposal must be made in writing to the admission authority, which must either reject the proposal in writing within two months, or implement it. If implemented, the change again refers only to the admission limit for the year and age groups stated, the standard number being unchanged.

If, however, the admission authority rejects the proposal, the proposing authority may within twenty-eight days of the rejection make an application instead to the Secretary of State, for an increase in the standard number itself. He in turn may refuse to make an order according to the terms of the proposal, or agree to do so, or, after consultation with both the admission authority and the other authority, make an order for an increase smaller than that proposed.

The admission authority may also apply to the Secretary of State for a decrease in the standard number, on one of two grounds: that the school has lost teaching space since the measurement year, or that it has insufficient space on legal grounds, according to criteria set by regulations about school premises made under the 1944 Act. The admission authority is required to keep the standard number under review, so as to take account of changes made to the school which might affect its capacity in either of these ways.

There is no provision for the other authority to apply for a decrease in the standard number; there is nothing to stop them from asking the admission authority to do so, but the request may, of course, be refused.

The admission authority must prepare a detailed case for any reduction in the standard number. In an aided school, the governors will need to find out the DES standards for space requirements, perhaps with the assistance of the LEA. It will be of some interest to find out whether DES recommended standards for playing fields and outside play areas, which many schools fall short of, are an allowable factor in any request for a reduction.

Proposals to reduce a standard number must be published, as well as sent to the Secretary of State. Objections may be made within two months, and the Secretary of State may (as for the case mentioned earlier) refuse to make an order according to the terms of the proposal, or agree to do so, or, after consultation with both authorities, make an order for an increase smaller than that proposed.

The onus of proof is quite clear: the Secretary of State will allow a request for an increase, and refuse a request for a decrease, unless the reasons for the lower value of the standard number, in the strict terms specified, are compelling.

The immediate consequences for schools

The changes in admission numbers during the main period of falling rolls were well known in advance, within reasonable limits, and some advance planning was therefore possible, both by the school and by the LEA. Under open enrolment, the results are less predictable, and the time available for action will be very much less. But even small changes in admissions may have rapid and perceptible effects on staffing and resources, requiring an immediate management response; with larger movements the consequences may be catastrophic.

The total numbers of pupils nationally, both primary and secondary, have dropped since the base year of 1979, though actual closures of schools account for only a small proportion of the school places no longer needed. So the number of school places available in many areas will for a few years to come be well above the number of pupils waiting to fill them. Most schools will therefore have to compete for pupils, as indeed many have been doing for some time. But the rules of the contest have changed: no longer now a friendly game of bowls, but croquet at its most ungentlemanly. The consequences of making tactical errors may be severe, and the ultimate penalty - closure of the school, not by governors or the LEA but simply because it has no pupils - by no means unthinkable.

The right tactics for the head and governors of a school to adopt thus depend first on their estimate of the likely nature and extent of the local pressure on admissions. If the school is highly regarded, and admission requests likely to increase, the way ahead is reasonably clear, though by no means without its problems. If future popularity is not so certain, and requests for admission more likely to drop, the problems loom large, and will quickly get worse if they are not tackled at once. Estimates of the popularity (whether merited or not) of other local schools will also have a bearing on these assessments.

The way forward if admissions are buoyant

First check to see what the 1979 admission number was, for this normally becomes the standard number. If the school has had a formal change of designation, due perhaps to a change in the age range, this will have made it technically a new school, and the first year of the new arrangements replaces 1979. Again, the 1989 figure takes precedence if larger. Then multiply this figure by the number of year groups, and in the case of a school with a sixth form or a nursery add an appropriate figure for that. (Nursery pupils are not counted against the admission number, but space still has to be found for them in a school which has a nursery.) The result is the capacity implied by the Act.

The number of pupils set by this capacity limit will probably be larger than the present number, perhaps by a wide margin. But if the school's popularity remains high, neither governors nor LEA will be able to refuse admissions to any year group until the standard number is reached.

It may be that this will place a strain on the school in several ways, most obviously on its accommodation. As schools have lost pupils over recent years, many have lost teaching spaces as well: temporary buildings have been removed, and classrooms have been converted into parents' rooms, youth clubs or community areas.

Space requirements too have changed over the decade: newer teaching methods require more space in all of the primary years, and in secondary schools the subject areas particularly affected include humarities, foreign languages, and mathematics. Many new courses such as technology and child care are expensive on space. Also, many classrooms have been converted for different specialist uses such as computers. At the same time, teacher-pupil ratios have generally improved. The combined effect of these changes has been that a space which used to be sufficient for a class of 30 can now be assumed to hold only 25, and perhaps as few as 20. This, however, is an estimate made on practical grounds, and a calculation based on legal rules may produce different results.

If it is expected that the school will be popular, allowance has to be made for the full number of years involved - five for an 11-16 school, and so on - and for their present space requirements per pupil. If, before the number on roll levels off, the school will have run out of space, there will be (at least in the case of county and controlled schools) no ready means of creating more. The Act places no more obligations on the LEA to provide extra accommodation in these schools than did the pre-1988 legislation.

The way out of this dilemma may be for the LEA (or the governors of an aided school) to make application for a reduction in the standard number, as described in the section above on the requirements of the Act.

Otherwise, the school will require more accommodation if it continues to admit the full standard number. In this event the governors of a non-aided school will no doubt ask the LEA to provide it, inviting the response that the LEA has other priorities, and sees no need to provide extra school places when the area as a whole has sufficient. How this situation will be resolved is far from clear, but there is no doubt that the governors of overcrowded schools will have to fight hard for extra teaching space. The most likely outcome will be a return to the rows of mobile classrooms from which most schools have in recent years freed themselves.

Aided schools may find the acquisition of extra spaces rather easier, since the DES will be directly involved and will presumably (at least while policies remain as they were in 1988) want to make the new system work.

The rapid growth of pupils in popular schools will also, of course, make corresponding increases necessary in teaching staff, in support staff and in other expenditure. This may bring considerable benefits: opportunities to inject 'new blood', long-delayed promotion for existing staff, flexibility in providing for growth subjects, and cushioning of the effects of the lower demand for others. Problems will arise if specialist staff are difficult to recruit - and long-standing shortages in physics, technology of various kinds, mathematics and foreign languages are unlikely to ease. If the school is overcrowded and short of specialist rooms, good staff may be difficult to attract. All this time, too, governors and senior staff will be asking themselves how long it will be before growth turns to decline. As with accommodation problems, the LEA may not, in the new conditions created by the local management scheme, be able to give much assistance.

The way forward if admissions are declining

The first and perhaps unnecessary advice is to do everything possible to keep admissions up, at least to current levels. For many schools this has been for some years an essential part of the job of management: the difference now is that the stakes are higher.

The immediate effect of a low intake will be a fall in the budget share allocated by formula to the school. In so far as this implies directly that the school will need to lose teaching and support staff, it is familiar enough, and so are its implications: key staff who leave cannot be replaced; staff for whom there is no longer a place have first to be identified and then redeployed; delays caused by this process mean that other vacancies cannot be filled when candidates are available; revisions are needed to timetables long after the optimum completion date, and so on. But, under the combined effects of open enrolment and local management, this is by no means the full extent of the problems.

First, the need for staff to be off-loaded may be greater than in earlier years when the main pressure was from falling rolls. Most schools which have gone through this process have found that a loss of more than about 7% of the total number on roll per year has been very difficult to manage. This has been so even when the figures have been known with reasonable accuracy well in advance.

Under the Act, falls of the order of 10% per year may not be exceptional, and the figures will probably be known only in the spring of the admission year.

Second, there will be no LEA redeployment arrangement of the kind which helped many (as individuals, as school managers and in the LEAs themselves) to overcome the human problems caused by falling rolls. Under the local management provisions of the Act, governors of a school with delegated powers cannot be required to appoint to a vacant teaching post a candidate nominated by the LEA. A voluntary arrangement will no doubt be attempted, but without the power of compulsory transfer the LEA may be able to do little to help.

Third, before the advent of local management a school which found itself overstaffed, through no fault of its own, incurred no financial penalty, and the cost was borne by the LEA as a whole. Under local management arrangements, a school which has a teacher it does not need, costing say £15 000 for a year, will have to make matching savings elsewhere. Since salary costs will cover about 80% of locally controlled funds, the effects on the very few areas of expenditure which are for practical purposes within a school's immediate power to control may be dramatic. Schools may thus run out of paper or be unable to pay their heating bills, even though they have acted with due propriety.

If problems of this kind do arise, then the only way open for a school to avoid a worse repetition the next year - by improving radically the number of pupils admitted - may become much more difficult. The Secretary of State's guidance document has indicated that LEAs may provide some 'cushioning' against such situations. But it is clear that the new rules will create instability in the balance between the intakes of neighbouring schools. Even a small and routine movement, caused perhaps by a new housing development, may trigger a further, and larger, movement in the same direction the next year. The school which finds itself losing out may see the situation getting rapidly worse, in a way which neither governors, nor the LEA, nor even the governors of the school whose admissions are jumping upwards, may be able to influence.

The management of open enrolment

The education system of England and Wales has, at its best, provided outstanding examples of partnership, at the level of the Local

Authority with its county and controlled schools, its aided schools and their governors, and the local professional associations. The rules governing who pays for what in aided schools, for example, would probably be unworkable if both sides insisted on following them in every pedantic detail. The professional associations, and the governors of aided schools, have co-operated in redeployment agreements, showing a willingness to look beyond sectional interests. Problems related to individuals, whether staff or pupils, have been dealt with quietly and sensitively. Of course such procedures have not been universal, and those whose knowledge is based only on press reports may form a very different impression about the quality of management in the education service at LEA level. Partnership of this kind has, all the same, been a significant - indeed vital - feature throughout the period which the 1944 Act has dominated.

Now that the rules have changed, such partnership will be more difficult to sustain, but just as important. The management of admission policies, by agreement between neighbouring schools and with the benevolent intervention of the LEA where appropriate, provides a good example of the needs, the possibilities and the problems. The alternative is a prolonged period of confrontation, between schools and also between them and the LEA, in which all - and particularly the pupils - will be the losers. The last point is significant, in that it sets at risk one well-publicised aim of this section of the Act, to bring benefit to pupils by increasing the choices open to their parents.

The changes have two other aims, both of them fair and reasonable. The first is to encourage an element of competition between schools, because competition can, in the right circumstances, improve quality. The second is to encourage the economical use of school accommodation, through the closure of schools which fail to attract pupils. A school's response (and also that of the LEA) has to take account of these aims: to ignore them, and to hope that a weak or half-empty school will go on being protected, is no longer realistic.

So the first task for school managers is to make an assessment of the pattern of school places in the area. How large are the schools at present, in terms both of pupil numbers and of space available? What would be the practical consequences of a major change in the balance of admissions? Can a case be made for closing a school, and if so which one? What would then be the most likely pattern of admissions?

The response of one or more schools may, of course, be to opt for grant-maintained status (or threaten to do so). If so, the rules of the game become very different. For the present purpose, it is assumed that this does not happen; the opting-out tactic, which is not as simple as may appear, is discussed in Chapter 9.

If one school in an area is likely to close, then of course each will be fighting to ensure that the choice (if there has to be one) falls elsewhere. This is a familiar enough scenario: what is new is the ability of parents to determine the outcome, in certain cases within a few months. When this is likely, swift action is needed, and neither books of advice nor pious hopes about partnership can expect to be influential.

For the present purpose, it is of more relevance to look at the situation in which the balance of admissions is likely to change but only within manageable limits. Although closure may be the ultimate fate, lesser penalties may prove almost as bad - and may not be so mercifully swift. A single institution will not be able easily to operate an insular policy, and the LEA will not be able to exercise its traditional benevolent role if the schools do not acknowledge that it should be allowed to have one. Such a series of partnerships will be different from, and in many ways more demanding than, the traditional LEA pattern. But much will depend on such a system being made to work.

The school as a partner under open enrolment

The guiding principles arise directly from the preceding analysis. A school's long-term interests are best served by striving for quality, in competition with its neighbours but in a professional manner, not in a cut-throat fashion. If competition degenerates into unrestricted poaching, numbers may grow too fast for good management, bringing accommodation problems which the LEA is unlikely to solve in the time available. Closure of a neighbouring school will probably mean a further influx of pupils, and may generate much ill feeling, in the displaced teachers and pupils themselves and also among the families and the teachers of the whole area.

How, then, is this fine balance to be achieved, when so much of the power lies with the parents? If the management team of each school accepts that the school's own future health is most effectively ensured by not forcing its neighbours towards closure (or towards opting out), then the logical basis for planning and co-operation must lie in something very like the concept introduced in the 1980

Act, but lost in 1988: the planned admission limit. Since it cannot now be a limit, it is best described as an optimum admission level.

There is of course no reason why a school should not set such a figure by itself, and this is probably the right place to start. A range, rather than a spot target, may be better. The next stage of an action plan is more difficult to set down, because so much will depend on local conditions - how many schools will need to work together, what general state of relationships exists between them, and so on. In some areas, the practical constraints, even the sheer complexity of the total problem, may be too great for a comprehensive approach. But an attempt, even on an ad hoc basis, may be better than open warfare.

The LEA as a partner under open enrolment

If goodwill among schools is important under the new conditions of the Act, so also is goodwill between the LEA and its schools, aided as well as non-aided. The LEA still has a planning function; it still has some control over resources of cash and manpower, so that a little can be directed towards particular schools; and it remains for many purposes the problem-solver of last resort. So a school which has problems, whether human, financial or related to buildings, will still need to rely on the LEA. If these problems have been directly caused by a school's failure to allow the LEA its right to exercise a planning function, the school cannot expect more than the minimum of help.

The role of the LEA is therefore to work with its schools in ensuring that the various optimum admission limits fit into an overall plan. Again, it is assumed that co-operation, rather than rationalisation by closure, is the aim; if there is a case for the latter, there will be little scope for co-operation until it is resolved. An LEA officer should, therefore, be on each working party of head teachers. When the going gets rough, the officer will be able to bring pressure to bear in a variety of ways - if he knows his job, he will need no advice on how this should be done.

The LEA, where it is the admission authority, has under the Act just one key function in respect of the control of admissions: it can apply to the Secretary of State for a reduction in a standard admission number. The sole justification for such an application is (as already noted) that the accommodation is only sufficient for a total number of pupils which will result from the proposed admission number. Objections may be raised, and so the sensible course of action is for the LEA to make such proposals only after obtaining the agreement of the schools involved. (The Act requires that governing bodies be consulted, anyhow.) If all schools accept that proper planning is in everybody's long term interests, agreement should be possible. The governors of aided schools, as the admission authorities, will have a part to play in the process.

The overall position will probably resemble what follows, if full co-operation is achieved. Optimum admission levels will be agreed throughout a given area, and will in most cases be less than the standard number as defined by the Act. Where the discrepancy is large, there is a possibility that parental requests will create the kind of pressures that all parties have been attempting to avoid. In many of these cases, the school will not have sufficient accommodation, on a basis of adequate space and freedom of movement for both teachers and pupils, for the full standard number in each school year. So the LEA should, with the agreement of the school, apply for a reduced standard number (or, in the case of an aided school, invite the governors to do so).

Again, too much depends on local conditions for this process to be followed through in detail. It may be, for example, that the LEA should deliberately take some accommodation out of use, or transfer rooms to community use, in order to reduce the discrepancy between the optimum admission level and the standard number. The designation by the LEA (after consultation with the governors), of some rooms as community areas may bring both advantages and disadvantages from the school's point of view, on account of the provisions of the local management scheme relating to community schools: this is mentioned in Chapter 5. Planning has to remain a joint exercise between LEA and governors, if the aims of each include a contribution to a coherent education service for the area.

If the strategy works, the twin aims of the Act will achieved, and the advantages will be shared within the education service as a whole. But the if' is a big one, and the alternative may bring problems as yet undreamed of.

Chapter 4 Local Management: general principles

A new approach to school management

In the early 1980s, several LEAs developed schemes which allowed schools to have more say in financial matters. Similar developments were taking place in a number of other countries. In a small number of LEAs, some control was permitted over the balance between staffing and other costs, the most significant single step towards full financial autonomy within an overall budget. The success of these schemes (particularly in Cambridgeshire) was noted by the DES, and led directly to the inclusion in the Act of a comprehensive programme of financial delegation.

But the real significance of the changes goes far beyond just financial matters, as the title of this section indicates: a new approach is required to school management as a whole.

Every LEA is required to have its own scheme, within the rules laid down. The scheme must provide for budget allocations to all primary and secondary schools, and for the delegation to the governors of all secondary and some primary schools of the power to spend those funds. Though this book is written primarily as a guide for schools, it is worth noting that the implications for the LEAs themselves are far-reaching. Since LEA budgeting and accounting systems are not in all respects school-related, they have had to be substantially reorganised to meet the new requirements, as foreshadowed in the 1986 Act. Financial delegation will in fact mean more work for LEA finance staff, at least during the changeover period and possibly afterwards. Liaison with schools, including trouble-shooting, will account for a substantial share of the extra burden. It is naive to suggest that more than a small part of the additional administrative staff costs in schools can be met through savings at LEA level.

The Act defines three terms which need to be understood very clearly. These are the LEA's general schools budget, the aggregated budget and the individual school's budget share.

The general schools budget

The general schools budget is defined in the Act as the amount appropriated for meeting all expenditure on the Authority's schools for the particular financial year. It includes, therefore, capital expenditure, and other items (outlined below) which are not to be delegated to schools. This definition leaves various boundary problems, which are mentioned later. Their resolution will mainly be a matter for the Secretary of State and the LEA, but the way in which this is done may give scope for arranging for particular items of expenditure to come on the LEA's side of the line. For the purpose of this definition, in particular, the term 'school' itself is interpreted narrowly, and is taken to exclude non-school activities such as adult education.

The aggregated budget

The aggregated budget is defined as that part of the general schools budget which relates to expenditure within the delegation scheme. The four types of expenditure not to be included in the aggregated budget are:

a capital expenditure and related loan payments;

b expenditure supported by central government grants;

c other items prescribed by the Secretary of State;

d items specified in the scheme approved for the particular LEA.

The last type are known as discretionary exceptions, and the others as mandatory exceptions; together they are referred to as excepted items.

Capital expenditure costs need no explanation at this stage, though the practical implications of the exclusion are quite wide. It will be difficult, for example, to allow fairly for the trade-off between capital and running expenses, in matters such as improvements to security systems and heat insulation. These points are covered in more detail in Chapter 7.

Items of expenditure supported by central government grants are mainly salary costs relating to education support and LEA training grant personnel, 'Section 11' teachers, TVEI staff, and expenditure related to education grants for travellers' children.

The items prescribed by the Secretary of State have been outlined in a guidance document sent to LEAs. They are:

a   central LEA services such as accounting, audit and administration;

b   inspection services;

c   advisory services (educational, financial, medical, legal and related to buildings);

d   pupil transport.

The discretionary items are:

a   school meals provision;

b   pupil support services such as child guidance and education welfare;

c   funds administered by education welfare staff for clothing and other allowances for pupils;

d   provision for statemented pupils, and for other pupils in special units;

e   salary costs of peripatetic teachers, and of advisory teachers other than those supported by central government grants;

f   supply cover, both long-term and in relation to teachers away for public service or agreed union duties;

g   the additional costs of salary protection for teachers who are moved to a post carrying a lower responsibility allowance following a school closure;

h   the costs of structural maintenance and repairs.

There may also be a central development fund, of the kind commonly used before the Act, so that the LEA can fund specific projects which it initiates.

The LEA may include in its scheme a provision for passing over to the governing body the funds allocated to that school in respect of certain excepted items, with the condition, however, that these funds are to be used for the designated purpose only, a system called 'earmarked delegation' in the DES guidance document. TVEI funds and in-service training allocations are two items likely to come within this arrangement; another possibility is a central service such as advice and inspection, where the advantages would be to make the cost of the service visible within the school, and to encourage each school to make full use of the service. However, the management problems at the LEA end might prove difficult. Conditions may be attached to any earmarked delegation, particularly when items supported by central government grants are involved. It is possible that these conditions might be so restrictive that the delegation gave the school little advantage, but more usually the indirect benefits may well be found quite useful.

A contingency fund may also be created, which counts as a discretionary exception. This has to allow for such items as unforeseen September increases in pupil numbers, for which the additional per capita amount will probably be less than (perhaps about 75% of) the average cost. The fund must also provide for the costs of dismissals, premature retirement and redundancy, other than in those few cases where governors take responsibility. It must allow for the expenses arising from emergencies such as major fires (other than those covered by insurance). There will also be a small sum to allow for error correction. The contingency fund will thus provide a safety net, to allow for any anomalies and unfairnesses which the formula creates, and for unexpected costs arising for reasons beyond the school's control.

School managers will need to take full advantage of this facility. But the DES guidance is that the contingency allowance should be small, and that the total of both the discretionary exceptions (other than school meals) and the contingency amount should be not be more than 10%, dropping to not more than 7% after three years. These figures may prove to be too low to allow the LEA to do its job, and as a result the Secretary of State will probably come under pressure to increase them.

It may be wise for the LEA to set the contingency sum at the highest permitted level initially, but to use it sparingly and to distribute the unspent amount back to schools. This would achieve both flexibility and fairness. It would also discourage the temptation, both among officers and in schools, to see the sum as available for ad hoc distribution, a practice which would tend to perpetuate what should be a short-term device.

Some of the excepted items are not easy to define, and the way in which this is done in the local scheme may give scope for a school to use the small print to its advantage. Three of the key items (capital expenditure, supply cover, and the distinction between structural and other repairs) are mentioned later.

The school's budget share

The aggregated budget, which is what remains of the general schools budget when all of the excepted items have been deducted, must then be divided into the schools' budget shares. Other than for special schools and units, this is done by means of a formula which is determined by the LEA. The rules are specified generally in the Act, and in more detail in the guidance document issued by the Secretary of State. The latter states that basic rules of the formula must be simple, clear, and predictable in their impact, so that the calculation of the budget share for each school can be understood by everyone involved. The formula has itself to be approved by the Secretary of State, and may only be significantly amended with his agreement.

It is important to note that all LEA schools (excluding special schools), not only those with financial delegation, have a budget share, and must be given information about it before the start of the financial year in question. The difference is that only those schools with delegated powers can control the way in which their budget share is spent.

Schools without delegated powers retain the facility to be given, via governors, control of running expenses - as written into the 1986 Act, and common practice long before. But if the LEA's actual expenditure on the school differs from the budget share, the difference must be carried forward. No doubt each school involved will blame any overspend either on LEA mismanagement or on the formula itself, but will claim at once that an underspend is totally unfair and that the balance should be added to the school's capitation. As so often under the Act, the LEA cannot win.

The initial provisions of the Act are that all secondary schools, together with primary schools having 200 or more registered pupils (including those of nursery age), must be given delegated powers. LEAs may extend their own scheme to include other primary schools and special schools. In the latter case, a formula need not be used and the LEA may use any suitable method to fix the budget share. The Secretary of State may extend the whole scheme by regulations, and will probably do so in stages, the special schools being delayed until more experience has been gained in schemes voluntarily extended to include them.

The Act provides for the LEA to withdraw delegated powers from a particular school, if the scheme is not being operated satisfactorily. It can act at short notice, if necessary, and various safeguards are built into the process. Such reserve powers are not likely to be widely required, and are not described here in detail. They are stated clearly in the Act, and direct reference to them can be made if necessary. (There is a further provision in the 1986 Act which allows an LEA to intervene in the running of non-aided schools.) Most operational problems will be spotted at an early stage, either within the school or through the LEA's routine monitoring, and will be resolved through advice or negotiation well before formal action becomes necessary.

The local management scheme has three purposes. The first is to ensure that parents and others know how the available resources are shared among schools. The second is to allow those involved in the management of schools with delegated powers to make decisions about the optimum use of those resources. The third is to ensure that any finance released by the more efficient use of resources ('efficiency savings') can be used for the benefit of the school. All very worthy, no doubt - but it begs a number of questions, and leaves plenty of scope for a school to benefit greatly (and perhaps even unfairly) through giving careful attention to the tactics of its management response.

The formula and what it leaves out

The formula to be used to calculate the budget share for each primary and secondary school is clearly of critical importance, and its construction is a matter of considerable technical difficulty. Its starting point is the aggregated budget. As noted above, this is what remains of the general schools budget after the allocations for which the LEA takes direct responsibility have been deducted. To summarise briefly, these deductions cover mandatory exceptions such as capital expenditure, discretionary exceptions such as peripatetic teachers, and also a contingency fund. Before the formula itself operates, the budget shares determined for each special school and unit are deducted from the aggregated budget. But no further deductions are allowed. Thus the whole of the aggregated budget has to be allocated, either to special schools and units by LEA decision, or to other schools by formula.

A formula is, by definition, specific and admitting of no exceptions or pragmatic variations; by contrast, schools are full of people and systems whose needs are not determined by simple rules. The DES guidance document makes clear that the term 'formula' may be interpreted quite widely, but it still has to consist of clear rules, and these have to be published.

However good the formula, and however fair-minded those who apply it, some schools are going to benefit from the consequent redistribution of resources and some will lose. For better or worse, part of the job of school managers will be to order those aspects of the school which are within their control so as to use the formula to their best advantage.

For those who want to be as well informed as possible, the best starting point is the report entitled *Local management of schools*, prepared for the DES by the management consultants Coopers and Lybrand. (It is free, if still available, from the DES information section at Elizabeth House.) This covers both principles and details, is highly practical and readable, and fudges only on three issues: the detailed trade-off between capital investment and revenue saving, the difficult matter of quantifying the effects of differing socio-economic factors, and the even more difficult problems of performance indicators. It does not claim to provide all the answers, particularly to what is perhaps the most difficult question of all - how to deal with non-statutory provision, especially in the integrated community school. The DES guidance document (also available free from the DES) is directed more to LEAs than to schools, but is equally valuable for detailed study. It fudges the same three issues as Coopers and Lybrand, but it does tackle some aspects of the community school problem, and this is discussed at the end of Chapter 5.

The Coopers and Lybrand report points out that anomalies are inevitable, which will make a safety net necessary to start with - and that this itself will be anomalous and difficult to phase out. The consultants' main conclusion - even after a study of the most successful LEA schemes - is that considerably more work is required on the nature of the formula. The school trying to cope with a formula worked out by its own LEA, in advance of such a development programme, must look very hard at what is being proposed. This chapter and the next offer a guide through this process.

The report notes that there are only two fundamentally different types of formula, though each may vary in its details. The first type is based on historical levels of actual or budgeted expenditure; the second is based on one or more indicators of the 'need to spend'. The report comes down firmly on the merits of the latter, and the DES guidance follows this lead. The reason is that reliance on historical factors is unfair. If two schools have similar heating arrangements, and one of them has operated its system economically while the other has not, the latter will benefit from a formula based on historical costs, not just for a year but permanently. When the formula starts to operate, the spendthrift school can economise (and spend the savings elsewhere) while the other cannot do so.

The main factor in the typical LEA formula is to be the number of pupils in each age group, with weightings chosen by the LEA for each group. These weightings will probably benefit older pupils in secondary schools, and perhaps also younger children in infant schools.

Of the smaller factors, the first will probably be some form of deprivation allowance, based perhaps on the numbers of free meals or on verbal reasoning or similar test results. (In due course, the data emerging from the assessment arrangements for the national curriculum may be used.) The numbers of free meals, however, depend on rules which vary from time to time, most recently in April 1988. It is possible that there will be an allowance for ethnic minority pupils, though the links between the actual need in this field and the possible measures of it are more tenuous than they once were. There may be an allowance for specific pupils who are the subjects of formal statements under the 1981 Act, though the LEA may take direct responsibility for these as a discretionary item. In addition to or instead of these, there may be an allowance for special needs pupils not subject to a statement.

Pupil-related data in addition to numbers and ages have long been used in some LEAs for the calculation of staffing quotas. But the process has never been straightforward: under the Act, more will depend on such calculations, and problems are to be expected.

This will be of the greatest significance in LEAs which contain schools from a wide range of average levels of deprivation. The requirement that the formula be simple will militate against the use of multiple or complex factors, to the further disadvantage of pupils who already carry the deprivation label.

The formula will include a fixed element (or something which is algebraically similar), to allow for the fact that some costs are not related by direct proportion to the size of the school. There may also be a factor related to pupil turnover. A high level of turnover (caused, for example, by the presence of a local base for armed service personnel) generates significant extra costs. A further possibility is a curriculum-related element for sixth forms, though this would be complex to administer and might be subject to misuse, if schools made decisions about the curriculum designed to maximise the formula-related benefits.

The formula may also contain, initially at least, an element related to the actual buildings occupied, taking into account their historical costs of heating, repair and maintenance, but disallowing as far as possible variations due to differing efficiencies of use. This element may be related to the floor area, fuel used, and type of structure. A further element, which if needed should be permanent, may allow for additional costs which result from the layout of the buildings, particularly those related to a split site. All of these will provide problems at LEA level, which are not relevant to the present discussion except in so far as the particular solutions chosen will determine the rules of the game - how to increase income and reduce costs - which is to follow.

All of these items, other than the basic element of age-weighted numbers of pupils, are to be kept to a minimum. The DES guidance document lays down that not less than 75% of the aggregated schools budget (after deducting the shares of special schools) must be allocated by the formula on a basis of pupil numbers. For LEAs with areas of high levels of deprivation, this may be difficult.

As already noted, no formula can take into account all the ways in which the needs of schools differ. But three matters which are significant in cost terms may be worth a mention at this point.

Calculating the costs

1 Some of the costs related to educational disadvantage, including pupils with special needs, may be different from those allowed for

- probably greater. As is well known, class sizes in schools with a high level of disadvantage need to be smaller, more specialist support is required, and pastoral care time per pupil is greater. This is in part offset by savings because fewer public examinations are taken by this group of pupils. How all this balances out will depend too much on local factors to be considered in any detail here. But it is almost certain that those pupils near the end of the scale of disadvantage (while falling short of being subject to a formal statement) will not benefit the school's balance sheet. Whether this is a desirable line of argument may well be questioned, but when so much is to depend on that balance sheet it cannot be ignored. These matters may well be among the most difficult to resolve, not just technically but because of the moral and ethical implications.

2 Some costs related to buildings may be very difficult to handle fairly. To take an example, the biggest single item (excluding staff costs) in the routine running expenses of a secondary school is probably that of the swimming pool - something that not all schools have, which makes it even more difficult to cost fairly. It is expensive in water charges, in heating costs, in rates, and in the maintenance of both the pool itself, its associated equipment, and the building containing it. It may develop faults, and be out of use as a result (perhaps generating consequential costs for pupils displaced). It may be shared with other schools (involving transport and supervision costs), or be used by outside groups. Not only is the equitable costing of all this likely to be difficult - it also provides an excellent illustration of the administrative costs (both for schools and LEA) which can arise under local management, concerning matters which previously no-one had to do much about except pay the bills. No doubt a greater awareness of the true costs of provision will be advantageous - but a very real extra cost is incurred in the process, for which direct additional resources are unlikely, in most cases, to be available.

3 The actual state of furniture and equipment in schools will vary, perhaps quite widely, at the time of the handover. A newly-opened school is likely to need less in the following few years than one 20 years old whose original furniture is wearing out. Also, the LEA may have partly completed a programme of installing technology rooms or computer suites, and some schools would therefore lose out if the programme was, in effect, halted.

The implementation schedule for the scheme

The consultation paper issued in July 1987 asked LEAs to submit proposals to the Secretary of State by September 1989, and this was confirmed in the guidance document. The Act requires that the scheme should start at the beginning of a financial year, and the Secretary of State has decided that implementation should commence in April 1990. A scheme may allow implementation to be phased over three years, so that the last group of schools must commence in 1993. The Secretary of State may extend the phasing-in period by order, and will probably come under some pressure to do so.

Each LEA is required to consult the head teachers and governing bodies of all schools before preparing its scheme. The guidance document sets out the information about the scheme which has to be submitted to the Secretary of State for approval, and this has to state the schools to be included and their place in the phasing-in sequence.

In addition to the phasing in, there is to be a transitional period before a needs-related formula is fully implemented. This will allow both for the weightings in the formula to be fine-tuned and for the change from the existing system to be made in stages. Schools are only able to respond slowly to a cut in resources (whatever the reason), and a formula-related cut of even two or three per cent would be difficult to manage in one year. Any simultaneous cut as a result of falling pupil numbers would make the problem worse, and for a few schools as long as five years might be needed. But, as already noted, the transition has to take place within three years of the entry into the scheme of the last group of schools to have mandatory delegation.

The phasing in may only be by schools. Phasing by heads of expenditure is expressly ruled out, because LEAs might leave the delegation of the staffing budget, the most important item of all, to the last. There are special rules specifying how new schools are to be brought into the scheme, to which direct reference should be made if required.

In the financial years 1988-89 and 1989-90, the LEA has to provide the governing body of every school with an itemised statement of expenditure for the school for that year. The statement does not have to be issued in advance (though from 1990-91 onwards the budget shares must be notified before the start of the financial year), merely at some time during the year. It must contain itemised information about the expenditure on the school, whether incurred already or budgeted for the year. This requirement is similar to that already in force by virtue of the 1986 Act, and it continues, for schools without delegated powers, after the scheme starts.

The local management of staffing costs

Since staff salaries and related expenditure cover such a high proportion of a school's running costs, this part of the local management scheme is of critical importance. The details as set out in the Act are quite simple, and are described in the remaining sections of this chapter. They allow governors who have delegated powers almost complete freedom to appoint and dismiss staff as they choose, under rules which differ slightly between aided schools and the rest. The resulting costs, including the employer's contribution to superannuation and National Insurance, and the direct costs of the appointing process (advertising, interview expenses, and relocation allowances if paid), come from the school's budget share.

These requirements do not cover long-term supply appointments, staff whose salaries are supported by central government grants, or staff appointed solely for the provision of school meals or midday supervision, for which in all cases the costs are the direct responsibility of the LEA (unless the LEA, in the case of school meals, uses its discretion to delegate). Where staff work at more than one school (as, for example, in the case of peripatetic music teachers), an appropriate proportion of the cost is met from the budget share, unless it is designated as a discretionary exception in the LEA's scheme. Costs arising from dismissal or premature retirement, and the costs of negotiated agreements leading to resignations, are met (provided governors have acted reasonably) by the LEA. When shared staff are 'dismissed' by the governors of one of the schools involved, the problem has to be picked up by the LEA.

Simple in outline the new system may be, but the reality will be very much more complex. The cost to an LEA of providing staff for all its schools includes various items which are of little significance in a large budget, but which do not fall uniformly on individual schools. When these items are transferred to a school's own budget, the effect may become highly significant.

First, staff may continue to be employed even when, on a cold economic calculation, they should not be. The teacher whose training was for a subject which has lost its place in the curriculum; the teacher who is suffering from a serious or progressive disability; the teacher lacking in competence but not to the extent that requires dismissal - all these have, in most LEAs, continued to be employed in schools, often with a compensating addition to the school's staffing quota. Sometimes such teachers have had to transfer schools; only the power to allocate resources flexibly between schools has made this possible, and under local management the power no longer exists. The resulting burden on a school (particularly a small school) may be considerable.

Second, requirements for short-term supply cover do not fall evenly between schools. For a small school, a run of minor ailments may have serious consequences.

Third, it has been normal to specify a school's quota of teaching staff without reference to the actual salary cost. Thus a school has been allowed a particular number of main professional grade teachers, without reference to the points on the salary scale of each one. Under local management this will no longer be so, and it will be advantageous (other things being equal) to appoint someone at the low end of the range. It will also be necessary to allow for the future costs of annual increments, for all staff not at the top of their particular scales. (There will, of course, be an increase to correspond with nationally negotiated salary rises; but whether the formulae used will be accurate enough to ensure a close match, bearing in mind that schools will spend different proportions of their income on staff salaries, remains to be seen.) For non-teaching staff, similar considerations will apply, and the complexity and unfamiliarity of the various salary structures will cause further problems.

Fourth, negotiations about conditions of employment will increasingly have to be carried out at school level, particularly in respect of non-teaching staff, because of the greater flexibility of their salary scales. This could have a variety of consequences, not least because most school managers will not be familiar with the legislative background. For example, an employee may request a salary upgrading, on grounds of comparability with others doing similar work - a likely growth area in any event, since it is a tactic considerably under-used by the various unions. Investigation of the case will be time-consuming, and if the employee is successful, as he usually will be, the extra costs will have to be met from the school's budget share. In respect of teachers' salaries, the 1988 percentage limits on the payment of incentive allowances may be cancelled as being inconsistent with the principles of the delegation scheme, and this would no doubt increase the pressures from teaching staff.

The ultimate stage of this process - an industrial tribunal - is for practical purposes beyond the capability of a school, other than with full LEA support. This is because of the time-consuming nature of the procedure, not just because of the cost of any award made. The bland assumption that governors would take on this responsibility when necessary, which was made in the DES information booklet about the Act and repeated in the guidance document, should be dismissed at once.

Finally, and in the long run perhaps most importantly, the LEA will not be able to take mitigating action when problems arise, at least to the same extent as in the past. No longer can a teacher be transferred when surplus to requirements, other than by agreement with the governors of the school to which he goes; no longer will an education officer be able to deploy resources to meet a specific and exceptional staffing need, at least to the same extent as of old. It may be that schools have not thought very much about such things in the past, but they may well do so when they discover that these powers no longer exist.

In the light of these various constraints, it is essential for school managers to prepare carefully for the introduction of this aspect of local management, representing as it does some four-fifths of the total costs covered by the school's budget share. It will prove to be a serious and costly error if, through a failure to use the flexibility which is available during the lead-in period, a school is left with salary commitments which it cannot afford under local management, and which it no longer has the ability to off-load. This exercise is considered in detail in the next two chapters.

One further implication of the Act's provisions about staff appointments requires a mention. In summary, the Act gives power to governors while leaving (in non-aided schools) the legal responsibilities firmly with the Authority. This may not matter too much when all goes well - after all, it is only a small step beyond the previous system as it applied to most staff in aided schools. But when problems arise, and a teacher is dismissed by governors or civil action is taken in the courts, the LEA is left to take full responsibility even though it was not involved in the appointment of the person concerned. Thus the governors have the rights of an employer, while the LEA has the responsibilities of an employer.

There is a clause tucked away at the end of the Act which allows the Secretary of State to reconcile the legal consequences of this anomaly; it may prove inadequate for such a purpose.

The appointment of staff in non-aided schools with delegated powers

In all schools with delegated powers, governors have an almost unrestricted right to specify a post which is to be funded from the school's budget share, advertise it, short-list, interview and appoint as they choose. The process is, of course, subject to general statutory and contractual requirements relating to non-discrimination, conditions of service, periods of notice and so on. Governors will also need to use the nationally agreed salary scales, and to keep in mind the balance between the salary levels of the various posts in the school. In relation to all their delegated powers including those concerned with appointments, governors cannot be held personally liable provided they have acted reasonably.

All this contrasts sharply with the situation in schools without delegated powers, in which responsibilities for staffing matters remain as they were before the Act. In non-aided schools, in particular, the LEA retains the right to appoint a redeployed teacher against the wishes of the head teacher and governors.

The provisions in the first paragraph above apply to all schools with delegated powers, both aided and non-aided. From this point onwards, however, the rules differ. The details relating to aided schools are covered in the next section.

When a teaching appointment funded by the school is intended, or is likely, not to be for a period of more than four months, governors (or, in practice, head teachers using powers delegated to them) may without any advertisement or interview recommend a person to the LEA for appointment. (LEA rules will probably be framed in such a way as to make the ratification stage a formality for temporary appointments, so that heads can give confirmation on the spot to the teacher concerned.) This provision is designed to allow heads to respond quickly when short-term vacancies arise, where such appointments are within the delegation scheme. If the costs are to be paid by the LEA, however, any authorisation for governors or heads to make direct appointments must be derived from the LEA's own rules, since the Act only provides for governors to spend out of the budget share, not from general LEA funds.

Other than for appointments of four months' duration or less, governors must inform the LEA when a prospective vacancy for a teacher becomes known, and must provide a copy of the specification for the post, before placing an advertisement. (Except in relation to a headship vacancy, the responsibility of governors in such matters is likely to be delegated to the head teacher.) Coverage of the advertising must include employees of the LEA, most obviously through the LEA's own bulletin. For a headship or deputy headship, national advertisement is mandatory. If a headship appointment cannot be arranged to commence immediately after the departure of the previous head, the governors must appoint an acting head; if this happens in relation to a deputy headship (or if a vacancy results from an acting headship appointment), governors have the option to appoint an acting deputy.

For a post other than head or deputy, the LEA may nominate one or more candidates for the vacancy, and governors are required to give consideration to such nominations. If governors decide to appoint one of the teachers so nominated, or if they decide to appoint from within existing staff, no advertisement is required. The latter point is a significant change from previous practice, which frequently required, to the embarrassment of all concerned, an advertisement and interview when there was a clear intention all along to appoint from within the school.

The Chief Education Officer or his nominee has the right to be informed of all actions taken relating to the appointment of a teacher in a non-aided school, from the notification of the vacancy to the final interview. He may attend all meetings, and give advice on every stage of the process. This remains so if responsibility is delegated, as it may be, to a sub-committee; the sub-committee has to number at least three for head or deputy appointments but is without restriction otherwise. The same applies if the delegation is to the head teacher, as it may be in any appointment other than those of head or deputy.

In respect of appointments below that of deputy head, the CEO's representative must give advice if so requested, but governors must still give consideration to advice given without a request. This should not normally cause any difficulty - the advice does not have to be followed, and anyhow most governing bodies have in the past come to value it highly. But if governors had rejected the advice out of hand (and particularly if the advice had been expressed in strong terms), a court might well decide that the legal protection afforded to governors who have acted reasonably did not apply.

The head teacher has a similar right to be involved at all stages of the appointment process, in every case other than the appointment of his successor, and his advice must similarly be given due consideration.

When governors, or those acting with delegated powers on their behalf, recommend a person for appointment, the Authority is required to make the appointment unless it is not satisfied that he meets any staff qualification requirements which apply. These requirements are couched in very broad terms: they relate to academic or other qualifications, health, physical capacity, and fitness 'on educational grounds or in any other respect'. (Similar powers were given to LEAs in the 1980 Act, and have rarely been invoked; under the new Act, however, the potential for disagreement is higher.)

In addition, the head teacher and governors both have the general obligation under the Act to exercise their functions with a view to securing that the national curriculum is followed. If either makes an appointment which unquestionably contravenes this, it may be possible for the LEA (which has the same obligation, in respect of maintained schools) to obtain a court ruling that it is ultra vires and void. Alternatively, either head or governors could take action against each other. Clearly it must be hoped that such things will never happen, but the Act allows plenty of scope for them.

When an appointment is not confirmed by the LEA, it causes embarrassment, delay, inconvenience and a loss of goodwill, and so it is in everyone's interests to prevent this from happening. Part of the reason for the involvement of the CEO's representative is to enable him to give informal warning that a particular nominee might not be acceptable, and so obviate the ill effects. There is a direct link, in that the officer attending would normally be the person who recommended that formal action by the LEA was desirable. As usual, the quality of professional co-operation will be the determining factor, for all but exceptional cases, with the Act's full powers kept in the background.

Under pressures resulting mainly from falling rolls, many LEAs have in recent years developed a system for restricting the freedom of schools to make appointments when vacancies arise. Typically, appointments to promoted posts have been restricted to those already employed in the LEA, and schools have been required to appoint a redeployed teacher when there was one available. These arrangements have never covered aided schools, though governing bodies of many such schools have co-operated voluntarily in LEA schemes. Under the Act, an LEA can no longer operate in this way: it may ask governors of non-aided schools to consider nominations for posts below deputy head, but no more. No doubt a voluntary scheme will be attempted where appropriate, and, with the traditional level of goodwill and high professional standards, this may well achieve some success. Nevertheless, the system has lost a valuable element of flexibility.

For the appointment of non-teaching staff, the requirements are much simpler. If the post involves work at the school for more than 16 hours per week, the CEO (in practice the designated staffing officer) must be consulted. There are no requirements about advertisement or interview, and the governing body merely has to recommend a person for appointment by the LEA in writing, giving full details. Where the LEA has regulations governing the pay and conditions for the type of post involved, or alternatively where the post is entirely outside their regulations, the governors may only make recommendations about the appropriate point on the scale, and the LEA may at its discretion override these. It is clearly desirable for the LEA to have clear policies on the matter, in order to avoid clashes of this kind.

The job specification, advertising procedure, short-listing and interview process may be carried out in any manner (consistent with general employment legislation) which the governors think fit. But it is to be hoped that in practice officers of the LEA will be involved in more than just a formal manner. At the very least, their local knowledge may help to avoid the occasional serious error; rather more often, their specialist knowledge of personnel matters will be valuable as it frequently has been in the past.

The Act makes specific reference to the appointment of the clerk to the governors of non-aided schools with delegated powers. For this, governors are required first to consult the Chief Education Officer, and may then appoint as they choose. No mention is made of the existing practice, common to many LEAs, in which the CEO himself, acting through a nominated representative, is the clerk. Clearly there is no reason why this should not continue; equally, there is no reason why governors should not appoint their own clerk, unless the school's articles of government preclude this. One factor will be the mechanism by which the clerk's salary and expenses are met: should these be covered by the LEA only if the CEO remains as clerk, a change might be costly. Under the LEA's particular local management scheme, however, costs relating to the clerking (whether incurred by an LEA officer or otherwise) may be charged against the school, and if so it would probably be advantageous for the governors to appoint their own clerk - perhaps an unpaid volunteer. However, governors used to having an LEA officer as clerk may feel that the resulting direct link with the LEA has benefits which will offset the extra cost.

The Act provides that the governors shall have responsibility for the discipline, suspension and dismissal of staff. When dismissal is envisaged, the person concerned may make representations to governors, who are required to consider them. Governors must also, before they formally notify the LEA of their decision, allow the person to appeal against it. Governors are also required to establish, and to publish within the school, a statement of the disciplinary rules and procedures of the school, and must make provision for the redress of grievances related to the employment of staff.

As all involved in personnel matters are well aware, matters which might involve the possibility of dismissal require a full knowledge of general employment legislation, sometimes including case law, and very extensive consultation. Whatever the wording of this Act, therefore, any governor or head teacher contemplating such action should seek advice from the LEA. The only exception to this general rule, in the current context, is that a governing body wishing to change from having the CEO as clerk to appointing its own will probably be able to negotiate such a change without great difficulty, if the school's articles of government allow it.

At the risk of stating the point too often, it should be added that good professional relationships will ease matters all round, particularly when things are in danger of going wrong. A high proportion of the problems arising at the level of the individual school are the results of bad appointments: time spent in ensuring that such problems are avoided, within the limits of human fallibility, is time well spent. The point is given further emphasis by the fact that, if things do go wrong, the main responsibility for putting matters to rights will lie with the governors, not with the LEA and its greater resources, experience, and ready access to legal advice.

The appointment of staff in aided schools with delegated powers

In aided schools, most of the above rules do not apply, and staffing matters are governed by the simple statement that a governing body with delegated powers shall have the power 'to appoint, suspend and dismiss staff as they think fit'. When an employee of the governors is dismissed, governors merely have to inform the LEA of the reasons for the dismissal; but LEA employees dismissed from aided schools are subject to the rules outlined in the section above on non-aided schools. Where aided schools do not have delegated powers, matters remain as they were before the Act.

Aided schools are not subject to any new rules concerning the appointment process, except that an officer of the Authority may have the right to attend meetings and to advise governors, subject to an agreement between the governors and the LEA about the details. Such an agreement may cover appointments, dismissals or both, and may refer to any specified types of appointment such as a headship or deputy headship, or to all promoted posts or all main grade posts. If such an agreement cannot be reached, the Secretary of State may impose one on the two parties, but in practice mutual co-operation on such matters will probably continue to be the norm.

Chapter 5 Local Management: implementation

Preparing the ground for implementation

The local management provisions of the Act require the LEA initially to work out, and to make known to those involved, the true cost of running each school (including capital expenditure allocated to the school for a particular year). This was, in outline, built into the 1986 Act, and schools should therefore have some experience of it already. It is the first stage of a process of which the ultimate aim, at least in the minds of some, is to run each school like a business. As with any business, it is intended that the inputs and outputs will be costed, and that decision making will be based on cost-effectiveness in parallel with purely educational considerations.

At this stage, however, all that is being attempted is a first look at the financial aspects of the scheme as a whole - that is, leaving the management implications (and the problems) until later. What is required, for the present, is an understanding that actual costings, current and committed, will from now on play a central part in the management process. This represents a major change, and so planning for it should start as early as possible. There is no reason to wait until the local management implementation date for the school is determined, or even until the details of the LEA's own scheme are known.

This exercise may best start by looking at the full costs of running the school for the current year, without too much attention to accuracy or detail at this stage. Where VAT is involved, it should be ignored for the present. (In the actual scheme, VAT will be reclaimed by the LEA and credited to each school, so the relevant amounts are the VAT-exclusive figures throughout.) The checklist below omits those items which have clear boundaries and which are outside the local management scheme: capital expenditure and loan charges, central LEA services, and pupil transport. Some items likely to be outside the scheme, however, are included where the boundaries are not so clear: in such cases there may be scope for moving the boundary line, in such a way as to improve the school's own balance sheet.

Annual running costs - a checklist

These figures should be known, for completed financial years starting in 1986-87, as a result of the provisions of the 1986 Act. However, it is most unlikely that the detail is all there. Some figures may well not be accurate: the salary of a teacher working at more than one school, for example, may not be divided pro rata, and costs for schools in the same building with a common heating system may not be accurate. There may well be errors, which have passed unnoticed because there has been no way of checking the figures.

1 Salaries - teachers

For all salaries, allow about 15% extra for the employer's contributions to superannuation and National Insurance. The items marked with an asterisk may not be costed against the school's budget share, or at least not completely so.

a Permanent teachers, who will be paid from the school's budget share, who are currently at the top of their salary scales and are not in any of the categories below.

b As *a* above, but below the top of their scales and so qualifying for an increment next year. This is separated from the category above in order to make it easier to allow for these increments - an effect known as incremental drift.

c* As *a* or *b* above, but supernumerary or on protected salaries, so that some or all of their salary costs may in the future not be paid from the school's budget share.

d Teachers on temporary contracts with the school (who may or may not have a permanent contract with the Authority).

e* Long-term supply teachers, whose salaries will be paid by the LEA, not the school. These should be defined in the LEA scheme; if this is not yet published, count those who remain in post for four or more weeks. (It is also important to note whether the LEA pays for these four weeks, or only from the fifth week onwards.)

f Short-term supply teachers.

g* Teachers not based at the school but with a timetabled commitment (eg peripatetic music teachers).

h* Teachers funded, wholly or partly, by central government grants (eg TVEI and Education Support Grant teachers, teachers funded under section 11 of the Local Government Act 1966).

i* Teachers appointed to meet specific needs of statemented pupils.

j Teachers (or those with comparable professional status) not responsible for teaching school-age pupils (eg community and adult education professional staff).

k Fees paid to other institutions to cover the costs (mainly salaries) of instruction given within that institution to pupils from the school.

2 Salaries and wages - non-teaching staff

At a later stage, it will be necessary to allow for an increase in administrative staff costs, on account of the additional work load in the school caused by local management itself.

a Permanent staff, paid from the LEA aggregated budget, who are currently at the top of their salary scales and are not in any of the categories below; include all maintenance staff.

b As *a* above, but below the top of their scales and so qualifying for an increment next year.

c Temporary contract staff, including foreign language assistants.

d* Supply cover staff.

e* Staff funded wholly or partly from central government grants (eg TVEI support staff).

f* Staff appointed to meet specific needs of statemented pupils.

g* Staff with responsibilities not directly related to school-age pupils (eg community staff or youth leaders).

h* School meals and midday supervision staff. These are likely to be outside most LEA schemes, initially at least, and it may not be worth looking at costs at this stage.

3 Buildings and grounds (school)

For this purpose, the school should be defined as that part of the whole organisation whose function is the education of school-age pupils. This will in some cases be difficult, and the whole matter of community schools is considered in the last section of this chapter. Some parts of the buildings may be shared with other organisations, for example the school library if it doubles as part of the public library service. The costs of some parts, for example the swimming pool, may need to be shared with other schools or organisations, in a manner which will have to be more tightly costed than in the past.

a   Rates.

b   Maintenance - necessitated by wear and tear.

c   Maintenance - necessitated by vandalism.

d   External decoration.

e   Internal decoration.

f   Maintenance - planned maintainance of heating equipment, swimming pool machinery, PE equipment etc; window-cleaning.

g   Heating and lighting.

h   Water charges, swimming pool and other.

i   Cleaning equipment and materials.

j   Insurance, excluding LEA responsibilities. (This may need to be re-examined when delegation starts.)

4* Buildings and grounds (community and other non-school)

This covers the same areas as section 3 above. Many items will be shared, since this is part of the reason for having community schools; again, the actual division of costs will be important under local management even if it was not in the past.

5 Running costs related to the teaching of school-age pupils

a   Textbooks, computer software, audio-visual materials.

b   Exercise books, paper.

c   Printing, photocopying.

d   Materials to support teaching (expendable).

e   Field trips and other essential curricular activities outside the school.

f   Fees for, and expenses of, external examinations.

g   School library: books, periodicals and other materials.

h   Careers support, funded by the school: books, leaflets and other materials.

i   Materials specified for the support of statemented pupils.

j   Protective clothing, laundry.

6 Running costs related to school administration

a   Stationery, printing, duplicating, photocopying.

b   Postage and telephone charges.

c   Repairs, maintenance and replacement of office equipment.

d   Hospitality.

7 Running costs related to other activities

a   In-service training of teachers (where met or supported from the school's budget share).

b   In-service training of other staff (where met or supported from the school's budget share).

c   Vehicles: tax and insurance, running costs, maintenance and repairs.

d   Travelling expenses.

e   Advertisements for staff, interview expenses, relocation expenses if applicable.

f   Non-expendable equipment and materials to support teaching, and their repair and maintenance.

g   Furniture, routine replacement.

h   School trips and visits, other than in 5*e* above; Duke of Edinburgh's Award scheme.

*i**   Running costs of non-school activities: adult education, youth work or community.

j* Running costs of school meals provision, including equipment replacement. (See note at 2*h* above.)

8 Special projects

Include under this heading anything of a special or non-recurring nature, such as a locally-funded improvement to the buildings, a major purchase of equipment or the replacement of a minibus.

Income other than from the school's budget share

To offset some of these costs, the school will have an income from various sources, in addition to the major amount which the LEA provides. The sources and amounts will mostly be well known, in contrast with some of the costs. But some care will be needed with income from lettings - a key factor in local management. Use of the premises by the LEA for activities organised by LEA staff should be allowed for, because governors will be able to charge for this. Also, allowance may be made for income arising from charges to parents as permitted under the Act, which are outlined in Chapter 11.

In many cases the various items in the expenditure list will provide a checklist, as the income will be related directly to a particular category of expenditure. While thinking about these sources of income, it will be helpful to look at other possible sources: when local management is fully implemented, increasing the school's income will be as important as reducing unproductive expenditure.

Note that there is no mention of extra-district charges. The DES guidance document is not very clear on the matter, but the arrangements are likely to be as follows. Where pupils travel across LEA boundaries, the recharge process will be carried out between the two LEAs, and the school's only involvement will be to inform the LEA of the details of the pupils concerned. The formula which allocates funds to the school will not distinguish extra-district pupils from the rest.

A first look at the costings

Salaries

It is not difficult to guess some readers' reactions to the checklist above, for this is not a field in which all teachers and governors will feel at home. Many items will be known about only vaguely; many will not be separately costed (even by the LEA); many offer plenty of scope for argument about who pays; at least one (rates) may be unexpected. However, allowing that the need at this stage is only for some very rough estimates, the principal conclusion so far is that the complexity of the list is a measure of the size of the problem which local management presents.

The first section, covering teachers' salaries, takes up the major part (typically about two-thirds) of the total. It includes long-term commitments, some of which may not match well with the school's long-term needs, either because the specialisms of the teachers concerned do not fit in with current needs or simply because the person's level of competence is low. Commitments to employing staff are for most practical purposes as inescapable as those related to buildings, and so it is important to know very precisely what they are. Many a secondary head teacher, faced with 25% falling rolls over four years, would have been able to maintain the quality of the education offered in the school with 25% fewer teachers - but only if he had been allowed to choose the 25%. Invariably he was not, and the actual losses due to redeployment or chance were for the most part not the ones needed. As local management is introduced (with or without some fall in the nominal roll), the details will be different, but the underlying problem is the same.

It is mainly for this reason that the salaries sections of the checklist are split up into what may seem to be several closely similar categories. In accepting delegated powers under local management, school managers should not, where they have any choice in the matter, take on any commitment when it is not in the school's interests to do so. The levels of commitment related to staff employment vary, in ways which as far as possible correspond with the subdivisions above. Though it is clearly necessary to separate teachers from non-teachers, the comments below relate to both together.

The first two categories will probably account for the majority of staff, and therefore for most of the costs also. This underlines the need to take advantage of any flexibility which remains.

The reasons why a particular teacher (or, less frequently, non-teacher) is not counted, or not counted in full, against the school's staffing quota may well be somewhat obscure. A long time may have passed, or the head teacher who agreed to the arrangement may have left, with nothing on file to show the details. But if there are any such protected posts in the school, it is vital to establish the facts clearly before local management begins. It is very proper that an LEA, as a good employer, should offer a job in another school to an existing employee who has experienced problems, by an agreement with the receiving school which may allow that he does not count fully against the quota. But such matters are easier to deal with in a quota calculation than in an audited balance sheet. There is a danger that the school will be left paying the full salary cost.

The same may apply in respect of the protected salary levels of employees who have lost their original posts as a result of reorganisation of some kind. (Head and deputy posts are also protected for individuals when a school's group size falls, though LEAs may not accept that this qualifies.) Again, the facts should be clearly established, so that the extra costs continue to be paid by the LEA, and not from the school's budget share.

Questions relating to the contracts of some staff may be among the most difficult, as educational and personal considerations interact with legal and financial criteria. The balance between conflicting pressures must of course be left to the professional judgement of those involved: the discussion which follows is mainly concerned with legal and financial considerations, but that is not to imply that other aspects are less important.

The aim must be to ensure that the commitments which are accepted at the start of local management are known long-term requirements. Where an employee does not have a permanent contract at the school, it may be desirable not to act (even by default) in such a way as to create one. For example, there may be teachers on the staff who have LEA-related rather than school-related contracts, because at the time of their initial appointment the LEA wanted to be able to move them from school to school during a period of falling rolls. If the school will need every such teacher for the forseeable future, all well and good - but if not, it may be wise to ask the LEA to take over the commitment.

More commonly, an employee may have a short-term contract which is liable to become permanent, simply through the passage of time. Most of these teachers do an excellent job and meet a continuing need - but the rare one who does not will be even more of a problem under local management than in the past, if the salary becomes a permanent drain on the school's budget share. It would be most unwise to rely on the Act's provisions for dismissing staff, because of the extensive safeguards built into general employment legislation.

The legal position is that an employee has security of tenure after two years in post; part-timers have a longer time pro rata. But a post held in another school in the same Authority counts towards this time, if it terminated immediately before the current post began. Various devices have been tried with a view to circumventing these rules, but the courts have tended to disallow them when this intention was transparent. Even when no formal security exists, dismissal from a post which is then filled by the appointment of someone else on the same scale may well be open to question. When any short-term appointment is made, therefore, it is vital to record formally the conditions on which it will terminate, most commonly the return to duty of the person being replaced. But even then the temporary post may become permanent by default, should the person not return.

The management problems related to supply teachers and other staff are rather different. These teachers (they mostly are teachers) are required during a period in which the usual teacher is still being paid, and so the question of who foots the bill becomes vitally important. For sickness cover, the impact on schools is uneven and unpredictable, which may produce problems for the small school.

The general strategy is clear enough: get the particular absence counted as long-term if possible, so that the LEA pays; and if the school is to pay, keep cover to the minimum acceptable to all concerned. The principal factors here are the rules for cover set out in the conditions of service for teachers, in which teachers (other than supply teachers or those with less than a 75% teaching commitment) are required to cover only for the first two days of an unpredicted absence. But, given a high level of goodwill between teaching staff and management, a more flexible arrangement can be worked out to the benefit of everyone involved, particularly if the school's agreed procedures allow a 'bank' of permitted but unused days to be built up.

The day-to-day details will evidently be difficult. Whether a teacher off sick for three weeks will be quietly invited to take another week off so that the LEA pays; whether teachers will not always insist on the full amount of cover allowed so as to leave more money for books - questions like these will be resolved at school level, not by rules from on high.

According to the scheme, teachers not based at a school but with a timetabled commitment there count against the budget share. What actually happens may not be as simple as that, and the best tactics will clearly be to acquire as much time as possible from teachers paid centrally, such as LEA support staff.

Since expenditure met through central government grant does not come out of the budget share, it is worth attracting such money to the school. Although the grant itself will probably cover only 70% or 50% of the cost, the remainder will be a charge on the LEA rather than the school. But there are dangers in the longer term: the grant is likely to be only for a limited period, and the commitment may not end with it because the employee has security of tenure. Even if there is no commitment to employ the people concerned, the work they have done may need to be carried on. This example illustrates the long-term planning which local management will require.

Problems related to the staff of the fully-integrated community school are covered in the last section of this chapter.

Buildings and grounds

It will clearly not be easy to separate LEA responsibilities relating to buildings from those of the governors; the interests of other users such as community groups will complicate matters still further. As a general guide, it has been suggested that the relationship is analogous to that between landlord and tenant, and this has some merit. But it has limitations also, and in any event the legal problems relating to tenancy are notorious. As has been the case in the past in respect of this matter in aided schools, an approach based on good personal relationships, with informal negotiation concerned more with the general principles than the fine detail, will best meet the need.

The matter of rates will be important, even though in the past it has only been of interest to those involved in recharging the amount from the education budget into the central rates fund. It is to be included in the delegation scheme, even though the Coopers and Lybrand report recommended exclusion on the grounds that the school has no control over it. Thus the school's budget will have to allow for possible future increases; under the new Uniform Business Rate these may not be as great as some of those in the past, but this may prove an optimistic forecast.

Sometimes the rateable value may need to be questioned, since rules for carrying out valuations of school premises are not always clear and unambiguous. When the result was only of interest as a book transfer, anomalies were not of much significance; under local management they will be. Also, rates may still be levied on parts of the buildings which are not in use, and this also will matter more than in the past. It may be beneficial to take little-used parts of the school buildings formally out of use, and to seek a corresponding reduction in the rateable value.

Most other running costs related to sites and buildings are straightforward in principle, though with plenty of scope for argument over details. Major structural matters such as roof repairs will be an LEA responsibility, and pressure may be needed to ensure that they are done. Conversely, neglected minor repairs which are the responsibility of governors may become major problems, and the LEA may bring pressure on governors to ensure that standards of maintenance are high. The same applies to routine maintenance of heating systems. (If standards have not been high in the past, the debate should be interesting.)

Once again, all that is needed at this stage is a rough idea of the scale of the costs in the various categories. Preparing for the transfer of responsibilities is covered in more detail in the next chapter.

Running costs

This is the area most familiar to school managers, and to that extent requires little comment. But few would claim, even in the most generous LEAs, that capitation allowances have in recent years been sufficient to meet their school's reasonable needs. In particular, allowances for increased examination costs have rarely been sufficient - a large item, and likely to become a still higher proportion in the future. Hence one of the principal objectives of school managers as they implement the local management scheme must be to arrange the school's affairs so that increased expenditure in this area becomes possible. Indeed, such a possibility is one of the main reasons for commending the introduction of local management.

Penny-pinching has been so much a part of the routine that a significant reappraisal is needed here. Perhaps an objective of doubling the amount under this budget head would not be too high. The danger for schools is that of having too many major commitments in staff and buildings to allow the necessary flexibility in running expenses. The business of assessing these major commitments, and reducing them where appropriate at the earliest possible stage, is thus (in the literal sense) vital, for the school's financial health in subsequent years will depend largely upon it.

A checklist for action

Perhaps the clearest of all the lessons learnt from those LEAs already operating a local management system is that a complete and accurate information base is fundamentally important. Without it, confusion or worse is inevitable, as for example in the case of the school in Peterborough which found it had a £25 000 credit balance in its salaries account, and had no idea why.

It is the salaries bill, as the largest item by far, that most of all needs to be accurate. To those not involved directly, it may be surprising to find that such a simple matter could be other than accurate; to anyone with experience of the little sources of confusion about it which grow and multiply, it will be no surprise at all. So there is no better place to start than to attempt to balance the salary figures given in the latest LEA statement to governors (as required under the 1986 Act) against the actual salary costs for the financial year in question. This may be an easy or a difficult exercise, depending on the size of the school, the number of staff changes, the quality of the LEA documentation, and the number of difficult cases.

At the very least, the LEA detail should include the names of those whose salaries have been counted, together with (in the case of those not teaching full time at the school) an indication of the proportion of salary included for each. The standard extras (employer's contributions to superannuation and National Insurance) should be available as a separate total. Much better would be a full list, showing salary scales, actual salaries or points on the scale, a fraction showing the multiplier for part-timers, and starting or finishing dates where appropriate. Under 1986 Act arrangements, short-term supply teachers may well not be costed against the school. The full list should be requested if not available, but the LEA's own salaries files may not be coded in such a way as to enable it to be printed directly.

If all else fails, a list should be compiled from information supplied by the staff themselves, with due safeguards for confidentiality. Data for supply staff and others who have left since the start of the financial year in question will have to be worked out as accurately as possible. Of course, the results should agree (allowing for any inaccuracy in the methods of estimation) with the official LEA total. However, there are several ways in which errors may arise.

First, the actual head counts of permanent staff may differ. Teachers on secondment, long-term absence, or temporary attachment elsewhere, or those shared between schools, are the most likely causes of discrepancies. LEA salaries files have not in the past generally been linked to specific schools, other than for the purpose of directing pay slips correctly; school-related staff lists have been compiled separately, partly because they have had to allow for future commitments (resignations not yet effective, and new appointments still to be taken up), which are irrelevant for salary payment purposes.

Next, part-time teachers, peripatetic music or remedial teachers, or foreign language assistants may not be shown accurately. Staff paid partly through central government grant (for example additional manpower under TVEI, and 'section 11' teachers) may also not be counted correctly; when local management is operational, these will be excluded from the delegation scheme. Finally, supply cover - long and short term, related both to illness, secondment and in-service training - should be checked as far as possible; the timing of payment may need to be taken into account, as amounts paid by a claim procedure sometimes run a month behind the normal salary system.

It is not important at this stage that the costings are in accordance with the details of the LEA's own delegation scheme, even if these are known. All that is necessary is to understand what the figures cover and to bring to light any errors. The measure of difficulty of the exercise will provide a further indicator of the magnitude of the task as a whole.

As far as possible, the figures should be split up according to the various categories of the first two sections of the checklist on pages 77-80. This will make it easier, later on, to distinguish the permanent commitments (and those with committed growth through incremental drift) from those allowing some flexibility, so that management options can be seen most clearly.

The quality of the LEA response, both to requests for information and to suggestions that their figures are wrong, will act as another pointer. Whether it is tactically sound to attempt to clarify all the anomalies at this stage, particularly those in the school's favour, must be a matter for local decision; for one reason, it is by no means always obvious whether a particular error is in the school's favour or not. To the extent that a school's expenditure for one year will provide the baseline for next year's budget (a depressing feature of local government financial procedures generally, and a probable feature of local management initially), an item wrongly costed against the school may be advantageous.

The next stage is to go through the same exercise for as much as possible of the remainder of the checklist. Bearing in mind that the residual errors in the salary calculations will probably have been measured in thousands of pounds for a large school or hundreds even for a small one, accuracy in terms of the odd hundred pounds or two is not important. If the cost is largely beyond the school's control, as with rates, only rough figures are required at this stage. Small items, whether of conventional capitation expenditure or otherwise, can be taken together.

When all this is as complete as circumstances allow, the result provides a picture of what it actually costs (omitting capital charges and other mandatory exceptions) to run the school for a year. Balanced against it are the small sums raised locally for the school or provided through endowments, and income from lettings and fees, together with the main LEA funding.

Most probably, carrying through this exercise will not have led to any greater understanding of accounting or financial procedures - though there may well have a growing awareness of the complexity (and at times absurdity) of local government administrative systems. The principal benefit should be, quite simply, a greater understanding of what the school costs to run, and of the limited possibilities for using the flexibility which local management allows in order to increase spending in areas where it is needed. At the same time, it should have become clear that, in many respects at least, a background in accountancy is not essential in order to understand what is going on. A commonsense approach, combined with a degree of perseverance in questioning when anomalies appear, will prove enough for most purposes. As the Coopers and Lybrand report put it, school staff do not need to become accountants: the task should not be much more difficult than managing one's own bank account.

The next stage of the exercise - still before any directives arrive from the LEA - is in three distinct parts, which can be taken in any order. These are to consider the management information system required, the human resources needed to meet the new requirements, and the degree of flexibility which the new system will offer within the school.

Preparing for the new system

Management information needs

The system will need to cover all data used within the school, and the transfer of appropriate sections of it to and from the LEA. Every school will already have a system of some kind, covering at the very worst a file of basic pupil and staff information, a timetable pinned to a board in the staffroom, a box file full of copy orders, and a correspondence file for everything else. At the other end of the scale, some schools already have sophisticated computer-based systems covering a wide range of data-intensive activities. The system needed for local management will of course depend very much on the size of the school: what follows is written mainly with a secondary school in mind, but it would be wrong to conclude that smaller schools can get by with just a little alteration to their existing system. A computer-based approach is taken for granted, even in the 200-pupil primary school which is the smallest to have mandatory delegation.

The recommendation of the Coopers and Lybrand report was that each school with delegated powers should have a stand-alone microcomputer system, standard across the LEA, with data transfer either by telephone line or via a disc through the post. Whatever configuration is used, schools should be aware of the implications of the Data Protection Act. For non-aided schools, the LEA has responsibility for this, and ought to advise accordingly; in aided schools the governors have the responsibility.

The ideal requirements of a management information system can be set down as follows.

1 The system should be *fully integrated* - that is, with no technical barriers to data transfer between different aspects of the administration of the school. The pupil information file, for example, should be usable for a variety of purposes, from printing class lists to the compilation of LEA statistical data and the recording of school fund contributions. An LEA-imposed financial management package, together with a pre-existing suite of general administrative software running on a different computer, may be unavoidable at the start, but does not provide an acceptable long-term solution.

2 The system must be *compatible with the requirements of the LEA's local management scheme*. This is obvious enough, and may well be

achieved by the LEA installing a standard package of hardware and software in all schools with delegated powers. This requirement does not imply, however, that a standard package is the only way the job can be done. Most of the links between school and LEA under local management are straightforward transfers of data between files, and this can be achieved (perhaps with a little difficulty) between different computer systems. The required compatibility is between file structures, not between items of hardware or software, though some small software changes may be needed. One of the Coopers and Lybrand recommendations, incidentally, was that data transfer should be kept to a minimum (including returns to the DES), but it remains to be seen whether this is how it turns out.

3 As one aspect of the financial procedures involved, the package must be *capable of dealing with VAT* in a manner which someone without accountancy qualifications can follow. In the past this has been dealt with at LEA level, and schools have only had to keep track of capitation expenditure in VAT-exclusive form. But now the school will have to be involved.

4 The system should be *capable of expansion and modification*, to suit changing needs and to allow for optional facilities at the level of a school or department. This is closely related to the requirement for compatibility just mentioned, and is met most easily by using a package which has an industry-standard file structure such as that of dBase III, and which runs under a standard operating system such as MS-DOS.

5 The system should meet any other possible *data transfer requirements*. The most likely one concerns the administration of public examinations, with entry details going to one or more boards or examining bodies, and results coming back.

6 The system must meet all current requirements for *information storage, processing and retrieval*. In particular, it must allow for the entry and processing of commitments, such as orders placed but not yet received or paid for. The availability of historical data is also important, so that comparisons with earlier years can be made without difficulty.

7 Ideally, the package should include, for secondary schools, a

suite of *programs for constructing the timetable*; these are available but expensive, and the changeover from the conventional manual system is complex. An alternative is a program into which the completed timetable is entered as data, first for checking purposes and then to enable extracts and summaries to be printed as required.

8 Finally, the system should provide *compatibility with other information-processing applications* within the school. The three most obviously needing to be kept in mind are word-processing by teachers and pupils (on computers provided for curricular use); desk-top publishing; and database interrogation and information transfer systems such as Prestel. But computers used for management purposes should not be linked via a network to others used for teaching, in order to avoid Data Protection Act complications.

Some decisions about these matters will already have been taken in the school. Decisions about other aspects may be made independently of the school, perhaps by officials of the Local Authority whose main concern is the introduction of local management, very quickly and within existing resources. Nevertheless, overall compatibility (at least in terms of the transfer of data files) should remain the aim. Full compatibility has many other advantages, including the need for staff to be trained to use only one type of equipment and software. It is also useful to have a computer in reserve should the main administrative machine fail.

This is not the place for advice about detailed specifications, partly because schools are unlikely to have total freedom and partly because any packages mentioned would soon be out of date. At the time of writing, several systems are available which meet the requirements outlined above, and the introduction of local management is itself providing a spur for further development.

The human implications

The introduction of local management has implications for the running of a school in many ways: a changed role for heads and management teams, a need for a different kind of partnership (with the potential for conflict) between senior management and the staff as a whole, a new role for support staff, and a massive need for in-service training to make it all possible. At this part of the planning stage, the two main needs are for full preparations by the senior management team (the main purpose of these chapters as a whole) and a hard look at the new role of administrative support staff.

The idea of extending the support staff to include someone at management level is not a new one, even in maintained schools; in the private sector, of course, it has long been standard practice. The new scheme will involve both an increased workload and a higher level of responsibility than before, and at least in the context of a secondary school the creation of the post of bursar should be given high priority, unless it is clear beyond doubt that the particular local circumstances suggest an alternative approach. The idea of a bursar leads to several questions, whose answers are likely to vary according to circumstances.

1 How can such a post be funded? The question is all too obvious, and the equally obvious answer (to make do with one less teacher) full of dangers It is best not to attempt an answer in isolation, and to concentrate instead on looking at the management needs overall, in such a way as to involve the whole teaching and support staff. If all are convinced that the need is unarguable, it will be easier to allay fears on both sides: from teachers, that a job will be lost, and from administrative support staff, that their job conditions will be changed for the worse.

2 To whom should the bursar be responsible? To this, at least, the answer is clear - he should be responsible to the head teacher. The alternative, that he should be responsible directly to the governors, offers the potential for conflict, and would place a major responsibility on governors (particularly the chairman) which is clearly undesirable. However, routine reports on matters within the bursar's role would normally be submitted directly to the governors. The bursar may also act as clerk to the governors, as is common practice in independent schools.

3 What salary level should be offered for the post, and what qualifications should be required, particularly in accountancy? Some experience of accounting practice would clearly be useful, but in general the answers to these questions will vary; one factor will be the availability of applicants with appropriate background experience when the post is advertised.

4 What should the job description for the bursar include? This equally will depend to a large extent on local needs, particularly the financial arrangements for non-school use of the premises. It will depend also on the grade and status of the post. The ideal is a high

status post, at a level equal to, or a little below, that of deputy head. Whatever the formal qualifications, the bursar must have the status appropriate to, for example, handling negotiations with senior officers of the Authority. The bursar will also be responsible for the work of most other support staff in the school, and the status of the post needs to reflect this.

5 When should the appointment begin? Clearly this should be as soon as possible, because the first year of the scheme, and the preparations for it in the previous year, will be critically important. Even if an early appointment is not possible, the post should be included in the planning from the start, so that those who have carried the responsibilities during the preparation period can hand them over in an orderly way. It should not be necessary for the incoming bursar to have to create the job when he arrives, possibly upsetting the senior secretarial staff who have enjoyed the extra responsibility (as well as suffering the extra work) which the introduction of local management has brought.

6 What of the smaller school, which could not afford (and does not really need) a full-time bursar? A part-time appointment may well be possible. The LEA ought to be aware of the need, if only because the introduction of local management will be made easier by having competent and trained staff in the schools. The LEA may therefore appoint bursars to cover several small schools each. This may not be an unqualified benefit to the school: a good bursar will need to put the school's interests first when disagreements arise (as they certainly will), and an LEA-appointed bursar may not do this. Again, the point at issue is management, not just preparing a budget and paying the bills on time.

In addition to the main responsibility carried by the bursar, the work of other support staff may need to change, and salary adjustments be made accordingly. There will probably be an LEA system for dealing with such matters, which will include appropriate recognition of the use of computers and word processors. These are delicate matters, and need to be handled with care and sensitivity.

Investigating the flexibility of the new system

Local management will require extensive in-service training, particularly for heads and deputies, and also for governors. But it is most unlikely that LEAs will be able to meet these needs in full, because of the scale of the exercise and because there are too few people in a position to act as tutors. Even if a full training programme is implemented, it is unlikely to cover more than the basic rules of the scheme. The tactics - how to run a good school within the rules, through maximising income and cutting out unproductive expenditure - will have to be worked out at school level.

By far the best time for this is before the scheme starts. Look carefully at the figures from the checklists, and as a management exercise see how much flexibility they offer. If preparations for local management are well advanced, it will be possible to compare expenditure with income, with all that this implies. But it is much better to work out in advance how to respond to both of the possible situations which may arise: how to cut expenditure so as to match the expected income, or how to use most effectively an expected surplus. If the actual balance is very close, it will still be desirable to cut out unproductive expenditure, in order to allow more for responsibility allowances to teachers or for the purchase of books and equipment. But, if only to allow for the extra costs of local management itself, an excess of desired expenditure over estimated income is the most likely situation.

First look at the possibilities for increasing the school's income, as this is in general preferable to cutting costs. If the formula is known, it will need to be studied very carefully in order to use it to best advantage: this looks set to become a new and important skill required in a head teacher. Otherwise, the possible ways of increasing income will be much as they always have been (with the addition of lettings and charges to parents), and need little further comment here. A covenanted donation system, already used in some areas, may however be worth thinking about if the likely level of support is high enough, because of the tax benefits.

Since the greater part of the school's expenditure is in manpower costs, it is mainly here that the scope for economies will lie. The rest is still worth a look, particularly heating, lighting and water charges. (In Cambridgeshire it was found that tighter control of automatic flushing devices offered significant savings.) But the main task must be to ensure that every person on the payroll is fully justifying the expense of keeping him there. Clearly this should be done in a manner appropriate to a highly sensitive exercise, and even then the emphasis should be on estimating the extent of the flexibility which the school has, should the need to use it arise.

If it is felt that there are individuals who are not cost-effective, the next (still hypothetical) step is to see how best the costs falling to the school can be reduced. If a department is over-staffed, or if a teacher has skills only appropriate for teaching a subject no longer in the curriculum, is it possible to get the LEA to agree to take the responsibility centrally? Or can the person concerned be redeployed to another school, while the powers to do so (which are curtailed when the scheme is implemented) still exist? If a teacher's terms of appointment allow him to be moved from school to school, should the governors ask that the LEA take over the responsibility? Such matters are never easy to deal with; but the terms of the Act make clear that the best time for the school to deal with them is before local management is implemented.

The other tactic which may be feasible is to use services funded by the LEA. In respect of manpower costs, this principally means using for the benefit of the school the time of teachers whose salaries are met partially from central government grants. Scope for including other items depends on the terms of the LEA's own scheme.

Otherwise, the opportunities for reducing manpower costs will relate to resignations and day-to-day changes. The Act does not lay down a procedure for determining who pays for supply cover, which will be a key factor. The consultative paper suggests that the LEA should pay for long term cover (meaning a month or more), and the DES guidance document leaves the details vague. So the actual rules will vary between LEAs, and it is difficult to go into detail. But this category of costs is critical: if kept low, it will increase considerably the balance available for spending on books and equipment; if it goes over budget, there could be a serious shortage in the school's disposable income. A saving of only six per cent or so in the salaries bill will be sufficient to achieve the target suggested in the last chapter, of doubling the sum available for meeting running costs.

Local management of a community school

The extension of the local management scheme to cover the fully developed and integrated community school is more difficult than either the Act, the Coopers and Lybrand report, or the DES guidance document allow. The biggest of these schools remain open almost every day of the year, encompass a wide range of educational, recreational and sporting activities, have social facilities which include a club with licensed bar, and have an annual turnover measured in hundreds of thousands of pounds. The management of such a school is very much more complex than that required in a traditional school.

The changes resulting from the 1988 Act follow closely on to a change brought about by the 1986 Act, which became fully effective only in September 1988. In all county and maintained special schools, control of the school premises is now under the control of the governing body, other than between the start of the morning school session and the end of the afternoon session. The governors are required to exercise their control subject to the direction of the LEA, and in doing so must have regard to the desirability of allowing the premises to be available for use by members of the community served by the school. This seemingly innocuous change has in fact far-reaching implications, both for governors and for LEAs. The first result is that the income from lettings (calculated net, for a school without delegated powers) goes to the governors; but there is more to it than that.

The new Act mentions community schools only in one section. This defines a community school as one in which activities other than school activities take place on the premises, provided that all the non-school activities are under the management or control of the governing body of the school. The section allows (but does not require) an LEA delegation scheme to apply the same rules to the appointment and dismissal of staff responsible (or partly responsible) for non-school activities as apply to the school staff. In an aided community school, such staff if employed by the LEA may only be dismissed or withdrawn from the school under the same rules as those for school staff employed by the LEA.

The management system of a community school has to take other financial and fiscal matters into account, in addition to those involved in any large school. In order to avoid liability for corporation tax, the community side of the operation may find it advisable to acquire charitable status. This means that there has to be a degree of separation between the management structures of the two parts of the organisation, with the result that a governing body so constrained may be held not to have the full control which is required in order to come within the definition above. In other words, to manage a community school under the Act, governors must control non-school activities; to avoid high tax penalties, they may not control non-school activities. Whatever the means by which this dilemma is resolved, it has wide implications, not least for the appointment and conditions of service of community staff.

Further, some types of activity may require a formal separation. An LEA is not permitted (and neither is a governing body as its agent) to set up an activity whose mode of operation is primarily that of a profit-making business. Hence a bar, which quite clearly falls within this definition, must be kept entirely separate from the school as such, and the area it occupies must be leased formally from the LEA.

Also, the running expenses of some of the non-school activities do not qualify for the reclaiming of VAT, as is the case for expenditure related to educational courses. Again, the community school has itself to charge VAT on fees paid to it for non-educational activities. The boundary lines are by no means clear, and have been the subject of much negotiation between Customs and Excise, LEAs and the senior staff of community schools. This has consequences which are by no means clear at the present stage of development of the community school concept. The picture is thus fairly confused already, before further complications arise through the introduction of local management.

The DES guidance document says that delegation schemes should not in any way restrict an LEA from continuing to give directions in accordance with the provisions of the 1986 Act (as mentioned above), or from continuing to maintain existing community provision. Under the new Act, therefore, LEAs may fund community activities to whatever extent they choose. Where governors control the whole operation, the LEA may also delegate to them the management of LEA-funded community staff, provided that the requirement of separation for fiscal reasons does not prevent this.

Alternatively, if some of the non-school staff are employed other than by the LEA (for example the library service or the social services department), the day-to-day management of these staff may be kept quite separate. In both cases, extra costs will be incurred by the school in heating and lighting, and perhaps also in caretaking, cleaning and the maintenance of equipment. But, whatever the method by which this is paid for, the funding does not come within the delegation scheme.

All this presents immense problems for the LEA, both political, financial and organisational. If the LEA chooses to delegate its powers relating to non-school activities to governors, it loses direct control over the spending of funds which are politically sensitive and important; if it attempts to retain control, the whole concept of the integrated community school is set at risk. Governors and head teachers may have to wait for some time, with little opportunity to intervene, while these matters are sorted out.

Subject to the arrangements which are finally agreed, the income which the locally managed community school receives from the LEA will be in two distinct parts. First there will be the school's budget share, which is calculated by formula, mainly from data about the pupils, but also to a limited extent from the size and the heating system of the buildings. The buildings included in the calculation are only those which are used for school purposes; any used solely for non-school activities are excluded. But since the aim is to use all buildings as intensively (and thus as economically) as possible, it should be feasible to bring almost all buildings within the school into the formula calculations, thus maximising the formula income. This figure has to be made known, as a total and as a cost per pupil.

The second part is the LEA's contribution to the non-school activities, which will be determined by the LEA in any manner it chooses, and in principle does not have to be made known outside the school. The responsibility for deploying these funds may be delegated to the governing body, in much the same way as the delegation of the budget share - but with the difference that the non-school contribution is earmarked for that purpose alone. However, as noted above, objections may be made to such delegation on a point of principle.

If such delegation is granted, the degree of flexibility actually allowed to governors will be almost total. The whole rationale of the community school is that boundary lines do not exist: that the buildings and equipment are available for the use of all, that staff are deployed according to need (either on a formal basis or informally), that adults can attend ordinary daytime classes and school pupils can go to evening classes, and that the extra costs of heating, lighting and maintenance are met in any convenient manner. The two LEA incomes, together with the other sources of income from the various community activities, provide a framework within which a good bursar (even more a key person in the community school) can achieve great flexibility.

The unknown factor in all this, of course, is the size and degree of delegation of the LEA community contribution to the school. The introduction of local management generally will focus the attention of Education Committees on actual school costs, including comparative costs and costs per head. Although the LEA funding of non-school activities is formally excluded from this process, in practice it may well come under close scrutiny. When this happens, larger differences may be perceived in the scale of funding of non-school activities across an LEA than between the levels of funding of schools as such. Claims of unfairness may therefore be difficult both to avoid and to answer, and the result may be a pressure to cut back on non-school contributions. This might have little effect on a community school which was well established and with good facilities, as these two factors together should enable it to generate enough income to be viable. But a school trying to build up its community side, and with only limited facilities to offer, would find a cut in the LEA contribution a severe blow.

The strength of the concept of the integrated community school is threefold: the benefits of combining statutory education with non-statutory; the economic efficiency which results from using to the full its resources of staff, buildings and equipment; and the integration across the full range of ages of its social, cultural, recreational and sporting activities. The introduction of local management should provide a significant boost to its development, provided that the many problems at LEA level can be overcome. If so, the results will be to the benefit of all.

Chapter 6 Local Management in operation

Day-to-day management under the new scheme

Much has been written about school management in recent years, and it is not a primary task of this book to add to the list. It is nevertheless true that local management requires good management - indeed, one of the merits of a devolved system is that it encourages and rewards good management. The first part of this chapter is intended to provide some help to those who, using the freedom (and working within the constraints) of the new scheme, wish to change their management techniques in order to make real the potential benefits.

Management involves relationships in every organisation, but particularly one as labour-intensive as a school. The new scheme will place even further emphasis on this familiar theme, because it alters the basis for some existing relationships and introduces new ones. Consider first the relationship between the head and the staff as a whole - perhaps the most important single measure, as it is very rare to find a good school where this relationship is bad, or a bad school in which it is good.

When this relationship has come under strain, the immediate cause has quite often been the manner in which resources have been distributed. It is not important whether the particular decision was justified or not, or even whether the facts are accurately known: what is critical is that one teacher or more thinks that the decision was unfair. Under local management, the scope for such disagreements is very much greater, because of the wider range of resources now under management control within the institution.

Further, the decisions which cause these disagreements now involve the careers of teachers to a greater extent than in the past. When in the past an incentive allowance was awarded, the choice of the teacher to receive it might well have been questioned - but at least the process was reasonably open. Now that the options for spending a given sum of money include repairs to buildings and so forth, the possibilities for conflict and mistrust have grown considerably. So, at the same time, have the opportunities for special interests and pressure groups, who will attempt to influence management decisions for the benefit of the cause they represent. Even a strong and able management team may find that such pressures play a dominant role, if the underlying structure is not right. When pressures do arise, the complexity of the situation means that resistance will be more difficult to sustain than it was in the past.

The principles of sound management under the new scheme, therefore, should centre around good communication, openness, clear procedures for dealing with sensitive matters, and a well established management structure which ensures that policies for the distribution of resources are clearly set down and followed closely.

The management committee

Central to this process should be the management committee, whose function it is to take those management decisions which lie between the head teacher's responsibilities for the day-to-day running of the school and the matters of policy which governors reserve to themselves. The management committee may be the governing body itself; if it is not, it becomes an additional layer in the management structure, and as such requires a full justification.

First of all, then, consider the conditions necessary for the governing body itself to take on the role of management committee. In any but a very small school, it must reach decisions about priorities of a fairly detailed nature. Its members must know enough of what is going on in the school to be able to take such decisions, while retaining the general goodwill of the staff as a whole. If the governors meet just once or twice a term, mainly to endorse proposals made by the head, and are not otherwise very much involved in the normal work of the school, this condition is not met. When decisions are questioned. either the governors will be held to have acted in ignorance, or the head will be felt to have merely used the governors as a mechanism for endorsing his own decisions. Neither governors nor heads should allow this to happen. Such a system may work adequately as long as no serious problems arise; it will fail when they do, in conditions which will then make change more difficult.

Without a new tier of management, the alternative is a very full delegation of powers by governors to the head. Since these powers are so wide, they will in most cases (when added to the already very extensive executive powers held by head teachers) simply become too great for effective management. On the one hand, governors who acted in this way could be accused of delegating too much, and certainly would be if clashes arose; on the other, the head would have to take a variety of management decisions himself, and this would leave him open to serious criticism from within the staff. There has to be a buffer, and if it does nothing else the management committee performs this role.

But, once there, it should do far more, as the remainder of this section is intended to show. Before that, however, the constitution of the committee needs to be worked out.

It may be called a finance committee, but for the reasons mentioned at the start of Chapter 4 the emphasis should be on management. A title including the word 'finance' might indicate that in some way finance could be separated from educational matters, particularly if there were another group with a title such as 'curriculum committee'. In all but the smallest schools there will be other committees and working groups, but the management committee should be clearly seen as the senior.

If the management committee is not the full governing body, it may be a sub-group of governors, on its own or with the addition of members of the staff. It need not include governors at all, and in a small school it might even be the whole staff together. There are many possible arrangements, and both the size of the group and the membership will vary according to local needs.

The only unquestionable requirement is that the head teacher must have a major role. In the educational system of England and Wales the head has always had the dominant influence, and under the Act (not only this section of it) this will remain. The rights of a head teacher of an LEA school to attend and to speak at meetings of governors, and to be himself a governor if he chooses, are not changed by the Act. The nature of the influence of the head in the context of a management committee will no doubt be different, but will almost certainly not be less than it was under the old system.

In practice, although it may appear to be restricted by the introduction of a new tier of management, the power of the head is more likely to increase. It may be strengthened directly, for example by his being chairman of the management committee. Traditionally, the head has had a strong influence in meetings of governors, not only as the senior professional when others had only limited educational expertise, but as the person who knew most about the detailed background to what was being discussed. (Even those who had a similar vantage point, the teacher governors, were inhibited from using it to counter the advice being offered by the head.) Now that the head will also know far more about the new dimension in the decision-making process, the deployment of financial resources, his power base will become stronger still, both in the governing body and in the management committee. In the latter, however, the nature of the discussions will be different, because of the greater staff involvement.

The bursar (if there is one) may be a full member of the committee, or may attend its meetings as an adviser. In practice it may make little difference, just as has happened in respect of head teachers since they were given the choice to be a governor. But the matter of status is significant in this instance, and full membership may serve to underline the importance of the role. (If the management committee is the governing body, the bursar could not be a governor ex officio, and so he would have to be co-opted or, in an aided school, be appointed as a foundation governor.)

As for the remainder of the membership of the committee, and the extent of its delegated powers, the whole responsibility rests with the governors. Their decisions, made no doubt after careful advice from the head, should also make clear which powers are retained by the governing body. The principal ones are likely to be the approval of the budget, virement powers above certain limits, and the appointment of staff above stated grades. The governing body would of course retain the right to ask for reports on any aspect of the life of the school, and to cancel any of the delegations should this become necessary.

The formal position of the head teacher in relation to the management committee also needs some care. If the committee is the governing body itself, the traditional links will continue; if, at the other extreme, the committee consists solely of staff, then the head will probably also be the committee chairman. If the management committee includes both staff and governors, it is probably best for the head not to be chairman, on the basis that the governors should be seen, through their representatives, as the senior body. This arrangement would also ensure that the roles of chairman and chief executive were kept separate. If this is the procedure used, it is clearly essential that the professional relationship between the head and the chairman of the management committee should be the very best possible.

The ideal arrangement may well prove to be that the chairman of governors also chairs the management committee. It is to be expected that the change to local management will lead to new and unfamiliar situations, in which it is not immediately clear whether the responsibility for making decisions rests with governors, with the management committee, or with the head. If the chairman has the dual role, and if he has a close and effective relationship with the head, such problems should be resolved without too much difficulty. The relationships between head and bursar, and between chairman and bursar, are almost equally important.

The management committee in operation

The method of working of the management committee will vary according to local need. In particular, the timing of meetings requires some care: a daytime or late afternoon slot will help to ease the rapid calling of meetings when necessary, but governors may prefer an evening meeting.

In what follows, the tasks are set out as fully as possible, but many of them can either be retained by governors or delegated to the head, and if the latter then further delegated, where necessary, to the bursar or to other staff. However, such delegations have in the past often been a matter of custom and practice, and will need to be made more explicit as customs and practices undergo radical change.

The management committee needs first of all to know the extent and the limitations of its own powers. At least some of its members should have gone through the exercise described in Chapter 5, and should therefore know the approximate costs under each budget head, the areas in which some flexiblity is possible, and the likely pressure points. These matters should be fully discussed in the whole group, if not everyone has participated in the preliminary stages. The committee needs to look closely at the formula approved for the LEA, and at least the head and bursar (and preferably some members) should have analysed it closely in order to be able to advise on the particular problems and opportunities it is likely to present.

The management committee also needs to be aware of the current state of development of the national curriculum, and the consequent needs for change from the existing curriculum where these have resource implications, as they usually will. Similarly, it should know the current trend of admission numbers, and the consequences in terms of the probable change in the school's budget share. The committee needs to be made aware, likewise, of the governors' legal obligations, and of the consequent insurance requirements. It needs to be kept informed, also, of current and probable future expenditure requirements related to the repair and maintenance of the buildings and grounds.

The committee will also need to have advice available, when required, on a host of other matters. Many of these will concern the DES's own financial regulations and procedures, to the extent to which they apply within the scheme. These rules should be simple and few, according to the DES guidance document, and must be stated in the LEA's own documentation to schools. The LEA must include such information in its published scheme, together with guidance on curriculum planning, good employment practice, and the specification of contracts. Further LEA guidance will relate to the governors' legal obligations concerning health and safety, which will increase under the new arrangements. There will also be regulations about bank accounts, written estimates and quotations, and end-of-year procedures. The school should of course have a copy of the LEA scheme as approved by the Secretary of State.

Most of these matters are clearly the bursar's job - indeed, one of the reasons for creating the post of bursar is to have advice about them available on the spot. In advance of the appointment of a bursar, someone else will have to take the job on - but a transfer of responsibility to the bursar should be planned from the start.

When the size and constitution of the management committee is being considered, the main concern will be to achieve a balance between a committee large enough to be representative and a group small enough to meet the main requirements. These are: flexibility; a rapid response when problems arise; and a clear effectiveness in decision-making in the eyes of the staff. It is also important to decide whether to include non-teaching staff, and if so how. On balance it is best to keep the number on the low side, and to invite occasional attendance from others as required.

A related factor is the mode of appointment of members, other than those appointed ex officio, and governors who clearly have to be appointed by the governing body itself. If a pre-existing group such as the senior management team forms the staff group on the committee, these matters are simple enough. However, a representative group drawn from the whole staff may be able more easily to generate and maintain the necessary high level of trust.

Whatever the composition of the committee, the need for openness (save in confidential matters related to individuals) suggests that the minutes should be made available to all governors and staff. On matters delegated to the head teacher, it is also advisable to inform all staff in writing of the decisions made, where these involve points of general concern.

Once the committee has reached this point, it is ready for its main initial task: to lay down procedures, and in doing so to prepare for establishing its first budget.

The establishment of management procedures

The starting point for this process should be whatever system is already operating within the school, in order to make the manner of change as evolutionary as possible. The changes have to allow for the various new factors in the situation, the most significant being that the staff perceptions will be different. This applies both to individuals, to the staff as a whole, and to common interest groups such as main grade teachers, members of particular departments, ancillary staff and so on.

Until the start of local management, all these have looked on the LEA (or the even more distant DES) as the chief provider, and therefore as a major target for their discontent, if discontent there was. Rules imposed from above determined how much capitation the school was allowed, or how many teachers, incentive allowances or support staff. Only the allocation of resources in each of the various categories was a possible target within the school. Under the new scheme, however, the balance between categories is also open to variation at school level, subject only to a total spending limit (and of course to the other general constraints laid down). A target for criticism, on matters more complex than the award of an incentive allowance or the sharing of capitation, is now within the school.

It follows, therefore, that the critical decisions on how the school's budget share is to be allocated between broad categories should be made after full consultation, openly, and by a body qualified in every way to undertake the task. The objective should be management by consent, in an atmosphere which enables teachers to get on with their proper work, rather than frittering away their time and their abilities in order to gain for themselves or for their professional responsibilities a greater share of the available resources.

Clearly this body should be the management committee, and the task, which subsumes the approval of a budget for each year, is the principal task which it undertakes.

At this point it is necessary to consider the relationship between the management committee, the executive (with the head as its focus, particularly when tensions are high), and that less easily defined force, the teaching staff as a whole. It is of critical importance that a clear mechanism exists to tackle problems as they arise, so forestalling major disputes. Such a system has always been a feature of good management in schools, and has correspondingly been absent when local disputes have arisen. As with other aspects of local management, the principles are the same as ever, but the benefits of success and the penalties for failure are both far greater.

The process by which staff unrest circulates and grows varies from school to school. It affects non-teaching staff as well as teachers, but not usually in more than a single sub-group (secretarial staff, caretakers and so on) at once. In all but rare cases, therefore, it is the concerns of the teachers which are of central importance. Typically, the process by which these concerns show themselves is through the representatives of the various unions, and for the purposes of this discussion it is assumed that this is the case. Even if the details are different, the general principles remain the same.

Consider therefore a situation in which the bursar has reported that there is a significant credit balance available for distribution, and a decision about its allocation is to be made at the next meeting of the management committee. There will be competing claims, some well known within the staff and others not. These might include the recruitment of a part-time teacher to relieve pressure in one department, or the appointment of an ancillary in another; several departments might be asking for extra equipment to meet new examination requirements, while repairs are probably overdue in various areas. Whatever the management committee decides, some teachers will feel that their interests have been undervalued.

Though the details may differ, two points of principle can be stated with confidence. Most obviously, all major decisions about priorities must be made, and be seen to be made, by the management committee, for that is what it exists for. Less evident, but just as important, is the need for staff to know why. In part, this can be arranged by publishing the minutes of management committee meetings. But some matters cannot be set down on paper in this way, because of their complexity or sensitivity. This is where the link between the head and staff (through the group of union representatives) becomes vitally important. The effectiveness of this link is a possible measure of the quality of management in the school - perhaps an accurate one, though the point would be difficult to test by research.

The link should work both ways. The union representatives, individually or together, can ease matters by giving early warning of trouble: concessions are always easier when confrontation is threatened than when it happens. Conversely, the head can make effective use of this group in passing on, carefully and selectively, the sort of detail which could not be set down on paper and made freely available. It might simply be the background information which explains an apparently odd recommendation, or the tactics behind an unpopular proposal. Or the purpose might be that of informal negotiation, where each side gives way a little in order to gain an advantage elsewhere - just as has always happened in a well-run and healthy school in which many conflicting interests have to be taken into account. The difference now is that the possible areas of friction are more extensive, and the stakes correspondingly higher.

It may be expected that local management will assist good schools to become better, as happened in the early schemes; in the less well managed schools there will be problems, and not only those caused by failures to balance the books. Of the problems of other kinds, the origin in many cases will be a failure by the head to build up a relationship of trust and openness with his union representatives, and (partly through this group) with the staff as a whole. Such a failure of communication can easily allow a small problem to grow into a confrontation.

The relationship between staff and governors can also be critical, and depends very much on the rather more direct relationships involving the head, first with his staff and then with his governors. Informal contacts are obviously to be encouraged, and only become a problem if the head feels (whether rightly or wrongly matters little) that something is being done behind his back. If staff feel they need to tell the governors what the head is up to, or if a governor thinks that he is not getting a true picture from the head and asks a teacher what is really happening, nothing will go right. A head teacher who becomes aware of trouble of this nature needs to take action quickly. Unfortunately, however, the head in whose school this happens is the kind for whom teamwork is an unfamiliar concept, and who ought not to be let loose in a locally managed school, or indeed any other. Again, problems of this kind lie ahead in a number of schools.

The last, and to most schools a new, set of relationships involves the bursar. Since several thousand of them will (or at least should) be recruited, they will no doubt come from different backgrounds and with varied qualifications. But what each one will need, in addition to the obvious administrative ability, is a fine diplomatic skill. For the bursar will have to get on well with every group: governors, head, deputies, individual teachers, catering and other support staff, and (most importantly) the administrative staff who are responsible directly to him. He will also have to build up good contacts with the LEA, and with other agencies such as suppliers and contractors. It is often said of a school caretaker (with more than a grain of truth) that he is the second most important person in a school; the bursar, if he is the right person for the job, should merit a similar comment.

The central position of the head teacher in all of this needs little emphasis. It is nothing new: it has come to be something of a truism that a good head makes a good school, and this will not change. Under local management the balance of the job will change considerably, and since the pressures are already high some of the responsibilities previously carried will have to be delegated. Clearly the appointment of the bursar should assist in this process. But handing over parts of a job to others is never easy, particularly if it is to someone less experienced than oneself.

The time of greatest strain will be the transition period, in the preparations for the first year and the first full financial year. If the groundwork has been well laid, using among other things the exercise described in the last chapter, and if good relationships have been established throughout the school, the rest should fall into place. The change is too big to manage successfully without the level of teamwork which is characteristic of schools at their best; the feeling of corporate achievement, once the school is running smoothly under local management, will be worth striving for.

The experience of the schools in, for example, Cambridgeshire, bears this out: they were not all volunteers, and were to some degree hostile to the idea at first. But once the advantages became apparent the objections quickly faded. Indeed, the funds available for 'extras' in the first large group of schools grew sufficiently for the effects to be noticed by those in neighbouring schools, who questioned whether the schools in the scheme had been given more than their fair share. Of course, they had not, and there were few objections when the scheme was later extended to cover all secondary schools in the county. The Cambridgeshire model was, however, simpler than the one now specified, and it remains to be seen how equitable the latter proves to be.

The first budget

The exercise outlined in the last chapter should provide much of the groundwork for the budget for the first financial year of the scheme, which will need to be approved by the management committee (and thereafter by the governing body) as early as practicable in the spring term. Indeed, it may well be worth doing a dummy run on the figures for the preceding financial year (that is, the year which is already part way through), using as a guide the expenditure figures provided by the LEA for the year before that. In addition, it should be noted that the Act requires the LEA, once the delegation scheme is in operation, to prepare and to publish a financial statement, showing not only the allocation to each school but also the allocation per pupil. This figure will arouse considerable interest, and there will be pressure from the schools at the low end of the range to redress the balance, whether it is justified or not. It will be easier to resist these pressures (or indeed to bring them to bear) if the school's approximate position in the range is known in advance.

For all amounts which are affected by VAT, the figures actually used should be those which exclude the VAT element. When local management is operational, this will be reclaimed by the LEA just as it always has been, and all calculations related either to a budget or to actual expenditure should therefore be in VAT-exclusive terms. A separate column will have to be used to keep track of the VAT itself, in order to compare actual expenditure (some of which will, of course, include VAT) with estimates. The accounting method laid down by the LEA should make the procedures clear.

When looking at the figures, note the items which were unusual in any way, and try to estimate the costs both for the current year and the budget year. Look for items on which, if the governors had then had financial control, savings could have been made without detriment.

Finally, estimate the changes in staffing costs, taking separately the last five months of the current academic year and the subsequent seven months to the end of the financial year. (In addition to the likely staff changes taking effect on 1st September, increments for teachers not at the top of their scales date from this time.) The LEA should advise on any allowances which are to be made for the effects of national salary changes; some allowance should also be made for inflation in respect of non-salary items, such as fuel and water charges. The information needed to complete the expenditure side of the first budget should then be complete.

If there are gaps, as will probably be the case, it is best to use an estimate and then refine the figures later. When the school's budget share is known, it will then be possible to determine the general position at once - whether a surplus is likely, or a manageable deficit, or seeming disaster. Speed may well be important at this stage, particularly if the details of the budget balance will determine whether or not staff are to be recruited for the start of the summer term. Also, if the figures look very bad, it may well be necessary to seek LEA help under the safety net procedure, in which case it is clearly important to be able to act without delay.

The first financial year

As with almost any expenditure process, the actual costs will differ from the estimates as the financial year progresses. Clearly it is important to keep track, and this is also true for the LEA so that it can spot trouble at an early stage. But the school is much better placed to do so, because the bursar can allow for commitments - that is, for costs which have been incurred and will have to be paid out of the current year's funds, but which are not yet invoiced.

The process of keeping track of the figures in this way is known as commitment accounting, and is well worth attempting - indeed, at least a rough estimate of commitments is essential, particularly in the last two months of the financial year. All that is required is an extended use of the method which will probably have been employed already for capitation expenditure, in which rough figures based on orders placed are corrected later when invoices are received. Separate checklists may be advisable, since the pattern of payments varies: fuel bills, for example, come at known points in the year, and the final one can be estimated (at least with some tariff systems) by reading the meters.

Salary figures are as usual the most important, since they make up most of the total. Much will depend on the data provided by the LEA, probably on a monthly basis. If this is just a single total, perhaps with a further figure for the employer's share of superannuation and National Insurance, it will be difficult to check, and a full list with names (supplied separately and on a confidential basis) is very much better. The various errors which can arise were outlined in the last chapter.

The last two months of the financial year are the most critical. By the beginning of February, it should be clear whether the final figure is within acceptable limits. What those limits are will be set by the LEA - in the Cambridgeshire scheme, for example, the normal range allowed is 3% underspend to 1% overspend. If the permitted range is larger than this, it would still be prudent to keep well within the Cambridgeshire range. By comparison with a household budget, these percentages may seem small, but in the school context they are quite realistic. Balances of both kinds are carried forward into the next financial year.

Too great an underspend simply suggests that budgeting has been too cautious, and this is easy to correct; gross overspending may clearly require drastic action. Some schemes may allow for interest to be charged on amounts overspent, if these evidently result from bad planning. The aim should be to match the budget share closely, unless it is decided to underspend slightly in order to build up a contingency fund. An overspend reduces flexibility in the following year, particularly if it results from poor management, and in such a way that the true situation is not known until well into the new financial year.

Every effort should in fact be made to avoid mid-year economies - a piece of advice which is doubtless unnecessary in LEAs where such economies have been enforced in earlier years. The trouble is that there is such little scope for instant action. But to put a block on further expenditure of the traditional capitation type, starting in January and lasting until the new financial year, is not only unpopular but also gives the staff all too clear a measure of the quality of management in the school. Once again, there is no LEA to blame this time, though the formula itself may be used instead for this purpose.

The actual accounting procedures to cover the situation at the end of the financial year are quite complex - indeed, this is one of the few matters in which the detailed financial rules go beyond the requirements of a commonsense approach. The procedure ought to be made clear by the LEA, which of course has its own end-of-year rules; the school will probably have to observe these also. If it does not, the differences between the two sets of figures will cause disagreements, and this will help no-one.

The general principle of end-of-year procedures is that they should give a true picture of the situation, making allowance for commitments which have not been invoiced. Thus it is not possible, if the procedure is followed, to balance the books artificially just by delaying certain payments. The details may vary between LEAs, and in any event this chapter is not intended to be read as a handbook on accounting procedures. The responsibility for giving information and guidance in these matters must rest with the LEA.

If a problem of unexpected overspending does arise, it will need to be discussed with the LEA advisory team on local management. Tactically it would be much better for the school to initiate this action when danger signs are observed, rather than waiting until the LEA's own monitoring system picks it up. The involvement of the LEA in this situation is somewhat anomalous, in that if a school is at fault the first action the Authority has to take is not to impose a fine or other penalty, but to give advice. If this fails, more advice and assistance will probably be called in; only if the problem resists all this will the LEA be in a position to use its one real sanction, the withdrawal of delegated powers. It is not likely to happen very often, and the most probable causes are an unfair formula, a grossly incompetent head teacher, or a breakdown in the relationship between the school and the LEA.

The governing body in local management

There has in the past been a considerable variation across the country in the extent of the actual involvement of governors in the management of schools. On paper their role has usually included overall responsibility for the curriculum, but in many areas this has in practice been left to the professionals. Only in senior appointments have some governing bodies had any real influence. The Act gives governors much wider powers, which some will use effectively, others will delegate at once to head teachers where they can, and a few will probably try to use in a manner not conducive to good management. An early task for head and governors is to work out together, explicitly or implicitly, how extensive the involvement of governors is to be. If a head teacher assumes, wrongly, that governors will be willing to be involved very fully, problems will arise which a more realistic strategy would have avoided.

Perhaps it is better to take a different approach, and to suggest an annual cycle of three termly meetings in which the essentials of the governing body's responsibilities can be met. From this point, the remainder can be delegated or not as seems most appropriate, so that not only the full governing body but individual governors are involved as far as they are able. The management committee could not, given this starting point, be the full governing body, but might have any of the other forms of constitution suggested earlier.

The agenda of the first meeting of the academic year, in October or November, does not need to include major financial issues. There will be a review of the previous year, including examination results, and consideration of the annual report to parents, for which the meeting will follow later in the term.

The key meeting, in relation to the governors' delegated management powers, is that of the spring term, in late January or early February. The timing of this is quite critical, since it must be long enough after the school's budget share has been notified by the LEA to allow for the budget to be completed, and early enough to be able to plan expenditure (particularly on staffing matters) for the new financial year. The meeting will be concerned first with any major matters relating to the current financial year. It then has to approve the budget for the year ahead, which at the very lowest level of involvement is one of the two powers delegated by the LEA which the full governing body must reserve to itself.

The other formal responsibility of the full governing body has to be exercised at the last meeting of the academic year, which will probably be in June. This is the approval of the management committee's report and accounts for the financial year which ended in March. If the number of pupils to be admitted in September is different from that forecast, the governors will probably also consider any necessary adjustments to the budget. However, this is a responsibility which could be delegated if necessary.

Otherwise, the involvement of governors in local management is just that needed for staff appointments, and even this only to the extent that they do not exercise their powers of delegation.

The clear intention of the Act, and one that most in the education service would welcome, is that governors should be involved to a far greater extent than this minimum level. To extend the range by having more full meetings of governors is one way, but with the present size of governing bodies, at least in the larger schools, this may not be appropriate. A system of sub-committees, with a mixture of governors and staff, has much to commend it, as it can make good use of the qualifications, interests and available times of individual governors. Not the least of the advantages of such an arrangement is its flexibility, as it can be modified quickly and easily in the light of experience. The sub-committees may be given powers to co-opt, up to a stated limit, which further increases the flexibility.

Governors have always had a role outside formal meetings, and their greater involvement as individuals should make it easier for some to develop this role more effectively. Sometimes it has been difficult to take up the head's typical invitation to 'drop in any time', and involvement in sub-committee work should ease the way. Also, specialist skills, particularly in accounting procedures and in the care of buildings, can be used more effectively in this way than in a full meeting of governors.

None of this, however, should detract from the central importance of the management committee itself. Management of an institution as large, as complex and as labour-intensive as a school, cannot be carried out effectively other than by a small, cohesive and powerful group, most of whose members are intimately involved in its life and work. As the range of management responsibilities increases, as it does with the introduction of delegated powers, the importance of this fact increases also.

Whatever the balance of responsibilities between governors, management committee, and the head and his deputies, a sense of partnership and teamwork is vital. As already noted, the LEA and its officers should be involved in the same manner, as should the trustees in the case of aided schools. The last word on this may suitably be taken from the Coopers and Lybrand report, referring to the relationship between the LEA's planning team and those in schools: 'Without the agreement of those who will have to operate the scheme, there will be insufficient motivation for local management of schools to succeed'.

Implications for schools without delegation

Special schools, and primary schools with less than 200 pupils, are not in the mandatory scheme. Also, some schools within the scheme may have to wait for up to three years while neighbouring schools get started. It may therefore be worth summarising the changes which affect schools without delegated powers, after the scheme as a whole gets under way.

As noted in Chapter 4, all LEA schools, excluding special schools, must be told their budget shares before the start of the financial year. After the end of the financial year, the LEA has to provide for governors a statement of actual expenditure related to the school. The LEA is obliged, like the governing body of a school with delegated powers. to manage expenditure within the budget: under- or overspend has to be carried forward into the following year.

There is a significant difference in the rules which may affect schools without delegated powers, and which if it did would be greatly (and rightly) resented. The LEA will no longer have the power to transfer a redeployed teacher to a locally managed school - but it will still have this right in relation to other schools. Schools without delegation could thus find themselves saddled with teachers whom other schools had nominated for redeployment, including no doubt a small proportion of major problems. The LEA's position in such matters is not easy: as noted earlier, it has the full responsibilities of an employer but not the full rights. If the LEA does take action of this kind, it will not be done willingly. But the consequences could be most damaging, and it is very much to be hoped that more equitable methods will be found for dealing with the rare, but very real, difficult case.

Apart from that, matters remain in a formal sense much as they were before the Act. But if local management achieves what is intended, and the Cambridgeshire experience suggests that this will happen in most schools, the main effect on the schools without delegated powers is that they will feel left out. This feeling will be accentuated by perceptions of the increased amounts which schools in the scheme are able to spend where it can most easily be seen, by parents and hence by the local community at large - on books and equipment. The result may therefore be that pressure will be brought to bear on the LEA to extend its scheme to cover all schools, including special schools and units. Provided that the necessary administrative support can be made available (and this will clearly be difficult for small schools, particularly in rural areas), there seems no good reason why this should not be achieved.

Chapter 7 Future developments in Local Management

The rules governing local variations

The introduction of local management across England and Wales will be by no means uniform, nor will it in any LEA or school remain for long in its initial form. The Secretary of State's guidelines are quite detailed, but still allow much scope for differing approaches, and the traditional degree of independence both of LEAs and of schools will ensure that every opportunity is well used. The Act allows LEAs to make minor variations without the Secretary of State's approval, and the guidance document states that any change which extends the powers delegated (or which reduces the number of factors in the formula) comes within the definition of a minor change. Alterations which have the opposite effects require full local consultation followed by a submission to the Secretary of State, in the same way as for the original scheme.

The purpose of this chapter is to explore, in no particular order, some of the variations which may be considered, either from the start or as later developments. Each has implications also for the grant-maintained school.

School bank accounts

No clear view has emerged as to whether a school with delegated powers should control some of its LEA income directly, through its own bank account. Accounts relating to parents' association or similar funds are not in question, nor are the usual LEA arrangements for petty cash. At the other end of the scale, it is not envisaged that LEA schools will take over the administration of salaries. In relation to other expenditure items, the payment process may be either left in the hands of the LEA, or transferred into the direct control of schools through a normal bank account or something closely similar.

The Coopers and Lybrand report sets down very clearly most of the points for and against transfer. Separate accounts would cost more for the banks, and schools might have to bear this in the form of bank charges; there would be cash flow problems; accounting would be more difficult; and opportunities for mismanagement and fraud would increase. But, the report adds, a school-based system would be easily understood by school managers; it has a clear psychological attraction; and the cash flow problem and the end-of-year arrangements would become realistic parts of the management process. In addition, the ability to pay bills quickly or to send a cheque with an order would sometimes make discounts possible. Further, the ability to pay lecture fees and travelling expenses on the spot would be a significant public relations advantage. From the LEA angle, also, this is one of the few aspects of local management which would yield a direct saving in central manpower costs.

On the other hand, there might be some difficulty in ensuring that schools followed the LEA financial procedures specified in the scheme (not that the schools would feel the loss too keenly, for many such procedures cause extra work and expense even though they may have been intended to reduce both). Also, a head teacher might feel that the operation of the account would be just one more management chore, making him even less like a teacher and more like a finance director.

Of all these factors, the most significant is perhaps the psychological attraction. Local management is about feelings and perceptions as well as about responsibility and control, and the feeling of being able to pay a bill by the simple and familiar process of signing a cheque is important. The additional work involved might be less than that wasted in chasing late payments or lost invoices through the LEA, and the time would be spent in a manner which the staff responsible would feel to be more constructive.

A simple school-based account system would create problems of cash flow both for the LEA and for schools, but it ought to be possible to match the flow patterns together: a phased release of funds to schools (perhaps about 40% in April, and 20% at the start of each subsequent quarter) might be workable on both sides. This should enable schools to avoid overdrawing their accounts, so that bank charges would not be high. The accounting problems ought to be met without difficulty, if there is a good LEA management information system. The greatest difficulties may be those of audit and the prevention and detection of fraud: whether these are critical remains to be seen.

The preferred solution of Coopers and Lybrand (though they feel the argument to be finely balanced) is that the LEA should act as banker, providing monthly statements for schools but continuing to draw cheques on their own account. They suggest that schools might be able to initiate payments by on-line computer, though there are strong arguments against on-line links as they themselves point out; if this proved impracticable, the consequent need to arrange for cheques to be sent out by the LEA would destroy the advantages of a school-based system. The psychological benefit, in particular, would vanish completely.

A possible system for school bank accounts

But there is a school-based method better than these. It has all the advantages of a separate school account, and none of the problems except that of increasing the possibility of misuse. This system has become possible as a result of the development of automated banking services. It works by operating each school account separately, but with an automatically-operated link to the main Local Authority schools account. From the point of view of the school bursar, the account is used in the normal way for drawing cheques, paying in, and other banking operations as required. The only difference is that, at the end of each day's transactions, an automatic transfer of funds is made from the central account, in order to make the balance of the school account equal to zero. (If, unusually, more had been credited than debited that day, the transfer of funds would be the other way.)

From the Local Authority Treasurer's point of view, the only action necessary would be to ensure that the central account was kept in sufficient funds to cover the expected expenditure by schools. The daily figures (available via direct line to a terminal in his department) would enable him to keep track easily of both the total expenditure and that related to individual schools. He would also have access to the full transaction record for an individual school, should the total suggest that its expenditure was excessive.

This approach would retain the psychological factor; it would leave the control of cash flow to the Treasurer's department, just as it was before local management; and it would link the school's accounting process (other than the commitment aspect) directly to that of the LEA, so simplifying both accounting and auditing. It would also enhance the LEA's ability to pick up signs of trouble at the earliest stage possible. There would no doubt be an additional cost to the bank, as compared with a single account, which would have to be passed on to the LEA or directly to schools, but this should not be large. The problems of dealing with VAT should be no greater than by any other method.

There seems no reason why a payment process controlled by the school, by whatever method, should not cover all payments from the budget share, other than salary-related items. If there are any other direct LEA payments, they should be specified in the LEA scheme. A process analogous to a direct debit instruction to a bank would ensure that such payments were known to the school; this is essential, for an LEA which debits a school's account without telling it why will soon lose goodwill. Alternatively, the LEA might simply invoice the school.

The school's monitoring process, given a system of this kind, will consist of two parallel sections. The first will have to reconcile any items paid for by the LEA, which will mainly be salary-related payments, with the budgeted figures for these categories; the other will have to compare the total payments initiated to date by the school with the remainder of the budget allowances. To allow virement between salaries and the remainder, the LEA will have to be notified by the school; virement can otherwise be controlled from within the school.

Projects involving capital payments

Another major question relating to the financial links between school and LEA concerns capital expenditure and capital debt repayment. Debt charges related to the school buildings are clearly outside the scope of the local management scheme, and need no further comment. There may well be other such repayments being made, unknown to the school managers, as a result of capital expenditure on adaptations to the buildings, or on furniture, fittings or equipment. Again, these need not be considered. But capital projects implemented or proposed after the start of local management should not be dismissed so readily as simply an LEA responsibility, either by the school or by the LEA. As the rules stand, the only obligatory link between LEA and schools on capital expenditure is that, at some point before or during the year, the LEA must inform each governing body of the capital allocation to the school for that year. To preserve the concept of a partnership between the LEA and its schools, rather more is required.

It should be mentioned at this point that the question of whether a particular item of expenditure is capital or revenue (which means to be met out of running costs) does not always have an obvious answer. Coopers and Lybrand commented that capital financing in local government is 'a particularly arcane subject', and anyone who has tried to understand it will agree at once. Planning in a Local Authority is usually rather short-term, and problems well ahead can normally be ignored: hence there is in any elected council an inclination to borrow money to bring quick results, with little regard to the long-term repayment consequences. This inclination is curbed by means of rules laid down by central government, and these restrictions would have to apply at school level also; the omission of capital expenditure from the delegation scheme would probably be necessary for this reason alone.

But, as suggested earlier, capital expenditure also has implications for revenue expenditure, and this ought to be taken into account in the Local Authority's annual round of determining its capital programme. This process involves all departments, not just education, and tends (political considerations apart) to consider competing claims by reference to the expected capital cost and the need for the project, rather than the revenue implications.

This approach hardly meets the needs of schools with delegated powers. As it stands, it would require the finance committee of the Authority to make decisions about capital projects in schools, without reference either to the wishes of governors or to the costs which the governors will have to meet (or the savings which they will be able to utilise). How this anomaly will be resolved (if at all) remains to be seen, but the following three examples may be of interest in themselves, and also act as pointers towards a workable system. The landlord / tenant analogy, favoured both by Coopers and Lybrand and by the DES, is no help: if a family in rented accommodation grows too large for the number of bedrooms, a request that the landlord should fund an extension is not likely to produce a positive response.

1   Consider first a proposal to improve the heating efficiency of a school, by means of structural alterations and the installation of cavity wall and roof insulation, thus cutting heating bills. At the same time it is planned to modify the controls of the heating system, so that small areas can be controlled independently, thus making the hiring out of small areas for evening and weekend activities economically viable. This will benefit the school in three ways: it will cut heating costs directly, it will increase income from lettings, and it will to some extent make the buildings more pleasant to work in. The third point cannot be costed, but the other two might mean that the proposal was in straight cash terms a sound investment. But there is no benefit to the LEA at all, other than an increase in the capital value of its property, and this is not of immediate importance.

What is needed here is a mechanism for enabling the LEA to borrow money in the normal way, and then to lend it to the governors; they will then take on the responsibility (through the LEA) for the debt charges due on the loan. Whether the governors make a profit or a loss on the deal is a matter only for them; the only cost to the LEA is that the project uses up a slice of its permitted borrowing. But it seems unlikely that an arrangement of this kind would be acceptable under present rules.

2   Next consider a proposal to install a technology room, making use of an otherwise redundant space. Here the benefit to the school is clear, but there are revenue implications, probably small enough for the school to take on willingly in relation to such a valuable new facility. Again, the LEA benefits hardly at all, but in this case the significant point is that it is acting in accordance with its general duty to provide for the capital aspects of the school's curricular needs. The real problem for the LEA is familiar enough: given many demands and limited resources, which school should get the technology room? (Or, should one school get a technology room rather than another school an improved library?)

But the context is now rather different, because the LEA is in the position of making decisions about just one aspect of a school's development, while its governors are responsible for most others but have no say in the matter at issue. In the scheme as it is under the Act, there seems no way of resolving this dilemma satisfactorily. The direct solution - to pass the task to governors - is not only disallowed under the Act but also poses major practical difficulties, since it takes the responsibility for working within the highly complex borrowing rules into a group whose financial expertise is restricted to that of the numerate amateur. For the present, pragmatism will probably be the main guide.

3 The third example is one that was mentioned in Chapter 3, in the context of the school whose pupil numbers have risen sharply as a result of the new admission arrangements, and which therefore needs more classrooms. Here the LEA's position is very different. As with the proposed technology room, it may (depending on the legal advice it receives) have a duty to provide the accommodation needed. But it was not responsible for the problem, since it had no legal power to limit sufficiently the numbers of pupils admitted (and nor did the governors). At the same time there are in all probability many vacant places in neighbouring schools. Why should the LEA use its restricted borrowing powers and limited resources in order to meet a need which both it and the governors would have avoided, had they been allowed to exercise their respective planning functions? Revenue implications do not come into it this time, since the school's income will grow with the number of pupils. But there is no answer to the problem of capital provision.

The section of the Coopers and Lybrand report on capital financing is well worth reading. They point out the problems very clearly, and their comment on the the effect of existing capital controls is that they may act as a considerable disincentive to schools. They recommend some relaxation, though without much optimism about the likely response.

Central LEA services

At least initially, most services provided centrally by the LEA for its schools will remain outside the delegation scheme. In the case of one such service, that of audit, independence from the school is required as a matter of principle, and this needs no further comment. But there may be moves to include some of the others.

The central LEA administrative system clearly has to remain as an independent entity, and the DES guidance document excludes it from the scheme. Schools cannot significantly vary the extent to which they use it, so any sharing among schools would have to be formula-based, and the total effect would be neutral. The same is true of part of the work of advisers and inspectors, to the extent that their time is centrally directed and is not available to be used by schools on request; they also are excluded.

The meals arrangements for a particular school may be delegated, and some (notably the large community schools) may be well placed to take advantage of such delegation and so will press for it. But a further factor, the privatisation of services, is involved here, and is considered in the next section.

Where the service is provided in relation to the needs of individual pupils, there are strong reasons for preserving a centrally-directed service, even though the guidance document only requires home to school transport to be excluded. But that is, perhaps, the one pupil-related service which might with benefit be delegated to some schools: it has very real possibilities in rural areas in particular, where a school's ability to control its transport arrangements directly might have a positive effect on the range and timing of activities both within and outside the normal curriculum. However, it is within the powers of the Secretary of State to vary the excepted items, and an LEA which offered a scheme which included the delegation of this function to the governors of a number of schools might find a ready response.

In addition, the following are left as discretionary items, for LEAs either to delegate or not: the schools psychological service; the various special needs support services, including special units; and the education welfare service. But LEAs are not likely to delegate these, partly because the support would be difficult to plan and maintain if demand was to vary greatly from year to year, and partly because it would not be right to allow schools to take away support needed by specific individuals in order to meet a financial pressure elsewhere. If any of these are delegated, they may remain as earmarked delegations: that is, schools will receive an income for the use of a specific service, but may not transfer any of this sum for use elsewhere.

The case relating to advisory teachers is not as clear. The two reasons mentioned above (the need for continuity, and the danger that a school will not be willing to use the resources offered even though it does need help) apply in some measure. At present the schools which most need help tend to be the ones who ask for it least; this would certainly get worse if needy schools also had to pay for the advice received.

The picture is further confused by the fact that many advisory teachers are funded with central government help of some kind (mostly education support grants), and are therefore explicitly excluded from the delegation scheme. It is apparently inescapable that the line of argument which says that schools should be released from most LEA influences (which underlies this whole scheme) also requires that the LEA-operated services which remain must be subject to more and more restrictions laid down by central government. It is probable, therefore, that it will not be practicable to include in the delegation scheme the time of the minority of advisory teachers who are outside the ESG arrangements.

The result will be that the LEA will be providing a valuable and free facility, whose use in a particular school will depend mainly on the head teacher's willingness to ask for it. The thriving school, perhaps unfortunately, will ask and will receive more than its share, while the stragglers become even further enmeshed in debts and confusion. The advisory teachers concerned, and also their colleagues in the inspectorate, will need to take care that their time is spent where it is really needed.

Competitive tendering for Local Authority services

Local Authorities are required under the 1988 Local Government Act ('the LG Act' in this section) to go out to competitive tender for various services, and departments of the Council may themselves submit tenders. In the present context, the relevant services are school meals, caretaking and cleaning, the maintenance of grounds, the repair and maintenance of vehicles, and the maintenance of buildings. (The last item came within an earlier Act, but the distinction is ignored in what follows.) Of these, the provision of school meals is a discretionary exception, and may therefore be retained as an LEA responsibility; if delegated, this may be to all schools with delegated powers, to nominated schools or to volunteer schools. The other services have to be delegated.

The permitted duration of the various contracts required under the LG Act is laid down in the DES guidance document, and ranges from three to six years. Voluntary contracts, or contracts for delegated services not within the LG Act, are not to run for more than three years.

The guidance document sets out the rules for determining whether the requirements of the delegation scheme or those of the LG Act take precedence. These are as follows:

1 If an LEA has, before the LG Act comes into force, voluntarily contracted out a service, both the LEA and its schools are bound by that contract until it comes up for renewal, and only then do the new rules apply.

2 In advance of the publication by an LEA of a formal specification under the LG Act for which it is to invite tenders, governors of schools with delegated powers are free to make their own arrangements if they wish. If they do so, they must continue on their own after the new rules come into force. If instead they ask to join in the arrangements proposed by the LEA, they may specify the standard of service they require, and the LEA must include that in its specification.

3 After the publication date referred to in the last paragraph, the governors cannot change their minds until the contract comes up for renewal. Before the renewal date (whether the contract was voluntary or required under the LG Act), governors may again decide whether to make their own arrangements or ask the LEA to include their requirements in the specification. If the former, they are not bound (as the LEA would be) by the statutory requirements on competitive tendering.

4 The contracts required under the LG Act have implications for the employment of staff, both by the LEA and by governors, which could create a variety of problems. LEAs are required to include in their delegation schemes the arrangements they propose to make for dealing with these, so little more need be said here.

Privatisation and the school meals service

The most difficult of the various decisions about participation in LEA contracts, partly because it is the biggest in financial terms, concerns school meals (unless the LEA chooses not to delegate this, in which case the problem does not arise). The LEA has legal responsibilities for health and safety matters related to school meals, and for providing free meals for those qualified to receive them: if the governors take on the main task, they also take over these responsibilities, as agents of the LEA. It may seem a poor bargain, and indeed it is not something that any governing body should take on lightly.

However, for the governors of a school which is well into local management and is thriving on it, there are advantages in bringing school meals under their control - perhaps financial, but more likely the ability to develop the school's catering needs as a whole.

The Coopers and Lybrand report recommended that school meals should be included in the delegation scheme, with appropriate safeguards related to health and safety, standards of provision, and free meals arrangements. They did so mainly because of the general principle that a matter should be delegated unless there are good reasons not to do so. Free meals can be allowed for by means of a cash subsidy; the health and safety interests can be met without difficulty, in the sense that the problem will already have been solved in relation to the delegated powers concerning buildings. There may also be complications about shared arrangements, for example where meals cooked in one school are taken in heated containers to another, and clearly this can only be dealt with according to local needs.

But the school meals issue raises probably the most sensitive of all the problems which the new rules will create. When a service goes out to tender, the governors must decide in advance whether to stay in or out, and will have little opportunity to assess the relative costs. If they opt out of the LEA contract, they take on a responsibility which they may not have either the time or the skills to fulfil properly; if they stay with the LEA, and the contract is not awarded to the LEA's own workforce, staff who have served the school well may lose their jobs, and if so the effect on morale would be serious. If the governors give high priority to keeping the existing school meals team in the school, the course of action most likely to succeed is to ask for its management to be delegated to them. However, it may prove difficult to convince the school meals staff themselves that this is so.

Privatisation related to buildings and plant

The merits of taking over responsibility for caretaking and cleaning, and the maintenance of buildings, vehicles and grounds, are clear enough to need little comment. With the mandatory delegation of these, and a deliberate decision to take over school meals (and perhaps also pupil transport, as mentioned earlier), the delegation principle will have developed far enough for the school to see itself as a single management entity. The LEA will still be around to assist when needed, and there will be a few loose ends of which the most tiresome will probably relate to the observance of LEA financial rules. But apart from capital schemes and insurance, no major activity taking place at the school will be subject to direct LEA constraints. The whole of the school's assets - buildings, equipment both for teaching and otherwise, transport facilities, and of course the entire human resource - will be available to be used and developed fully, for the benefit of the school and its community. Whether formally designated as such or not, it will have grown into a community school.

The question then arises as to whether a school with such a full implementation of local management is significantly different from a grant-maintained school, and this will be considered in later chapters.

Performance indicators and specific grant funding

The subtitle of this last section might well be 'Dreams and nightmares'. Its purpose is to return to the supposed ultimate expression of local management, mentioned at the start of Chapter 4, in which schools are considered in financial terms as substantially free-standing economic organisations.

Using the conventional analogy, in which a comparison is made with a business concerned with manufacturing or with supplying a service to the public, the basic idea is that inputs, processes and outputs should be given an appropriate cost or value. If this really was possible, a balance sheet could be drawn up which would show on one side the direct costs, measured in the normal way. The other side would then show the gain to the community which has resulted from the school's work, in terms of the value of the education-related changes which have accrued to the pupils who have passed through the school.

The difference between the two totals then becomes a measure (as with a business) of the school's effective work; when related to the size of the input factors, the result is analogous to a percentage profit. Thus far, no serious attempt at such a balance sheet has been made. There are some (mostly outside the school-related parts of the education service) who would like to rectify matters, and it is not hard to see why. As a public service, education has to compete for resources, with others such as social services and health. Is it not right to attach a notional value to a hip replacement, to the benefit resulting from a disabled person made mobile and thus able to do a normal job, and to a set of GCSE passes? An objective decision can then be made about the optimum use of resources at the national level.

Of course, it is not as simple as that, for any public service. The social and economic benefits to the community of these three examples alone would not be readily agreed, even within a factor of five or ten; to bring into the discussion the far more complex factors involved in defence matters, prisons and so on, would widen the range of the figures still further.

Nevertheless, the feeling remains: should there not be some way of assessing the true value to the community of the various aspects of the work of the education service? Clearly, this has to cover inputs as well as outputs, if it is to be used in resource allocation. A slow learner who is helped to read, use money, and take responsibility for himself in the community is an economic gain, just as much as a bright pupil's sheaf of examination successes. If these matters could be quantified, comparisons could be made between schools of different types and even of different age ranges.

Instead of a formula based largely on the number of pupils, resource allocation could then be decided on performance, by grants related to specific targets. After agreement between a school and the LEA of its input and current process measures, the school would agree that, given certain changes to its process measures and a particular level of grant, it would achieve stated values of the output measures. Its actual performance would later be measured, and subsequent grants altered accordingly.

Various extensions can be added to the basic principle. The school can be encouraged or forced to make curricular or organisational changes, in line with LEA or DES requirements, by making certain parts of the grant conditional on the school following policies and procedures laid down. From the school's angle, the idea of competition between schools on business lines suggests that they should be allowed to compete for the best staff, by offering salaries above the norm, on a basis of the effectiveness of their teaching in value-added terms. Also, the general grant formula will enable decisions to be made about admissions on a basis of input values, in the light of the output figures which the school's experience shows that it should be able to achieve. It might prove better to take only bright children; but the opposite might equally be true, if that was how the input and output value calculations worked out. The likely profit, supposedly as a measure of the educational benefit to the individual and to the community, would be the criterion.

For those who dream of this ultimate balance sheet, the Coopers and Lybrand report provides a guide. For each pupil of the yearly intake, a quantitative assessment has to be made of the following: his background, both socio-economic and cultural; his innate ability (a problem whose solution has eluded psychologists for a century or so, but never mind); his handicaps; the level of expectation both of the pupil and of his parents; and his academic attainment on entry to the school. Also part of the input equation are details about teachers and support staff, parental support, provision of text and library books, technical facilities, and running expenditure. Add to that the process measures related to teachers and the curriculum, and compare with the output as shown by examination performance, other intellectual attainments, and a variety of oddments ranging from the views of potential employers to the number of indictable offences recorded (presumably in relation to pupils rather than staff, though the report does not specify).

To most within the education service - perhaps even to most who have experienced its qualities as pupils, and now as adults have an informed concern about its health - this may be more of a nightmare than a dream. Those who find it so may need to be vigilant, in case some day it should become a reality.

Lest this seem too distant a possibility to merit such words, a quotation from the DES guidance document may suffice. It shows the point these ideas had reached by the time the Bill was passing through its final stages. 'The Secretary of State will expect schemes submitted to him for approval to include the following elements.... (f) the monitoring and evaluation procedures to be applied under the scheme, including the indicators the LEA propose using to evaluate the performance of schools.'

Chapter 8 The features of a grant-maintained school

A new type of school

The Act makes provision for two new types of school. The more radically different from existing LEA schools, the city technology college, is also new in the sense of starting from nothing, and is described in Chapter 11. The other, the grant-maintained or GM school, is to be a school of a new type but developed from a former LEA school. The change takes place as a result of proposals, made by governors and approved by the Secretary of State, to opt out of LEA control.

The grant-maintained school is the subject of the next three chapters, of which this one looks first at the its distinctive features, and then at the actual provisions of the Act. The next chapter looks in detail at the sequence of steps needed to acquire GM status, and the involvement of the various parties (head teacher, staff, parents, governors, LEA and Secretary of State) in the process. Finally, Chapter 10 considers the end product, after the change of status has taken place.

The GM school has several features which distinguish it from a non-aided school with full delegated powers, most of which are also different from those of aided schools. First, its governing body has corporate status - it takes legal responsibility for its actions in a way which a body without that status cannot. Specifically, it can enter into contracts, and it can be sued. The governors of an LEA school with delegated powers cannot under the Act be held personally liable provided they have acted reasonably; there is no such protection for governors of GM schools. (The governing body of an aided school has corporate status and so is able to enter into contracts to employ staff, but in practice the LEA takes legal responsibility for most one-off problems which arise.)

Next, the governors of a GM school have control of admissions, subject to a top limit which is specified by them in the proposals and, if approved, is stated in the articles of government. This limit is not calculated from the 1979 admission number or by reference to the physical capacity of the school, as it is under the Act for county and voluntary schools. The governors' admissions policy must however be consistent with the school's previous character as an LEA school, and with any provision of its trust deed. The governing body may seek to alter the character of the school, by changing the admissions policy or otherwise, but this requires a detailed process of consultation and is subject to the agreement of the Secretary of State.

Next, the GM school is completely free of formal LEA direction and influence, and indeed free of any obligation to relate to the LEA in any way, except in connection with the transport of pupils and in other pupil-related services. Note, however, that this is the formal position: GM schools will not be popular with LEAs, who will almost certainly apply pressure with the object of making life difficult, both for a school seeking GM status and for one which has actually opted out.

There may be an LEA involvement in providing for the additional needs of individual pupils who are the subjects of statements under the 1981 Act, to the extent specified in each statement. The provisions of the 1981 Act give the responsibility for this matter to the LEA, and the governors of a GM school are required to assist in implementing its decisions. In particular, the LEA may name a GM school in an attendance order for a pupil subject to a statement. But in the new situation, it is by no means clear how the responsibility will be shared between two bodies who are no longer partners in the manner assumed by the 1981 Act. The number of pupils involved is, however, likely to be small, if (as may reasonably be surmised) the admissions policy of the GM school is operated in such a way as to discourage acceptance of pupils known to be the subject of a statement. Of all the controversial issues related to the GM school, this is likely to be among the foremost.

The loss of the LEA link means that governors will take responsibility for the administration of salaries, including PAYE, superannuation and so on, in addition, of course, to all the financial matters mentioned in the section on local management (other than capital debt repayment and those pupil-related services retained by the LEA). Governors will also have to look after insurance, and any legal matter which may arise, particularly in relation to terms of employment, dismissal, and redundancy.

The only explicit difference for the head teacher, other than (in a former non-aided school) becoming an employee of the governing body, is that he is a governor ex officio, instead of having the choice. However, the actual change in his role may be very much greater, and this will be mentioned later. For the other teaching and ancillary staff, the position is similar: they also become (if they are not already) employees of the governors, who take on all the contractual responsibilities of the former employer. Again, what actually happens may not be as simple as that. There are still to be either one or two teacher governors; the Act gives the option, but all eligible schools will already have two, as a consequence of the 1986 Act, and so will probably keep them. During the process of acquiring GM status, the teachers have almost no influence over the course of events; to deprive them of one of their two possible seats on the governing body would be little less than insulting.

In respect of capital grants, the provision is similar in principle to that for aided schools, in which a grant of 85% of the total cost of approved projects is paid by the DES. But the level of grant to the GM school is, remarkably, 100%.

The governing body of a GM school may acquire or dispose of land or property, or invest its available funds; it may not however borrow money.

These are the main differences, as they appear on paper. A GM school has to follow the national curriculum, and the provisions for religious education are similar to those applying to the school before its status changed, modified in the same way as those for LEA schools, as described in Chapter 1. But there is much to be added in detail to this outline of the structure, starting with the status and powers of its governing body as defined in the Act; more still needs to be added about what the Act implies but does not state.

The GM school and its governing body

This section contains a complete account (except for some points of legal definition) of the provisions of the Act under which an established GM school operates. In the next section, the transitional provisions are described, by which the governing body of the former school becomes the governing body of the GM school. After that the other rules for changing the status are outlined, starting with a request for the change and ending, after its approval by the Secretary of State, with its implementation (after which further minor changes take place). The rest of the chapter describes the remaining provisions: the transfer of property and staff, the funding arrangements, the requirements for RE, and the rules for changing and closing a GM school.

All this is not easy reading, and much of the detail should be skipped over fairly lightly - unless, of course, it is intended to make a full assessment of the merits and disadvantages of the change, in which case a close reading should be accompanied by similar study of the actual wording of the Act. There is little here by way of comment, which is kept mainly until the two chapters which follow.

Under the Act, the Secretary of State is given the power to approve proposals, made in the required form by the existing governing body of an eligible school, that the school should have grant-maintained status. Any LEA secondary school is eligible, and any primary school with 300 or more registered pupils (including those in a nursery which is part of the school). The size limit for a primary school may be reduced or removed by order of the Secretary of State. But a school is not eligible if proposals to close it have been approved by the Secretary of State (or, in a case not requiring his consent, have been confirmed by the LEA), or, in the case of a voluntary school, if the governing body has served notice that it intends to discontinue it.

If, however, an application to close or to change the character of a school has been published by the LEA, or if an application to change the character has been published by the governors of a voluntary school, but has not in either case received the required approval, the eligibility of the school is not thereby affected, and the Secretary of State has to consider both proposals together. He must first suspend the proposal to close or change the character of the school, either through issuing regulations or in relation to a particular proposal. The suspension period is to allow time for a proposal to be made that grant-maintained status should be sought.

If such a proposal is duly made, and the two proposals then come up for consideration together, the Secretary of State must rule first on the proposal for GM status, and only if he decides not to approve it does he have to rule on the other application.

From the date specified in the approval, the governing body becomes incorporated (given corporate status) in a manner and under a name specified in the proposals, or in the proposals as amended by the Secretary of State if he so requires. On the incorporation date, the governing body becomes known as the initial governing body.

After giving his approval, the Secretary of State may by order give to those who are at that time known to be members designate of the initial governing body, who form what is called the prospective governing body, certain powers enabling them to prepare for the transition. Such powers may be used from a date to be stated in the order until the incorporation date, and may include the powers of appointing staff, entering into contracts, and making arrangements for the first year of admissions to the new school. No appointment or contract may, however, take effect until the incorporation date.

The order may specify that the LEA and the existing governing body must consult the prospective governing body, before taking any decision in relation to the school during this period whose effects might last beyond the incorporation date; if any such decision was nevertheless taken, the prospective governing body could then take action to ensure that the effects were negated. The order may also give to the prospective (instead of the existing) governing body the right to negotiate the handover of buildings and property. The Secretary of State may give grants (which may have conditions attached) to the prospective governing body in respect of expenditure incurred by them; the LEA has no liability in respect of such expenditure or of any other action taken by them. The Secretary of State may also consult with the prospective governing body on matters concerned with the new school, including its instrument and articles of government.

On the incorporation date, all decisions made by the prospective governing body remain valid unless and until the initial governing body varies them, and their effects in legal terms are taken to be as if they had been made by the initial governing body.

There are plenty of seeds of conflict here, partly because some of the prospective governors are likely also to be members of the existing governing body. More importantly, perhaps, the voting strengths within the prospective governing body will be determined to some extent by chance, since some places will be more easily and quickly filled than others.

After the incorporation date, there is a further transitional period, during which there are separate rules which are outlined below. At the end of it, the instrument and articles of government come into force, the governing body formally takes the powers defined in them, and the GM school becomes fully operational.

The powers thus given to the governing body require that the school shall remain of the same description as it was as an LEA school, unless changes are authorised (under a process described in the last section of this chapter). Changes requiring such authorisation are those affecting its general character, for example the introduction of arrangements for selective admission by academic ability, an increase in the size of the premises, or a move to new premises.

The instrument and articles are made by order of the Secretary of State, and may only be varied or revoked by his order. Both initially and in relation to later changes, the Secretary of State is required to consult the governing body. Between the date of incorporation and the date when the instrument and articles come into force, which is the transition period of up to six months designed to allow for these consultations (in so far as they have not been completed through the prospective governing body), the Secretary of State may give directions to the governors. These may cover any matters relating to the government and conduct of the school, within the general provisions of the instrument and articles as set out in the Act. These are described below.

The instrument of government

The instrument of government, which lays down the constitution of the governing body, must comply with any trust deed relating to the school. It will state the membership of the governing body, which is: five parent governors; a specified number of teacher governors, which may be either one or two; the head teacher, ex officio; and a specified number of governors of one further category, defined below, equal to at least nine (or eight, if there is only one teacher governor). The reason for the last number is that this group of governors must outnumber the others, by at least one.

In the case of a GM school which was formerly a voluntary

school, this category has the same name as the corresponding group in the existing governing body, the foundation governors. In a former county school, these governors have a new title, that of first governors. (This does not imply first in time; it is rather a description of the precedence of this group as the one which can outvote all the others.) At least two of the first/foundation governors must, at the time they take office, be parents of pupils at the school.

The Secretary of State has the power to appoint either one or two additional governors, if it appears to him that the governing body is not adequately carrying out its responsibilities. If he does so, further governors (equal to the number of such appointees) may also be appointed: in a former county school, they are to be first governors who are appointed by the governing body, and in a former voluntary school they are to be foundation governors, who may not be ex officio and are appointed by those who otherwise appoint foundation governors, acting together if necessary. Such extra governors have a term of office determined by the appointing body, of not more than five years. The Secretary of State may also appoint first governors, to a governing body which has them, if there are vacancies in this category which cannot be filled (or which the governing body refuses to fill).

These are in the nature of reserve powers, the first of them to be used when serious concern arises about the conduct of the school, and the second being designed to cover the possibility that the first might not work - though this power does not exist in a GM school which was formerly a voluntary school. It may of course not be sufficient even if available, and later provisions of the Act allow for the possibility of the governing body ceasing to function.

The parent and teacher governors are known together as the elected governors. They hold office for four years, and may stand for re-election. Teacher governors are elected by the teachers at the school, as under previous legislation. Parent governors are elected likewise by the parents, the difficult matter of setting the rules which determine who has a vote (or more than one, where there are siblings) being left to the governors themselves. Neither a teacher governor who leaves the school, nor a parent governor who ceases to have a child at the school, is required as a consequence to resign from office.

A foundation governor is a person appointed (otherwise than by an LEA) 'for the purpose of securing, so far as practicable, that the established character of the school, at the time when it becomes a grant-maintained school, is preserved and developed and, in particular, that the school is conducted in accordance with the provisions of any trust deed relating to it'. This is quoted in full because the matter is highly sensitive, particularly in the context of a church school. Grant-maintained status will have attractions (not only that of the 100% capital grant) for a church school whose governors have different priorities from the diocesan authorities - not a common occurrence, but by no means unknown, and very worrying to the diocese when it happens. The wording here may help to avoid a declaration of independence (from both LEA and diocese) in these circumstances, but only if the trust deed is very tightly worded.

Foundation governors are appointed for a term to be stated in the instrument, which is at least five years and not more than seven, and may be reappointed for further terms. The person or body who has the right to appoint each foundation governor is to be stated in the instrument; alternatively, the instrument may specify that a foundation governor is to be the holder of a stated office (and the requirement as to the term of office does not apply). An appointed foundation governor may be removed from office by the person or persons who appointed him.

First governors are appointed by the governing body itself, once the school is in full operation. The arrangements by which the initial governing body is formed are different, and rather complex: these are described in a separate section below. The term of office of first governors is not less than five nor more than seven years, and they also may be reappointed for further terms. A first governor is to be 'a person appearing to the persons appointing him to be a member of the local community who is committed to the good government and continuing viability of the school'.

It is also the duty of the governing body, in appointing such governors, to secure that they 'include persons appearing to them to be members of the local business community'. This is similar to a provision made in the 1986 Act for the appointment of co-opted governors in county schools; the term 'business' is not defined, but may be assumed to include such activities as farming, where this is the principal economic activity of the area. The number of governors to have business links is not specified, but the use of the plural implies two or more.

If insufficient parents stand for election as parent governors, the governing body may appoint the requisite number, preferably from those eligible as parents of a pupil at the school, or otherwise by choosing the appropriate number of people who are parents of at least one child of school age.

Any governor of a GM school may resign from office at any time. This may appear to be a superfluous provision, but in view of the fact that the governing body may get into financial difficulties, for reasons which could be claimed to be their own fault (either through mismanagement or by being sued for damages without adequate insurance cover), the unrestricted ability of a governor to resign is a valuable personal safeguard. A foundation governor who is appointed ex officio (including the head teacher) may only resign as a governor by resigning from the qualifying office.

The instrument of government may state the circumstances which disqualify someone from holding office as a governor. The only disqualification specified in the Act is that a member of staff (teaching or other) at a school which has first governors may not be such a governor.

The instrument may also lay down the procedural rules for the governing body: the offices of chairman and vice-chairman, committees responsible to the governing body (which may allow for them to include non-governors), powers of delegation, and provisions under which business may be transacted by sub-groups of governors such as first or foundation governors. The requirements about committees may, alternatively, be in the articles rather than in the instrument, or may be shared between them; but if any committees are referred to in the articles, their functions must also be stated there.

The instrument may refer to the appointment and duties of the clerk to the governors; there is nothing laid down in the Act on the matter, and it may well be left entirely to the governing body.

To the extent that neither the instrument nor the Act specifies procedures, governors may regulate their own: these rules may cover such matters as voting and the number to form a quorum. When there is a vacancy for a governor, or if it later transpires that the election or appointment of a governor was invalid, any decisions made remain valid.

When an action of the governing body has to be formally recorded, as for example in the signing of a contract, the signature of the chairman, or alternatively that of another member who has been authorised to sign, together in each case with that of a further member who needs no special authorisation, is sufficient.

The articles of government

The articles of government start from where the instrument leaves off. They lay down the rules under which the governing body, as constituted by the instrument, carries out its task. They state first the respective powers and duties (including those of delegation) of the Secretary of State, the governing body, any committees it sets up (as noted above), and other parties involved such as the head teacher.

The articles also set down the means by which the governors and head teacher are to comply with the requirements of the national curriculum, and with any complaints which may be made concerning the whole curriculum of the school. The governing body is required to consider any representations it receives from people connected with the local community, on curricular matters other than religious education; the Act makes specific reference in this respect to the chief officer of police for the area (as does the 1986 Act for LEA schools).

The articles must provide for the admissions policy and related practical arrangements, and for an appeals committee to deal with complaints concerning admissions; these have to be published. The appeals mechanism may be arranged jointly with one or more other GM schools. Similar arrangements apply to appeals about the permanent exclusion of pupils; there is no provision requiring a mechanism for appeals against temporary suspensions, but equally nothing to prevent one from being included.

The articles must provide also for disciplinary rules and procedures applicable to members of staff, and for a staff grievance procedure. When dismissal is proposed, provision must be made for the person concerned to state his side of the case; arrangements must similarly be made, after dismissal is decided on but before it is implemented, for the person to appeal. The details are not laid down in the Act, and should therefore be clarified during the consultations with the Secretary of State - as also should other matters, such as the question of appeals against pupil suspension mentioned above.

The articles must require the governing body to prepare, and to send free of charge to all members of staff and to parents of registered pupils, an annual report, the contents of which are to be specified in the articles. The report must be open to inspection at the school. Governors must also hold an annual meeting for parents, to which they may invite other persons, and the articles must set out the procedures for the meeting and for the actions governors or others are required to take as a consequence of resolutions passed at the meeting. These are similar to the corresponding provisions in the 1986 Act which apply to LEA schools, though in this case there is no quorum requirement at the meeting for a resolution to be valid.

Unless the Act, the instrument or the articles make provision otherwise, the governors have the power to do 'anything which appears to them to be necessary or expedient for the purpose of, or in connection with, the conduct of the school'. Specifically, governors may: receive the property (and associated rights and liabilities) which is transferred to them on the date of incorporation; acquire land or other property; enter into contracts including those relating to staff employment; invest sums of money not immediately required; and accept gifts of money, land or other property and use them in any appropriate manner for the benefit of the school. Governors may dispose of property, and may also dispose of land with the written consent of the Secretary of State. These powers do not confer the right to borrow money, or to grant any mortgage, charge or other security in respect of land.

Governors may also, unless the instrument or articles specify otherwise, provide education at the school, as the agents of an LEA and under arrangements agreed with them, other than primary or secondary education. This would allow, for example, the GM school to administer an adult education unit, on its own premises but under the auspices of the LEA. However, the relationships between LEAs and the governing bodies of opted-out schools are unlikely to be good enough for this to happen very often, even if such activities had taken place when the school was maintained by the LEA. Where it does, those responsible will need to be aware of the rules related to charges for such activities, which are laid down in the section of the Act relating to charges for school activities generally.

Governing bodies may also pay allowances to their members, to cover travelling, subsistence or other expenses, in accordance with a scheme which may be devised by them but for obvious reasons is subject to the approval of the Secretary of State. This power is similar to that given to LEAs under the 1986 Act to pay allowances of this kind, and any existing local scheme might provide suitable guidance as to what was acceptable.

The governors have an obligation to publish information about the school, at times and in a manner specified by the Secretary of State. They also have to make any reports and provide any information required by him. Information has to be provided similarly for any LEA having an interest, to the extent that the LEA needs it in the exercise of its functions, whether in relation to the school itself or to individual pupils. No doubt some ingenuity will be applied by each LEA in this matter, in order to keep a close eye on a school whose maintenance costs it pays but over which it has no shred of control.

The transition between governing bodies

The composition of the governing body of a GM school is independent of the size of the school, and is (as already noted) five parents, one or more probably two teachers, the head teacher, and eight first / foundation governors (or nine with two teacher governors, or more than eight or nine if the instrument so specifies). But the actual numbers, as stated in the instrument, are still to be decided at the time the proposals are made, and may initially be different in two categories (teachers and first / foundation governors) from the final composition. If the final number in any stated category represents an increase from that in the initial governing body, an election or appointment is held or made so as to take effect at the same time as the instrument, or as soon as possible afterwards; if the stated number represents a decrease, matters remain as they stand until (through resignations or the ending of terms of office) the numbers fall into line.

The numbers of governors of each category in the existing governing body will depend also on both the size and the type of school. Some transitional provisions are therefore necessary, and are defined in such detail in the Act that they are by no means easy to follow. But if the proposed change of status is not agreed by all parties concerned, as is likely to be the case, the small print of the provisions may be of considerable importance in determining the answer to the vital question of the balance of power.

This section describes those provisions, and to avoid undue repetition some short cuts will be used. First, the head teacher is unaffected by the change, in that he is a governor ex officio in the GM school, as he has the right to be in all LEA schools. His membership is therefore taken for granted.

Also, the only parents and teachers referred to in this section are (except in one case) those who are governors, and so the word 'governor' is omitted in this connection. The exception is the case of the first/foundation governor who is also a parent, and this category is stated specifically when relevant. Next, the only schools in consideration under present rules are primary schools with 300 or more pupils, and secondary schools which in all but rare cases will be at least as large; the composition of the governing body in LEA schools, which depends on the number on roll, is therefore assumed throughout to be in the range appropriate to a school of 300 pupils or more.

A further small point is that the 1986 Act provides that the rules for the governing bodies of special agreement schools are the same as those for aided schools, and this means that the transitional procedures are the same as well; special agreement schools are therefore not mentioned separately.

Finally, the numbers of teachers and of first/foundation governors are assumed to be two and nine respectively. The changes needed, if the proposals or the instrument specify different numbers, should be reasonably clear.

There are seven key dates during the transition period:

1   The date on which the governing body becomes obliged (as a result of a process described in the next section) to hold a ballot of parents.

2   The date of the ballot, if it shows a majority in favour of seeking GM status. (At one point the significant date is that of the count.)

3   The date when the governing body publishes proposals for acquiring GM status. (At one point the significant date is that on which the proposals are sent to the Secretary of State.)

4   The date on which the Secretary of State approves the proposal, and on (or after) which he may also make orders about the powers of the prospective governing body.

5   The date of incorporation, when the initial governing body of the GM school takes over from the former governing body.

6   The date when the instrument of government is published (which may be either before or after the incorporation date).

7   The date when the instrument becomes effective.

These seven dates define eight periods of time, starting before the governors decide (or are required) to seek GM status and ending with the fully operational grant-maintained school. In some way or other, the rules for each of these periods differ.

The main changes take effect on the date of incorporation (which is referred to at some points as the implementation date, or as the transfer date). But the procedures for determining which of the existing governors are to continue, and for filling any places not taken up by those who do so continue, must as far as possible be completed before the proposals are published. The responsibility for securing this lies jointly with the existing governing body and the authority responsible for any elections or appointments which become necessary.

Where the authority which is responsible for an election required under this provision is not the existing governing body, that authority must be informed by the governors in writing of the need for the election and of the proposed date of publication (in order that the electing authority shall be aware of its obligation to act speedily if time is short). If not completed by the publication date, the election or appointment must follow as soon as practicable.

The persons who as a result of these various actions are to be members of the initial governing body of the GM school (if the proposals are approved by the Secretary of State) have to be named in the proposals. If at the time of publication there are unfilled vacancies, this also must be stated, together with the reason for it.

In the existing governing bodies of non-aided LEA schools, the number of parents is either four or five. In aided schools, there must be at least one parent (in addition to any who are foundation governors), the actual number being laid down in the instrument. The change of status may thus require more parents, or leave the number unchanged, or possibly require a reduction.

In respect of teachers, the number in non-aided LEA schools is two, and in aided schools is at least two. If it is more than two (or if there is to be only one teacher), a reduction will be needed.

For these two (the elected) categories, the rules for the transition are as follows. First, the teachers and parents whose terms of office are due to end after the proposed incorporation date have to notify the governing body that they are willing to serve on the initial governing body. (If they are not, or if they later withdraw their statement of willingness, they continue to serve on the existing governing body until the incorporation date.)

If the new number is then the same as the old, the existing office holders become members of the prospective governing body. If a reduction is required, those to continue are chosen by agreement between them or, in default of agreement, by drawing lots. If one or more additional parents or teachers are required (either because of a change in the number needed, or because of a known vacancy, or both), elections have to be held for the requisite number, following the rules which apply under the 1986 Act. A person so elected becomes a member of the prospective governing body, and of the existing body if there is a vacancy.

If the existing governing body includes any elected governor whose term of office is due to end before the proposed date of incorporation, and at such a time as to make it their view impracticable to fill the vacancy between that time and the proposed publication date, the governors may themselves terminate his appointment, on a date of their choice.

They may do the same if the relevant term of office is due to come to an end after the proposed publication date and before the end of the period of six months beginning with the proposed incorporation date. If a period of office is thus terminated, a governor who is subsequently elected or appointed under 1986 Act arrangements holds office for four years, starting with the date on which his appointment becomes effective - whether this is before, on, or after the date of incorporation. (When a closely contested proposal is being put forward, the facility to remove an awkward parent or teacher at a critical time may be a useful tactic, which can be controlled by a careful choice of an apparently neutral factor, the date of publication of the proposals.)

The terms of office of elected governors on the initial governing body of the GM school depend on the time and nature of the election. A governor who was elected to the existing governing body before the publication date, and who transfers without further election to the initial governing body, serves the remainder of the term for which he was elected. A governor who is elected, after the publication of the proposals, to a vacancy on the existing governing body, and who will transfer to the initial governing body on the date of incorporation, serves for four years from the date his appointment to the existing governing body becomes effective. Finally, a governor who, before the incorporation date, is elected to serve on the initial governing body, but without being in the intervening period a member of the existing governing body, serves for four years from the incorporation date; time as a member of the prospective governing body does not count.

The changes which are the most sensitive, because they affect the group which holds the majority vote, concern the first or foundation governors. Because the modes of appointment of the two catagories differ, they are here taken separately.

The number of foundation governors in an aided school must be at least seven, but there is no upper limit and the number in a secondary school may well be more than the nine specified as the minimum for the GM school with two teacher governors. In a controlled school there are four foundation governors; in addition there are four or five governors appointed by the LEA (who may be but need not be members of the Education Committee), and either one or two co-opted governors.

One or more of the foundation governors of the existing school may (under the instrument of government for that school) be appointed ex officio in relation to a stated office. For any such governor, the transfer to the initial governing body is automatic, unless he leaves the qualifying office. If, when the new instrument of government comes into force, the office again qualifies for ex officio status on the governing body, he remains a governor; if not, he ceases to be one.

The person or body responsible for appointing the initial foundation governors of the GM school (other than any ex officio governors) is the same as that relating to the existing governing body. He is (or they are) not required to appoint any of the existing foundation governors, though this will probably be the norm. The appointments must take account of the requirement that two foundation governors (including any who are ex officio) have to be, on the dates of taking office, parents of pupils at the school. Where the appointment has to be made by two or more persons, they must act jointly; if they fail to agree, the Secretary of State has to resolve the issue. The appointment must take place before publication of the proposals, and the existing governing body is responsible for securing that this is done.

This leaves the LEA governors and (in controlled schools) the co-opted governors out in the cold, as far as the prospective and initial governing bodies of the GM school are concerned. They remain on the existing governing body until the incorporation date, but the power of this body is confined to matters which affect the school only for the remainder of the time before that date.

The mode of appointment of the initial first governors, to be named in proposals that a county school should become a GM school, is simply stated: the existing governing body must appoint them, before the publication date. Since this is done at a time when the prospective governing body does not exist, it is the last major opportunity for the governors of the former school to influence the way in which the new GM school will operate. In making these appointments, the governors must take account of the need for two to be parents, and of the requirement to include persons who are members of the local business community. Taking these factors into account, the process will be far from simple, unless there is substantial consensus - which is highly unlikely.

The arrangements have now been described, as far as the membership of the initial governing body is concerned, up to the point where the proposals have just been published, and a summary may be useful.

The situation on the publication date

The process of consultation and voting will already have taken place by this time, and this is described in the next section, together with a statement of the information to be in, and the mode of publication of, the proposals themselves.

On the publication date, the old governing body is still in existence, perhaps having lost an elected governor or two if their periods of office have been cut short because they were due to end within the specified interval during the transition period.

Any vacancies which have arisen in the existing governing body, either by this process or through normal terms of office having ended, will have been filled if time has allowed.

The proposed terms of office for the first/foundation governors (other than ex officio foundation governors) in the initial governing body will have been agreed.

The numbers of governors in the teacher and first/foundation categories in the initial governing body will have been agreed by the existing governing body, and those members of the existing governing body who are to transfer to the new one will have been named, both for these categories and for the parent governors.

Where this process has left places unfilled in the initial governing body, elections or appointments will have taken place if time has allowed.

For each person who has been appointed or elected to serve on the initial governing body (other than the head teacher and any foundation governor who is appointed ex officio), the date when his term of office ends will have been established.

Finally, if the appointments of foundation governors or (as appropriate) the elections of first governors have been carried out correctly, at least two in each case should be parents of registered pupils at the school, and at least two first governors (where relevant) should be members of the local business community.

The build-up to the incorporation date

The next phase of development of the initial governing body is when proposals for the acquisition of GM status are pending - that is, when they have been published and before the incorporation date. The 'pending' period may also end by the Secretary of State declining to approve the proposals, or by their being withdrawn with his consent.

During this period, and unless and until the Secretary of State gives powers to the prospective governing body, the existing governing body continues to operate normally, and any meetings which are held by the members of the prospective governing body have no formal status. When any such powers are given, those of the existing body are of course reduced. The membership list of the initial governing body must be kept up to date through this period, and any vacancies outstanding on the publication date must be filled as soon as practicable.

Further vacancies may arise, through a member of the prospective governing body becoming unavailable to serve on the initial governing body itself, for any one of five reasons: he may cease to hold office on the existing governing body by resigning from it, thus removing a necessary qualification for transfer to the new body; he may notify the existing governing body that he is no longer willing to serve on the initial governing body; he may die; he may leave the office which qualifies him as an ex officio governor; or there may be a change in his circumstances which disqualifies him from membership of the initial governing body.

Changes which might disqualify in this way are: for a teacher, ceasing his appointment at the school before the incorporation date; for a parent, ceasing likewise to have a child at the school; or, for a first governor, ceasing to be a member of the local community or being appointed to the staff of the school. Any governor may also become disqualified from membership as a result of a provision in the instrument of government when this is published.

If a vacancy is created in this way for a first governor, the existing (or prospective, if so ordered) governing body has to nominate a replacement. If the vacancy is for an appointed foundation governor, the foundation governors on the existing (or prospective) governing body, including if he is still such a governor the one holding the place to be vacated, have to elect a replacement. This is done at a meeting called for the purpose, by a simple majority vote, the chairman of the meeting having also a casting vote.

If the vacancy is for an elected governor, an election must be held under 1986 Act arrangements, if there is time to do so before the incorporation date; if in the opinion of the Secretary of State this is not practicable, the existing (or prospective) governing body may nominate someone, who must be eligible to stand for election to the office if such an election were held. The rules for this process are not stated here (in view of the probable infrequency of the event) but are set out fully in the Act. So, likewise, are the provisions for a repeat replacement.

When such a new appointment is made, the details have to be sent to the Secretary of State and are included by him in the proposals, replacing where appropriate those of the person no longer available. Similarly, if an ex officio governor (presumably including the head teacher, though this is not stated) changes, the proposals are changed accordingly.

The process of applying for GM status

The initiative may, in formal terms, come from either of two sources, and is only valid if the school is eligible for grant-maintained status. (The school must still be eligible at the time the Secretary of State gives his approval, and so a proposal relating to one having only marginally more than 300 pupils will not go through if the number falls below that.)

The first method is through direct action by the governors. A resolution must be passed at a meeting of the governing body, the terms of which must be that a ballot should be held on the question of whether GM status should be sought for the school. As soon as it has been passed, the governing body must consult with the LEA and, in the case of a voluntary school, with the trustees. The decision (if not varied as a result of the consultations) must then be confirmed by a resolution similar to the first, at a further meeting held not less than 28 days and not more than 42 days after the first.

Since the proposal is important, and probably controversial, care needs to be taken at each of these stages (and indeed at every subsequent stage for which rules are set down) to observe very precisely the procedures required, for example in giving the necessary period of notice in calling each meeting.

The alternative method of starting the process is through a request for a ballot, by a sufficient number of parents who have children at the school. Who in turn initiates this is not important, but it must be a person or group prepared to carry out the steps laid down; for the present purpose this is called the organising group. Its first task is to ascertain from the governing body the answers to two questions: first, in what form they require the requests from parents and, second, what rules are to govern the voting arrangements. This is a somewhat odd requirement, for the organising group will presumably only want to carry out the task if the easier route, by the two resolutions procedure, is not available because the governors do not want to seek GM status. The group is still required to ask the governors, even though they will not wish to be helpful.

The first answer is simple enough, and commonsense suggests that a signature on a suitable form provided by the group would meet the need. But if the governors are trying to be awkward, they might devise some way of specifying how each parent had to endorse his request which was designed to discourage.

The response to the second question is not so easy, because of problems relating to single parents, absent parents, step-parents (legally recognised or otherwise), foster parents, and voting rights in respect of children in local authority care. But in this instance at least, each parent has only one vote, irrespective of the number of children in the family who are pupils at the school: the reason is that the requests are counted by the number of parents, not the number of pupils. This number has to be 20% of the number of registered pupils at the school on the date the request is received - in other words, 10% of the maximum possible number of parents, if no child has a sibling at the school and each child has two eligible parents.

In determining their rules, the governors may be able to use or adapt the existing rules which the LEA is required to have for elections of parent governors under the 1986 Act. Aided schools should already have their own rules. But whatever the method, the accuracy and completeness of the list is the responsibility of the governing body, and it could prove a heavy one.

The Act allows any parent having a child at the school to see at the school, and (on payment of a fee not greater than the direct costs) to be given a copy of, a list containing the names and addresses of those who are known by the governing body to be parents of registered pupils at the school. The request must relate either to a proposal to hold a ballot or to the actual holding of the ballot. (In the former case, there is a clear danger of misrepresentation, by a parent seeking the list for other reasons.) This facility allows the organising group to contact parents in order to request their signatures in favour of a ballot. (It also enables both supporters and opponents of the proposal itself to canvass for votes at the ballot stage.) There is a further provision allowing a parent not wishing his name to be made available in this way to have the name removed from the list, though it is doubtful whether many will know of this in time.

But it is to be hoped that the route to a ballot through a request by parents will rarely be attempted. The difficulties of acquiring GM status are great enough already, without trying to do it over the heads of the existing governors who are to be so much involved in the process. Whether the grant-maintained school is a good idea at all may well be questioned, but that is not now the point. If a school is to become one, it will need a first class management team; it will also need a structure to enable it to work effectively, which includes within it the governing body, the head teacher and his senior colleagues, and the bursar; and they will all need full support from both present and future parents. A clash between parents and governors would be the worst possible start.

The ballot on a proposal for GM status

The next stage begins, either when the governing body passes the second resolution, or when the necessary number of requests by parents has been sent to the governors. Since the former will be the usual route, this point will be referred to as the time of the second resolution. Within three months of this date (or in the case of a request by parents, during the second or third month following the request), the governors have to arrange for a body designated by the Secretary of State to carry out a ballot on their behalf. This body will initially be the Electoral Reform Society (ERS), which has wide experience of conducting ballots on behalf of trade unions and other organisations.

Before arranging to hold the ballot, the governors must send a written statement of the details to the LEA, and in the case of a voluntary school also to the trustees. The diocese ought also to be consulted where relevant.

Governors have no choice in the matter. They cannot refuse a request from parents if has been presented in the correct form, and if they have passed the second resolution they cannot go back on it, other than with the consent of the Secretary of State. But neither form of requirement is valid if an unsuccessful ballot on the issue has been held within the twelve months preceding the second resolution or the request. This is to avoid a situation in which either governors or parents, favouring a ballot while the other party did not, used attrition tactics by forcing repeated ballots at short intervals. The Secretary of State has the power to waive the twelve month limit, but it is probable that he will only do so if there has been a significant change in the school's circumstances.

The ballot must be secret and postal. All or part of the cost may be paid or reimbursed by the Secretary of State: this payment is conditional on the governors observing the rules (including any guidance published), and in practice will go straight to the ERS. Governors have to take all reasonable steps to provide the ERS with all the information it needs, and the ERS then sends it to the parents, together with a ballot paper and details of where, and by what date, it is to be returned. As noted above, the responsibility for determining the list of eligible parents lies with the governors. These matters are to be the subject of guidance published by the Secretary of State, and to avoid problems later such guidance should be followed to the letter. It has been suggested that a child could have up to four 'parents' for the purpose of the ballot (two divorced natural parents, and the current spouse of each), but this is so clearly unfair that it cannot be regarded as binding.

The information to be sent out is comprehensive, to the extent that there must be some doubts as to whether it will be understood by a fair proportion of parents. It starts with a general explanation of the procedure for acquiring GM status, the constitution and powers of the governing body, and the conduct and funding of a GM school. The proposed membership of the initial governing body will only be partially established at that time, but the names and addresses of those members who are identified at a specified date are to be stated, together with an explanation of the election and appointment procedures which will be required to fill the remaining places. Finally, parents must be told the intended date on which the GM school will come into being, given a positive vote and the approval of the subsequent proposals by the Secretary of State.

A copy of the information sent to parents must be made available for inspection by every person employed to work at the school. It would be a reasonable courtesy to ensure that each received a personal copy.

The Secretary of State may lay down conditions relating to the ballot, either generally or in particular cases; he may require that a second ballot be held within a specified period if errors have been made, or if he considers that governors have acted unreasonably.

The publication of proposals for GM status

If the ballot shows a simple majority in favour, and if over 50% of the parents qualified to vote have done so, the governors have to publish proposals for acquiring GM status within six months of the day the votes were counted. If the number voting is 50% or less, a second ballot must be held within 14 days, and a simple majority in this ballot is sufficient to require the governors to act (again within six months), irrespective of the number who voted.

Before the publication date, the governors must also take the steps needed to provide the remaining information which has to be included in the document. The most important such step is securing that elections and appointments are carried out so as to fill the remaining places on the initial governing body of the GM school.

The proposals have to contain information about the membership of the initial governing body, similar to that sent to parents with the ballot papers, and of course brought up to date. In addition, the proposed date of incorporation must be stated, and the name of the school as it will be from that time. The provision to be made for pupils with special educational needs has to be stated, and the intended admissions policy including the maximum number to be admitted in each year group. The admission number is calculated for this purpose in relation to a school with infant age pupils by ignoring nursery admissions, and counting admissions at reception level whether from the nursery or not.

Finally, the proposals must outline the intended arrangements for in-service training, for the professional development of teachers, and for the induction of probationary teachers. (The above is not intended to be a full statement of the requirements, and when drafting an actual proposal it is essential to work from the Act itself.)

A copy of the proposals must go to the Secretary of State, and clearly ought to be sent also to the LEA, and in the case of a voluntary school to the trustees. The actual publication mechanism is specified as follows. A copy must be posted by each entrance to the school, and in another conspicuous place near the school. Copies must be available for inspection at the school, and at other convenient points such as the local library. A summary must be published in a local newspaper, stating the key points such as the proposed transition date and admission arrrangements, details of where complete information is available, and the procedure for making objections. The costs of preparation and publication of the proposals are the responsibility of the governing body. The Secretary of State may by regulations make modifications to all of these arrangements.

In the interests of good public relations, it might be worth sending copies also, of the full information or of the summary, to the parents of each child at the school, to all members of the staff, to all other schools which might be affected, to councillors for the area, and to the local press on its merits as a news item.

Once published, the proposals may not be withdrawn except with the Secretary of State's consent, and in giving consent he may impose conditions, which may require the governors to publish revised proposals by a given date. Alterations to the proposals (whether as the result of additions and changes to the list of initial governors or otherwise) are formally made by the Secretary of State and not by the governors themselves; what happens to the document after alteration is not specified, but governors should at least make copies available at the school in an up-to-date form.

After publication, two months are allowed for objections, which are to be sent to the Secretary of State. He may extend this period if he thinks it desirable to do so. Anyone may of course make an objection, but the Secretary of State is only obliged to consider objections made by ten or more local government electors, by the governors of any school affected, by any LEA affected, and by the trustees of the school if it is a voluntary school. There is no explicit provision requiring the Secretary of State to consider objections made by the staff of the school, but it may reasonably be assumed that he will do so.

The decision of the Secretary of State

The Secretary of State then makes his decision. How long this will take remains to be seen; it is to be hoped that the guidance papers will give some indication of this time, because governors have to know how long to allow when deciding what date for implementation to include in their proposals.

The decision of the Secretary of State may be to approve the proposals, to approve them with modifications (in which case the proposed modifications must be discussed with governors), or to reject them. If he rejects, he may require a re-submission, which may have conditions attached and must be sent within a specified period. After approval, the Secretary of State may give powers to the prospective governing body as explained above. On the date stated in the proposals (or the proposals as modified), the initial governing body becomes incorporated, and the GM school comes into existence under the name chosen.

As mentioned earlier, the instrument of government will not have come into force at this point, and the Secretary of State may give directions to the governors to enable them to do their job until it does. These directions will probably take the form of a standard document conveying the general powers of the instrument and the articles.

In the period before the instrument of government comes into force, the governing body must inform the Secretary of State of all changes to its membership, relating to vacancies arising as well as appointments made.

After the transfer date, the governors are allowed six months' grace before the provisions of the Data Protection Act apply in respect of personal data for which they become responsible on that date.

The transfer of property to the new school

On the incorporation date, the initial governing body formally takes over all the rights and responsibilities relating to the management of the new school, including those affecting property and the employment of staff. They also take formal responsibility for any actions already taken by the prospective governing body, if it has used any powers given to it by the Secretary of State. This section describes the transfer of property, and the next that of staff.

The arrangements are complex, and the details will only be of interest to those who have to manage the process. The following is a summary of the main principles. On the incorporation date, the property of the former maintaining LEA, or where relevant of the governing body, is transferred to the initial governing body. The 'property' includes all land, buildings and other items used or held for the purposes of the school (including a house provided for the use of a member of its staff), and the rights and liabilities associated with it. The definition is wider than that used for house purchase transactions, and includes fittings as well as fixtures; what happens about exercise books and such like remains to be seen. The Act provides for the setting up of an Education Assets Board, whose function is (in relation to GM schools) to act as broker and arbitrator in these negotiations. Disputes unresolved through negotiation may be referred to the Secretary of State. The whole process is likely to be time-consuming and difficult, particularly for the senior staff of the school.

Any liabilities in respect of the principal or interest on any loan are not transferred. The transfer of ownership also excludes any land or other property vested in the LEA or in the former governing body as trustees. But the trustee rights are transferred instead to the initial governing body, on the same terms as before, and so the practical effects in day-to-day terms are the same.

The Secretary of State is given power under the Act to modify any trust deed relating to the school, if this appears to him to be necessary. The reason might be to bring the trust deed into line, either with GM status as such, or with a provision of the new instrument of government, or with approved proposals to change the size, site or character of the school. The Secretary of State must, if he thinks necessary, consult the governing body, and any other person or body who has an interest as a trustee, before using this power.

The transfer of staff to the new school

In summary, any person (with certain exceptions) who on the day before the transfer date has a contract of employment specifically at the school becomes on the transfer date an employee of the governing body, under the same conditions in every respect. The exceptions are: any persons whose contract at the school terminates on the day before transfer; any persons employed by the LEA solely to work at the school who are withdrawn by the LEA on that date; any persons who are employed by the LEA to work partly at the school and who are withdrawn by the LEA on that date, if they are designated for this purpose by the Secretary of State; and any persons employed at the school by the LEA in connection with the provision of school meals, unless the meals are provided solely for consumption at the school. The matter of LEA staff who are employed partly at the school and partly elsewhere is clearly best resolved by negotiation, rather than by (in effect) leaving it to the Secretary of State to arbitrate.

The contracts of employees falling within these exceptions remain with the LEA. Any person who has been appointed or assigned by the LEA to work at the school starting on the transfer date has the same rights as if he had, immediately before that date, been employed at the school by the LEA to do the same work.

If, after transferring to the GM school, an employee considers that a substantial and detrimental change has been made in his working conditions, he has the same rights to take action at law as if the change had been brought about in the course of continuous work for the same employer. But the change itself is explicitly excluded from this provision: to qualify for consideration, the change must be in the actual conditions of employment, whether related to the job itself or to the terms of the contract other than the change of employer.

When proposals for acquiring GM status are pending, special rules about appointments apply. This period is defined as that starting with the receipt by the LEA of notice that a ballot is to be held, and lasting either until the ballot fails to show a majority in favour or until the proposals are published. During this time the LEA may not appoint anyone to the staff of the school (whether the contractual terms include reference to the school or not), or dismiss anyone from the staff, or transfer anyone who works at the school to another establishment, other than with the consent of the governors.

Such is the formal provision. In the Act itself, the relevant sections convey no hint of the human concerns which will undoubtedly underlie them; even the title above these sections, 'Transfer of property, staff, etc', conveys all too clearly that legal niceties, rather than the professional lives and careers of teachers and support staff, are under consideration.

Much is at stake here, for teachers and other staff will be affected by the change in ways that go far beyond the legal protection of a contract. How it will all work out will depend more on the professional associations and on local conditions than on the terms of the Act, and further comment here is unnecessary. But one point does merit special mention: the job of the head teacher will be very different, and most probably more exacting. To many head teachers, the LEA is slow, fussy, often tiresome, sometimes arbitrary, and occasionally downright unfair. But, in spite of all this, it is valued highly - not least because it is there, staffed by professionals, when problems arise. In many an opted-out school - if many there are - it will be sorely missed.

The funding of a GM school

The payments made to the governing body for the purpose of running the school may be of three kinds: the maintenance grant, the special purpose grant, and the capital grant. These payments are governed by regulations made by the Secretary of State.

The maintenance grant

The maintenance grant is to meet the normal running expenses of the school, and it is the duty of the Secretary of State to pay it. It is calculated, for each financial year, by means specified in the regulations, which are to include: the time and manner of payments; the arrangements for rectifying any overpayments; any special conditions relating to the payments; and the power to require governing bodies to comply with these conditions. Governing bodies must apply the funds solely towards the exercise of their functions, as defined in the Act, in the regulations, and in the articles of government.

The stated initial intention is to match the payments to the amounts which would be paid to the school as an LEA school, with the addition of the appropriate share of the costs of central services. Before the start of the LEA's local management scheme, the basis is to be the school's actual running costs; when the scheme is in operation, the formula approved for use within the former maintaining LEA will be used, again with a supplement to cover the former central services costs. Bearing in mind the extent of the changes likely to arise in the school during the transfer process, and the probable tensions between the school and the LEA, these arrangements contain the seeds of a great deal of trouble, even in the short term.

When the maintenance grant is fixed, the Secretary of State recovers the amount of the grant from the LEA; he may do this in advance using estimated figures.

There are further provisions about grant-related expenditure calculations, and about inter-Authority payments, which are of no particular relevance to schools. The governors of a GM school must, however, provide the LEA which formerly maintained it with information about pupils not resident in that LEA area. Having made the payment to the Secretary of State, and having completed any cross-boundary transactions, the LEA is deemed to have satisfied its statutory duty to educate those of the pupils resident in its area who are registered at the GM school.

The LEA is required to prepare and publish, before the start of each financial year of the local management scheme, a statement of its intended expenditure on all schools in the scheme (as mentioned on page 111). This statement has to include details of the share of excepted services for each school, and the basis on which these shares have been calculated.

The maintenance grant for a GM school is to be based on these figures, according to the first set of regulations published by the Secretary of State In addition to the equivalent of the budget share, the school will receive an amount corresponding to that spent by the LEA on central services related to the school, since it will no longer make use of (or have access to) most of these services. The figures in the LEA statement are intended to enable the grant to be calculated. No doubt the LEA financial staff will do their calculations within the rules, but in such a way as to benefit a potential GM school as little as possible.

Capital-related expenditure is excluded from the grant calculations, since outstanding capital liabilities do not transfer to the governing body on the incorporation date. In other words, the LEA goes on paying debt charges on buildings it no longer owns or controls.

Note also that the Act does not say that there must be any link between these figures and the maintenance grant as calculated by the Secretary of State. A particular Secretary of State may indicate an intention to link them, but that is not the same thing. The Act itself does not specify anything about the calculation, except that it is subject to regulations which are written, and may be altered, by the Secretary of State. The governors of a school contemplating GM status would do well to reflect on the implications of this, if they are planning for a future which may at times be under a government whose education policy differs from that which held sway in 1988.

Special purpose grants

The regulations may (not must) also allow for special purpose grants, to be paid by and at the discretion of the Secretary of State. They are not recoverable from LEAs. They may be one-off, for a specified period, or on an indefinite basis, and are for a variety of purposes - indeed, the provisions seem to have been worded in as wide a manner as possible. The purpose of such a grant may be: anything coming within the grant regulations; any special needs (not defined, but apparently not restricted to special educational needs in the 1981 Act context); and anything which it appears to the Secretary of State cannot reasonably be met through the maintenance grant. Who takes the initiative is not specified, and so governors may apply direct if they choose.

The initial intention of the Secretary of State is that special purpose grants will be used to ensure fair treatment of grant-maintained schools, by comparison with LEA schools. They may, for example, be used to fund support similar to that given to LEAs through education support grants. They may also be used to assist with premature retirements or other severances which the governing body may initiate during the first year of the school's life.

Capital grants

The grant regulations may (not must) provide for capital grants, and for defining the kind of expenditure which these grants are to cover. Any capital grants allowed are to be sufficient to cover the whole cost. But there is nothing in the Act itself to indicate how grants are allocated, which will clearly be necessary in view of these generous terms. Approval of individual projects will have to be considered in the light of the total resources available nationally for capital projects at all maintained schools. Once again, the Secretary of State is in total control.

It would, however, be tactically sound for the governors to request a capital allocation, for equipment and for alterations and extensions to the buildings, where a case can be made for them in order to meet the requirements of the national curriculum. If the case is strong, which in view of the greater emphasis on science and technology should be possible, it might be difficult to resist. Also, if it was turned down there would be an opportunity to make a little political capital instead. A matching request for a special purpose grant, to cover extra running costs and to provide the necessary specialist staff, might be worth putting in at the same time.

Religious Education in the GM school

The legal background to RE in maintained schools was outlined in Chapter 1, and does not need repeating here. The provisions for the subject in a GM school follow the same general lines, and vary according to the type of the former school. A GM school which was a county school will follow the same agreed syllabus as it did immediately before the change of status. For a former controlled school, the same applies but with added provisions for denominational teaching corresponding to those of the former school (provisions which have not in recent years been widely used). Schools which formerly had aided or special agreement status will continue the arrangements which existed before the change.

If, after the change of status, an LEA changes its agreed syllabus, a GM school which has used the previous syllabus is (rather surprisingly) required to follow suit; the conference convened under the terms of the 1944 Act to draw up the new syllabus must, however, consult the governors of any GM school which uses the existing syllabus before making a recommendation. If the change produces more than one agreed syllabus in the LEA, the governors of the GM school may choose between them.

The LEA Standing Advisory Council on religious education, which could be set up under the 1944 Act but under the new Act is now mandatory must include a representative of those GM schools in the LEA area which use such an agreed syllabus.

There is no direct provision for a GM school which was previously a county or controlled school to change its own syllabus, other than by asking the LEA to act on its behalf, and this is hardly practicable in the circumstances. The only possible method is for the governors to follow the procedure laid down for making a change in the general character of the school, for which the rules are outlined in the next section.

This part of the Act also refers to the arrangements for a daily act of collective worship, in terms similar to those above. They reflect the changes in the Act which affect all schools, which were also described in Chapter 1. In summary, the arrangements for a GM school will be the same they would have been, following the changes made in the new Act, in the former school.

Change and decay in the GM school

A major change to an LEA school may arise through a policy decision of the LEA, or through force of circumstances which leave the LEA with no choice but to take action. That is equally true of the GM school, and the Act makes provision for both kinds of change, with one important exception.

If governors wish to make a significant change to the character of a GM school, or to enlarge its premises significantly, they must consider the matter and pass a resolution; this must be confirmed by a second resolution not less than 28 days later. No change may be proposed to the religious character of a school which has trustees without their consent in writing. The proposals then have to be published, in accordance with regulations to be issued by the Secretary of State, and must state the intended timing of the change, the proposed admission number, and the effects of the change on pupils with special educational needs. If the premises are to be altered, access for disabled persons must be provided.

The governors must also send a copy of the proposals to the Secretary of State, together with details of any new premises (or alterations to the existing premises) which are referred to in the proposals. Two months are allowed for objections, and then the Secretary of State considers the proposals together with the objections, and either gives his approval, with or without conditions, or rejects the proposals.

There is no restriction in the Act on the timing of an application to change the character or premises of a GM school. These may be included in regulations issued by the Secretary of State, and the initial intention is to keep changes to a minimum within the first five years of the school's life. But if a later Secretary of State were willing to allow it, a school could change its admissions criteria, in order to select by academic ability, within a few months of the change of status. A justification could easily be found: foundation governors of a former voluntary school have a duty to develop as well as to preserve the character of the school, and a change to a selective admissions policy would (in the eyes of some) come within the scope of that term. Likewise, first governors of a former county school have to be committed to the good government and continuing viability of the school, and that is open to a similar interpretation. The trust deed of a former voluntary school, together with the attitude of the trustees themselves, will also affect the outcome of such a proposal.

A small change in the admission number, not so great as to imply a change in the character of the school or to require a significant enlargement of the premises, does not require any formal procedure other than the consent of the Secretary of State. The governors do not even need to inform the LEA.

There are no direct provisions for a governing body to seek a return to maintained status, and this is the exception mentioned above. It would be easy for the Secretary of State to allow this, however, because his powers are so wide: he would need only to issue regulations which cleared the way.

A change brought about by force of circumstances may well happen for much the same reasons as in an LEA school, but the actual sequence of events is quite different. The four possible triggers (singly or more likely in some combination) are: a fall in admissions so great as to make the school no longer viable; severe financial difficulties; a catastrophic event such as a major fire; and a multiple resignation by governors which leaves a body too small to be quorate, combined with a lack of candidates willing to be appointed or to stand for election.

Any of these causes would allow the Secretary of State to use the first stage of his reserve powers, to appoint two governors and also (in a former county school) to appoint further governors to fill any vacant places for which candidates have not been found. If these are insufficient to put matters to rights, the next stage is that the Secretary of State issues a notice to the governors, specifying what is wrong, the measures needed to remedy the situation, and the time he is allowing the governors (which must be at least six months) to take these measures. The notice must also state that, unless matters are remedied, the Secretary of State intends to cease to maintain (that is, to close) the school.

He may issue this notice without consultation, if he is satisfied that the school, in its current state, is unsuitable to continue as a GM school. The grounds on which he may do so are:

a   that the number of pupils is too small for viability;

b   that the governing body has failed to carry out its duties in respect of the national curriculum for a significant period of time;

c   that the governors have been guilty of substantial or persistent failure to observe the provisions of the Act or of any other enactment.

Clearly these conditions are wide enough, in the light of the Secretary of State's general powers under the Act, for him to catch even an adequately-managed governing body with whose policies he happened to disagree.

There is, perhaps regrettably, no procedure allowing the Secretary of State to take over the running of the school as a going concern, with a view to returning it to some form of local control when the current problems had been resolved. Such a procedure would reduce, if not wholly remove, the effects of a threat to close the school because of declining public confidence in it. If the Secretary of State thought that direct temporary control was the right course of action, he would therefore be forced to use the notice simply as a tactic, even though he had no intention of carrying out the threat to close the school which must be stated in it.

Equally regrettable is the fact that the LEA has no rights whatever in the matter, even though it is still paying the bills. If a GM school which used to be maintained by the Authority is having problems, both members and officers will know through their local contacts what is happening. The LEA will also have to find school places for any pupils who wish to transfer away from the GM school on account of its problems. If the problems prove too great and the GM school closes, the LEA will have a much bigger problem on its hands. But until a late stage in this sequence of events, the LEA can do nothing, except of course ask the Secretary of State to take action, and ensure that he is kept fully informed.

If the Secretary of State considers that the matters referred to in the notice are irremediable, he may also (again without consultation) state in the notice that he not merely threatens, but intends, to cease to maintain the school on a date specified. He may do the same if, after a notice which contains just the threat, the measures required by that notice have not been taken within the period specified (unless he chooses to extend this period); in this case he must act within two months of the end of that period, and after consulting the former maintaining LEA - the first time that it is formally involved.

If the Secretary of State decides to close a GM school without using as a reason any of the concerns mentioned above, he must give at least seven years' notice, and must first consult both the governing body and the former maintaining LEA (and also the LEA for the area, if different). This might appear to mean that an incoming government could not close down all GM schools within the time between elections. However, a school known to be closing in a few years' time would be unlikely to attract new admissions, and so the closure process would most probably be irreversible well before the end of the seven year period. This is so, not only because of the lower number on roll, but also because of the effects the reduction would have on the maintenance grant for the school.

The procedure for changing the character of a school, outlined above, also covers a decision by the governing body to close a GM school. The Secretary of State and the LEA for the area (and not in this case the former maintaining LEA, if it is different) must be informed after the second resolution, and proposals have to be prepared within six months. Bearing in mind the likely effects on public confidence of even the first resolution, a process carried out at such a leisurely pace sounds a little unrealistic.

When proposals made through this process have been approved by the Secretary of State, or when he has decided to close a GM school, he must issue an order to cover the legal and financial arrangements required. Since the governing body has corporate status, it is formally described at this time as a governing body in liquidation. The provisions are complex, and are not described here in any detail. They allow for a new school to be created using the same premises, and for this school either to be an LEA school (county, controlled or aided) or an independent school. In respect of buildings, the general principle is to return buildings to the LEA which are comparable to those which were transferred to the school on the incorporation date.

Otherwise, the rules are concerned solely with details about property and money. The only reference to staff is that the governing body may be required by the Secretary of State to terminate their employment, and there is no mention whatever of pupils. Comment would be superfluous.

Chapter 9 Moving towards GM status

The tactics of opting out - or of avoiding it

In each part of the Act a set of rules is described on paper in legal terminology. From this will follow some actual changes which will affect real schools and the people who learn, teach, and otherwise work in them. Nowhere in the Act will there be a greater contrast between these two aspects than in the changes implicit in the process of acquiring grant-maintained status. There will, throughout its course, be a world of difference between the precise legal and financial priorities set down in print and the wider considerations which ought to guide the development of an educational institution. The last chapter set down the rules for acquiring GM status, concentrating mainly on the legal side; in this chapter the emphasis will be on people, and on their likely priorities in a school for which GM status is sought, and for whose well-being they each have a concern.

The sequence of events can be split up into distinct stages, as a play divides into acts. The first act opens when someone suggests that GM status for the school would be a good idea, and continues until the idea spreads far enough to qualify for a ballot. The next act starts with a favourable vote in the ballot, and continues until proposals made by the governing body are published and sent to the Secretary of State.

Then follows an interval, in which the Secretary of State and his officials consider the proposals off stage, and neither actors nor audience have much to do. The second half opens with the receipt of the Secretary of State's approval, and continues until the new school comes formally into being. The final act, of little interest to those off stage or in the audience, is a transition period before the new governing body takes over its full responsibilities. But events may cause the curtain to come down prematurely.

The drama also has several groups of players, some of whom (most obviously the pupils) remain in the wings throughout. One formerly powerful player (the LEA) has to fight for a share of the action all through. The group which is central throughout the action is the governing body, though some of its members drop out in various sub-plots and others emerge to replace them; those that stay the course undergo various changes of title, from existing governor to prospective to initial and back to just governor again. There is one crowd scene (the ballot itself), but the parents who take part in it have little to do after that.

Both the plot and the action are likely to be confusing to the actors, to the audience, and to press reporters whose task is to interpret the action to the community as a whole. The problem is that many different interests are interacting with each other, so that no single thread is dominant throughout. Perhaps it is time to drop the metaphor, and try to analyse the situation in more conventional terms.

In all, either seven or eight groups are involved, apart that is from the pupils. They are:

1 the governors;

2 the head teacher and his senior management team;

3 the teachers and support staff at the school;

4 the parents of pupils at the school;

5 other parents in the area who may be affected, and ordinary citizens who have a concern;

6 the LEA, represented in particular by the members of the controlling group in the Council;

7 the LEA officers whose responsibilities relate to the school;

8 in the case of a voluntary school, the trustees.

These groups overlap (for example governors who are also parents or teachers) and also subdivide (most importantly the governors).

Given seven or eight groups, many pairings are possible, and most of them could be clashes of one kind or another. The groups which are themselves divided confuse the situation still further; the force of public opinion in the area, and its expression through the press, may do the same. The teacher unions will also be letting their voices be heard, reflecting the views of teachers both in the school directly concerned and in nearby schools which will be affected.

Analysis is therefore difficult, and may best be attempted by considering the situations in which the various groups of participants find themselves.

The standpoint of the LEA

The analysis should perhaps start with the group whose situation is clearest, the LEA. Whatever its political complexion, the LEA has a great deal to lose and nothing whatever to gain. If a school becomes grant-maintained, the LEA loses whatever measure of direct control it had. It can no longer influence admissions (even to the extent possible under the open enrolment provisions of the Act). It loses a share of the funds which pay for its central services. It will still have to pick up problems which the GM school chooses to off-load, such as pupils it expels. The school's system of funding may well enable it to poach the best staff from the remaining LEA schools, particularly specialist teachers and technicians. If eventually the school closes, the LEA will have to make arrangements for the education of pupils still at the school at that time. If the school has problems, the LEA can do nothing to avoid the consequences, some of which will certainly come its way. Finally, the LEA has to go on paying whatever the Secretary of State fixes as the running costs.

The LEA also loses a capital asset without compensation, but has to go on paying any debt charges which are outstanding on the transfer date. (If the school closes and the buildings are sold, an appropriate repayment is made, but this is little consolation.)

With so much to lose, the fact that the LEA is substantially excluded from the decision-making process will be felt very keenly, and the resulting opposition will transcend most political allegiances involved. The actions of the LEA-appointed governors are of critical importance, from the first whisper of possible change right up to the incorporation date. From the LEA point of view, it is important to ensure that these governors are fully aware of the rules which operate at each stage, and that they act in accordance with the interests of the LEA, as far as it is possible to exercise control in this way. A change in its appointees, to ensure that LEA influence is the most effective possible, may also be worth considering.

Whatever the type of school, the LEA appointees will be in a minority on the governing body. They will nevertheless be able, at least in the early stages, to exert an influence far greater in proportion than their numerical strength, because of their position in the system, their political links, and their access to the professional advice and support of the CEO and his staff. However strong the desire to bring about change, both among the governors not appointed by the LEA and among the parents, a determined LEA will be a force not easily overcome.

The standpoint of LEA staff

One consequence of the above is that the involvement of LEA officers will be severely circumscribed. A conflict between the interests of a school and the interests of the LEA is not in itself an unusual problem for an LEA officer, but it is rare for it to be so clear-cut and so public as in this situation. No officer could possibly give advice to a head teacher or a governing body on how best to counter the LEA's declared intention (as it would no doubt be) of keeping the school within the LEA. The influence of the LEA inspectorate and administrative staff, as a force distinct from the Council as the main policy-making body, can thus be effectively discounted. If the governing body needs advice, other than from within its own membership and the staff of the school, it will have to find and pay for that advice itself.

The standpoint of the Secretary of State

The Act allows the Secretary of State considerable scope for supporting a school which is seeking, or has acquired, GM status. As soon as he has approved any proposals, he can give considerable power to those who will become governors of the new school. When the school is operational, he can fix the maintenance grant as he chooses, and he can give special purpose grants and 100% capital grants. He can alter many of the other operational constraints, particularly by modifying the requirements of the national curriculum for the school. He can give direct advice (and also convey advice through HM Inspectors, to the extent that he works within, or can circumvent, their cherished but threatened independence). He can also impose conditions on the governing body, in such a way as to ensure that the advice given is followed. Less formally, he can ensure that direct advice and support is available, and by the time the Act was passed he was already doing so.

But Secretaries of State can change. A new one could cut out special purpose grants and reduce maintenance grants (both to take effect at the start of the next financial year); he could, on an easily-found pretext, appoint two governors; he could impose new conditions on the governing body, relating to the requirements of the national curriculum. All this could be done within a few weeks of his taking office. Within a slightly longer time, he could change the articles of government. By threatening to close the school (for which again a pretext could easily be found), he could destroy public confidence in it, and thus ensure that the staff who were in a position to seek promotion, or who taught subjects in demand elsewhere, would quickly move to schools whose future was clearer. This loss of confidence would also result in a loss of pupils, and thus cause a further drop in income. The Secretary of State could, in short, destroy the school by using the same widely-drawn rules as were used to create it, subject in practice only to the need to consider, as far as he felt bound to do, the interests of the pupils and staff of the school.

He could ease this process (for himself, that is, though in the circumstances the benefit might be shared with the school and its pupils) by working in partnership with the LEA, which would no doubt be ready to assist. It is doubtful whether a smooth transition back to maintained status would be possible, but at least the danger of open conflict would be reduced.

Anyone considering whether to support a proposal to acquire GM status needs to take into account the possibility of this kind of intervention by a hostile Secretary of State. There exists only one effective way to counter it - to become an independent school, as many former direct grant schools did in similar circumstances in the mid-1970s. If the governors do not have the level of backing which would make such a move practicable at short notice, they change to grant-maintained status at considerable risk.

The standpoint of the staff of the school

All staff at the school have a dual interest when GM status is proposed: a concern for the interests of the school as they perceive them, and a concern for their own professional position in terms of job security, working conditions, and opportunities for further advancement. Both of these kinds of concern will be enhanced for those involved, as a consequence of the fact that there is no formal mechanism for taking them into account, other than through the influence and the votes of the teacher governors and the head in meetings of the governing body. The staff do not even have the right to have their objections formally considered, unless they make them under the provision which requires the Secretary of State to receive objections made by any ten or more local government electors. In these circumstances, concerns about job security are unlikely to be allayed by assurances from the governors. Also, the attitude of the various professional associations will be almost uniformly hostile to the proposed change, and no doubt this will make itself felt through the staff.

For some staff, on the other hand, the possibility of a selective admissions procedure (formal or more likely tacit) will be attractive. Promises of capital investment, more to spend on books and equipment, and higher salaries for all grades of staff, would no doubt be talked about, and perhaps even written down.

But each of these points is less significant than another local but critical factor - the perceived alternative to opting out. The balance of the main arguments (particularly in relation to the long-term future of a GM school in that form) is so one-sided that it would be an act of folly for the staff of a good, popular and secure school to assent to casting themselves free of LEA constraints. If it is not a good school under the LEA, it is most unlikely to become better as a GM school; if it is unpopular, its popularity may decline still further. But if it is a good and popular school facing an insecure future, then the acquisition of GM status offers, at least in the short term, a way forward. In these conditions - to take the simplest case, with a threat of closure imminent - the level of staff support (despite likely union opposition) might become very high. This situation has its own peculiarities, and is considered later in the chapter.

Otherwise, staff opinion may be too divided to have much effect on the course of events, and the divisions themselves will be unsettling for the school as a whole. But if the staff are united the effect may be considerable: though it is technically possible for a school to acquire GM status even if every member of the teaching and support staff is opposed to it, this is hardly likely for several reasons. Quite apart from their influence in the process itself, the unions could bring pressure to bear by the selective withdrawal of their members, and the experience of those involved in the disputes of the mid-1980s shows how damaging this can be. Also, a Secretary of State might be thought irresponsible if he approved proposals which were known to be unacceptable to the staff as a whole.

The standpoint of the head teacher

As a member of the staff himself, the head teacher will share in the concerns outlined above, and at times will act as the senior member of the staff in giving expression to them. But for him there is the further consideration that the nature of the job itself will change, and to some extent the same holds for other members of the senior management team. The job of a head teacher, as the senior professional in the school, is sometimes lonely: he holds the final day-to-day responsibility, however much he delegates and however close the link with governors and the LEA. But in an LEA school the feeling of being on one's own is tempered, both by the availability of LEA support when it is needed and by the ability to talk with other head teachers, informally or through whatever local groupings exist.

Not least of the changes brought about by a move to GM status is that these links will come under strain. No local schools will benefit from the change, and most will lose out, particularly those which have to compete for pupils both numerically and in terms of ability. For the head of a new GM school, the support of his fellow head teachers as a body will vanish, and even friendships may be at risk. Also, the attitude of the LEA will be reflected at every level, and previously supportive LEA staff will become less so.

At the same time, the governing body will be taking on various additional tasks, many of them complex and time-consuming. An important one to get right is the administration of salaries, including tax and superannuation. The LEA has specialist staff to do this work, assisted by a computer with powerful software; at least at first, the governors of the GM school will probably have neither specialist staff nor adequate computer support, and it is unlikely that they will be prepared to do the job themselves. So (unless the bursar is able to take on the task) the responsibility will come to rest, as will so many others, with the head teacher, and he will have to respond in some way. If in consequence the staff are not paid properly at the end of the first month after the transfer, the situation may be close to crisis. The head therefore needs to think through well in advance what his attitude is to be, and to warn governors at an early stage of what they are taking on.

The head teacher is also in perhaps the best position to assess the long-term risks, and to advise governors (and also, if appropriate, a group attempting to raise enough signatures to require a ballot) accordingly. The risks are of three kinds: management failure, a fall-off of admissions too great to sustain, and actions of the Secretary of State. The various modes of management failure, and the possible causes of low admissions, are wide enough to need no further comment; the attitude of the Secretary of State was mentioned above.

The issue for the head is primarily one of confidence in the governing body - to the extent that this can be regarded as a single entity under the new conditions, given the likely changes in its membership and the possibility of a prospective governing body in conflict with a powerful section of the existing governing body. If he believes that those in control know what they are doing, that they can override the expected opposition from the LEA and its appointee governors, and that they can carry through the whole process smoothly, then the change may take place with few short-term ill effects. Before that point is reached, however, the perceptions of other groups will have affected the process.

The standpoint of the governing body

In terms of power rather than influence, it is the existing governing body which holds the key position, up to the time of the ballot. Again, it is technically possible for the parents to force the issue: they can require a ballot, and if they do the governors have no option but to submit proposals. But the proposals could be drafted in such a way as to point out the dangers. In effect, the governors could say: 'We are required by law to make these proposals although we don't agree with them; if you support them in the ballot, the school will probably change status but the next Secretary of State could close it down; and in the meantime we will do what we can to oppose the process, first within the governing body and then if need be by resigning'. It would be a rash parent (or one whose motives were open to question) who voted in favour after that.

The actual balance of power will depend first on the numbers in the various groups, then on the attitudes of the Secretary of State and the external bodies which the groups represent, and finally on the individuals concerned. The balance will change, during the lengthy course of the formal process, as a result of these various interactions and because of changes in the membership.

If any elections to the governing body happen to take place when the acquisition of GM status is no more than a distant possibility, the appointing body would do well to ensure that a candidate was put forward who was able to give strong support to their views, since every vote will count. The head teacher, if not already a governor, should consider using his option to become one: some heads have felt, with reason, that their influence will be greater, and their political independence more visible, if they do not use this option, but in the situation faced here the vote may be more important, particularly if the two sides are closely matched. The head will need to bear in mind, however, that he will have to continue to work closely with the governing body, whatever the outcome of the application, and a measure of detachment might be advantageous.

In the midst of all these changes, it may not be easy for the members of the initial governing body of the GM school to assess their own competence to handle their new responsibilities, or to know in advance how much of their own time they will have to devote to the task. Further, changes in membership, during the two years or so that the process will take, will mean that groups within the governing body who have worked well together in the past may cease to do so.

When the battle commences in earnest, the outsider can only express the hope that the proposed change of status carries a sufficient measure of agreement - preferably near total, with only the LEA interests in opposition - for it to be feasible without serious detriment to the school's main task of educating its pupils. But the most probable way of bringing about this agreement is a threat to close the school or to merge it with another. As noted above, this is considered later.

The standpoint of the trustees of a voluntary school

The trustees have the right to be consulted, as mentioned in the last chapter. They also have the power to remove from office any foundation governors who are appointed by them. Thus, the dangers from their point of view are twofold: either a conflict between the parents and the governing body, or a conflict between the trustees and sufficient of the governors to place the voting strength of the trustees at risk. The influence of the trustees in such a situation will be strong: in an aided school there will be a majority of foundation governors, and in a controlled school a powerful minority. But the nature of the factor which unites the parents in opposition to the governors is, sadly, most likely to be either religious or ethnic, and if so the problem will need very delicate handling by all concerned.

There is a further possibility of conflict, when the proposals have been approved by the Secretary of State, as a result of his power to alter the trust deed relating to the school. Such action may be taken in the interests of the school, which by that time may not be identical with the interests of the trustees. How this would work out can only be guessed; it is not difficult to predict that the only real beneficiaries would be the lawyers on each side.

The standpoint of parents and the community

In a sense, there are three groups to be considered here. The only one with any formal involvement is the group of parents who have children at the school at the time of the ballot. But one year cohort at least will have moved on before the change takes place, and probably two. The second group, the parents of children who by the transfer date will have entered the school, have no say at all, other than by making objections. The third group, who have a more distant interest, either as parents of children who will later be of the relevant age, or simply as concerned citizens, have no direct say either. Since the ballot is just one step on a lengthy journey, only of real significance because it marks the point of no return, the formal involvement of parents and the community is in reality quite small.

In the absence of any malign influence, in fact, the whole process (in so far as it is determined by the ballot) depends almost entirely on the level of confidence which the parents as a whole have in the governing body. In any good school, the parents will for long have had substantial confidence in its leadership, and it is not important whether that leadership is perceived to be the governing body or the head teacher and his senior staff.

It is clearly essential to retain this confidence, both during and after a change to GM status, since it is a key feature of any good school. But it is also important because of the sheer complexity of the issues. As will have been evident from a reading of the last chapter, this is such that the detail will not be fully understood by most parents. When the ballot point is reached, therefore, a vote in favour of seeking GM status will be far more a vote of confidence in the governing body (and in the senior management team) than a considered opinion on the issue itself.

If GM status is sought when this confidence is lacking, disaster is almost certain. On the one hand, a vote of governors which a substantial number of parents opposed (notwithstanding the ballot result) might lead to a drop in admissions or perhaps to transfers away from the school. On the other, a governing body which was forced against its will to submit proposals could not be considered qualified to take overall charge of the school, and the resulting need to delegate almost total responsibility to the head teacher would be most undesirable.

There must be similar doubts if the governing body does enjoy a high level of confidence but, in the light of the different conditions which will exist after the change of status, does not really merit it. That will not be easy for anyone to be sure about at the start; as noted above, even the members themselves may not know.

Opting out as a tactic against a closure threat

Nothing unites those involved in the life of a school - the governing body, the staff, the parents and the local community - so much as a threat to close it. Even the LEA representative governors whose political allegiance is to the controlling group on the Council may waver a little. When there is such a threat, the idea of opting out may seem very attractive, particularly to those who have not read the small print. The clamour for a ballot might grow too much for the quiet voice of reason to be heard, and a positive vote in the ballot itself, instead of being an indication of confidence in the governing body, would instead be more of a vote of no confidence in the Local Authority.

The LEA itself, aware of the threat to its own freedom of action which such a vote would present, could not avoid it by stealth. If any change is proposed for a school eligible for GM status (even if there is no suggestion that the change of status is under consideration), the LEA must under the Act first consult its governing body.

Given a ballot result in favour of the change, the tactical position of the governors would at that point be very strong. Whatever the LEA does, its intentions will be frustrated. If it attempts a minor change, of a kind which under the 1980 Act does not require the consent of the Secretary of State, under the new Act it has to seek that consent. If it moves fast, the Secretary of State is bound by the Act to delay consideration of its proposals in order to allow time for the governing body to submit its own, and when he does consider them both together he is required to rule on the opting-out proposal first. If he approves it, the LEA proposal falls. On the face of it, the position of the governing body seems unassailable.

But there is a snag. It is a sound general rule for a parent or a teacher not to make a threat that he is not prepared to carry out, and the same holds in the world of politics and diplomacy. Once the ballot has been held, and if the vote is positive, the process of change to GM status is unstoppable unless the Secretary of State so consents (in which case the LEA could take over control again). Further, the second resolution of the governors, which will have preceded the ballot unless the ballot was brought about by the signatures of a sufficient number of parents, is similarly irrevocable.

Thus, if the governors are to remain in control of the situation, without taking a step towards GM status which they themselves cannot reverse, the only period for which they can hold off the LEA is the time between the first resolution and the second, which is a maximum of only 42 days.

If the governors do not perceive the danger in which they may find themselves, and in due course become forced to carry out their threat, the situation is likely to become very confused. The responsibilities of the governors of a GM school, as outlined above and in the last chapter, are very wide, and require a high level of personal commitment. Some governors, having reached this position by accident, might well resign, and if so public confidence in the school would be in danger of declining to the point where the Secretary of State would have to intervene. He would probably do this by formally rejecting the governors' proposals; alternatively, if proposals had not been received by that time, he would have to indicate his intention of doing so, in which case the governors would have no option but formally to request that their obligation to make proposals be lifted. In this way the Secretary of State would effectively hand control of the situation back to the LEA.

The threat of opting out may well be tried as a tactic of last resort, but it is not as foolproof as has been suggested. If the LEA keeps its nerve, the ploy will only work if the governing body is prepared to carry through its threat to the point where the school becomes a fully operational GM school.

Chapter 10 Management of a GM school

Management during the transition

The last two chapters have suggested that the path to grant-maintained status will be far from easy for any school. Even if, looking back on it, only a few of the possible problems have arisen, continuity in the classrooms will have been difficult to sustain, because of the pressures on the senior management team resulting from the detail of the transition process. Nothing written down could provide answers to all the questions which might arise about the management of the school during the transition and afterwards, and so two assumptions are made at this point. These will enable attention to be centred on the principal factors which distinguish the established GM school from a comparable LEA school, and this in turn (if matters are still at the hypothetical stage) should help to determine whether the change of status would be in the long term interests of the school.

First, the long-term risk to a GM school, which exists by virtue of the powers which a future Secretary of State could use against it, is ignored. As noted earlier, this would only be practicable if the school had sufficient resources and support to go independent, should the need arise. Further, this is not simply a contingency plan, whose discussion can be restricted to the governing body and the staff unless it is actually needed. Prospective parents, for example, will need assurance about it, and also information about the consequences, particularly in terms of fees, for there will be voices from the LEA schools warning of doubts about the future of the GM school against which they are competing for admissions. Applicants for teaching posts, likewise, will (or certainly should) ask about it.

Second, it is assumed that the governors, the staff and the parents are substantially united in support of the school's new status, with only the LEA taking the opposing view and, after the transfer date, co-operating just to the minimum extent required under the Act. If there has been substantial dissension within the school and its governing body, it can only be hoped that this will gradually die down, and that, if this happens through teachers leaving and parents taking their children elsewhere, the school is left in a sufficiently healthy state to recover and thrive.

It is futher assumed, in looking at the significant differences between the two kinds of school, that the GM school has already as an LEA school made a successful transition to local management. If it has not yet come into the scheme, and if the change of status cannot be delayed until it has done so, the management task will be that much greater.

The task of the governing body of a GM school

An LEA school - even a large school with delegated powers - can get by with a governing body whose direct involvement in the running of the school is quite small, provided that the quality of the professional leadership is very high. It is hardly to be recommended, and the risk of serious trouble is great, but it can work. However, this is not true of a GM school, for several reasons.

First, the governing body takes ultimate responsibility for many of its actions, whereas in an LEA school (even one with delegated powers) it sits uneasily between the school management and the LEA. When the need arises, the head teacher can work with LEA officers to ensure that governors who are able or willing only to act as a rubber-stamp are given enough advice and the right pieces of paper to act on. In the GM school, by contrast, no such fall-back system exists, and everything depends on the actual involvement of governors in directing the school on matters of policy.

The extent of that involvement will be clear from a reading of the last two chapters. Further, the financial responsibilities of the governors increase after incorporation, because all the items previously excepted from the LEA delegation scheme (other than debt charges and most pupil-related services) now devolve to them. School meals, in particular, become their responsibility if they are not already. There will be an increase in income, representing the share (as determined by the Secretary of State) of central LEA services now taken over by the school; but the loss of economy of scale may produce problems for the governing body, as also will the problems of the transition itself.

After the incorporation date, the pace will otherwise probably slacken a little - but only a little. Governors still have the main financial responsibility and the ultimate legal responsibility, and in both respects they will need professional advice - from outside (at considerable expense), from the administrative staff of the school (if they are qualified to give it), or from within their own membership, which is asking a great deal of the governors involved. The governors also have responsibility for staffing, relating both to new appointments and to disputes about matters ranging from regrading to dismissal; in these matters independent professional advice will not be immediately available.

The demands on governors, therefore, will be considerable, in the level of responsibilty each has to take and in the commitment of time which each will need to give in order to do the job effectively. A sub-committee arrangement will help to spread the load; this has the further advantage of bringing individual governors into contact with one or more aspects of the day-to-day life of the school, and enables the various meetings and visits to be arranged at times best suited to the governors involved.

Many of the management issues mentioned below, while principally the concerns of others, may also require the attention of the governing body, particularly when things go wrong. The job is not for the faint-hearted, or for those who have full commitments elsewhere. Those who take it on should know in advance what it will mean. Although it is open to any governor to resign (other than one who is appointed ex officio), this will not be a good advertisement, either for the job or for the school, and if several resignations were to happen together the consequences might be serious. An LEA in the background can maintain continuity when such things happen, to the extent that staff and parents would barely notice anything wrong; it is not likely that the DES will be in a position to do the same.

Management in an established GM school

The management of an operational GM school need not, ideally, be any more difficult than in a locally managed LEA school of similar size. The GM school has the great advantage of an admission limit fixed by its own governing body, and substantial control over the choice should the list be oversubscribed. It will, as a result, have a more homogeneous intake than most LEA schools, and this will make it easier to match the curriculum to the needs of pupils. Also, such an intake will benefit the school financially, because there are likely to be fewer problems related to individual pupils, while the school's income will include a proportionate share of the cost to the LEA of providing for such needs.

Balanced against these benefits are the additional tasks and responsibilities which result from the new role of the LEA, the link with the DES, the new aspects of the role of the governing body, and the changed relationship between the school and the rest of the educational community. These are both complex and inter-related, and the total effect on the job of the head teacher and his management team will be difficult to predict at the outset, even when looking at a particular school. Anything written in general terms, therefore, must be regarded as somewhat tentative.

Clearly, however, the role of the bursar will become more important. It will be much wider than that of senior administrative officer, and closer to the very different job of the bursar of an independent school - having high status, almost certainly requiring a professional qualification of some kind, incorporating the role of clerk to the governors, and involving direct responsibility to the governing body. This change of emphasis will in turn have an influence on the role of the head teacher, in a manner which will depend critically on the relationship between the two of them before and during the change of status. If the bursar in post is not suitable for the new role, this also will need careful handling.

The task of management in relation to the LEA

The starting point in looking at the relationship between the recently established GM school and the LEA it has just left must be the recognition that it will be severely constrained at every level. Most of the reasons for this have been mentioned already, but two may be worth underlining.

First, the negotiations between the school and the LEA over the details of the transfer will almost certainly have been protracted and difficult, and the LEA staff will have felt the process to have been far from equitable. Perhaps also the LEA, seeing the transfer ahead, will have found ways of cutting back on the level of resourcing, particularly if the school had not at that time been given delegated powers. If so this will have caused equal resentment on the part of the GM school. It is assumed here that the negotiations have been formally concluded, in relation both to staffing matters and to buildings and other property, but it is most unlikely that the points of disagreement will have been forgotten on either side.

Second, the GM school will have taken with it a share of the costs of the central LEA services, of which it now makes no use. But the cost to the LEA of supplying these services to the remaining schools will not have fallen appreciably, and the cost to the LEA per school will therefore have increased. This will be much resented by the LEA, particularly if several schools opt out, or if the increased unit cost has made staff reductions necessary.

It is assumed here that the actual division of responsibilities between the school and the LEA will have been agreed in principle, on pupil-related matters such as the involvement of the medical and psychological services, school attendance, grants for clothing and other purposes, payment for free meals, pupil transport, and the provision to be made for pupils who are the subject of statements under the 1981 Act.

The responsibility for these matters rests with the LEA. Whatever benefits and services it provides for pupils at its own schools, then (unless the governors of the GM school have to provide such services and benefits themselves, which for the most part they do not) it has to do the same for pupils at the GM school, on terms which are no less favourable. This at least is the requirement of the Act, but it gives plenty of scope for something rather different to happen in practice. It would be most desirable on both sides, not merely to reach agreement in formal terms, but to develop links close enough for small problems to be resolved quickly.

The background out of which to develop such a working relationship is none too promising. Nevertheless the relationship will be needed, and not only for the matters related to individual pupils just mentioned. It would also be of great advantage to the GM school if co-operation were possible on admissions, and on arrangements for in-service training both for teachers and for administrative staff. There might be further advantages in still closer partnership, both to the school and to the LEA, particularly if the LEA were to act (for a suitable fee) as the agent of the governing body in administering the salary and wages system for the school. But it is unlikely that links as close as this would be acceptable to the LEA.

From the viewpoint of the senior staff of the school, there is scope for offering an olive branch or two. The way will be easier if their personal involvement in the opting-out debate has been perceived within the LEA as fairly neutral, rather than anti-LEA. Indeed, the preparation for an acceptable level of co-operation might well have begun during this time and continued during the transfer negotiations, if the head and senior staff had refrained from arguing too much about small details.

After the date of incorporation, the first major point of dispute will concern admissions, at least in the context of a GM comprehensive school. The LEA will be anxious to ensure that the GM school has a balanced intake, including a fair share of pupils with special needs; however, assuming that the GM school is high in popular esteem, it would be all too easy for it to manage its admissions so that the intake was anything but balanced. Further, the scope for the LEA or anyone else to correct any sharp practice on the part of the GM school is very limited.

Before the change to open admission, LEAs were able to plan the admissions arrangements for county and controlled schools quite closely, on an annual cycle ending in the early summer. At this time the schools knew what their intakes would be in September. Often the aided schools fitted in their own arrangements alongside these. Open admission has upset this, and the increased level of competition between schools is making it more difficult for LEAs to keep to a schedule. Those who manage the admission arrangements for the GM schools could gain advantage for themselves by setting a very early date for closing their application lists, thus getting first pick. The senior staff of the GM school, if they saw the long-term advantage to be gained from playing fair by the LEA, could take an important step in this direction by keeping to roughly the same timing as the LEA schools.

The LEA, for its part, could make the process more difficult for the GM school by restricting access to its primary schools for recruitment purposes, and would no doubt come under some pressure from competitor schools to do so; this would give the latter a big advantage in their attempts to make known the merits of their respective schools. It would therefore help the GM school if, by offering concessions elsewhere, it could gain LEA co-operation on this matter. Other examples of the benefits to both parties of a measure of co-operation will no doubt appear as time goes on.

The rules under which the GM school has been set up may appear substantially to remove it from LEA control, but the need for partnership - albeit of a more restricted kind - is as great as ever.

One further point concerning the LEA may be worth a mention. It has a role in relation to its own schools, which is little known about other than by the staff who are directly involved, and yet is important enough to be missed if it is not there. Also, no local or national network of GM schools which is formed is likely to be able to provide a substitute. This function is the system of LEA references. When an applicant for a senior post comes from a school in another LEA, it is usual for a reference to be requested by the appointing LEA. The reference is normally drafted by the inspectorate and signed on behalf of the CEO, and thus carries the full weight of the LEA. Though it may not be as full as a head teacher's reference, the staff of the appointing LEA can be fairly confident that a strong recommendation can be taken at face value. The kind of reference which is designed to get rid of a difficult teacher does, sadly, sometimes appear among those sent by schools, and the LEA reference is a valuable safeguard. Without it, a teacher seeking promotion from a GM school may be at a disadvantage.

The task of management in relation to other schools

The extent to which a popular GM school can control its admissions (and off-load its problems) will be greatly resented in the LEA schools affected. There are other factors involved, in addition to the level of ability of the intake which was mentioned above, because the system set up by the GM school will probably favour those parents who are the most likely to bring other benefits with them. The kind of parents who take the initiative and put in an early application, rather than wait for a letter from the LEA, will be just those who will be the most useful to the school, through their active practical support and their willingness to contribute financially.

It may happen, also, that the GM school will cause jealousy in the LEA schools in other ways. Its system of funding, in respect of the maintenance grant alone, may enable it to use the element relating to the share of LEA administrative costs more economically, thus releasing funds for books and equipment. Special purpose grants, handed out quite freely by a Secretary of State who has a vested interest in making the new schools a success, would widen the gap still further, and any capital grant would have similar effects. Some of the school's extra revenue might be used (as far as the regulations allowed) to increase incentive allowances for teachers, or to regrade other staff; this again would be resented in the LEA schools, both in itself and because of any movement of key teachers or support staff to the GM school which it encouraged.

The professional associations were almost unanimously opposed from the start to the proposals for GM schools, and it is to be expected that a measure of hostility will continue at least to the point (if it is ever reached) when a substantial number of their members work in them. How it will manifest itself will depend on local conditions, but it may well be sufficient to affect the day-to-day working of the GM school. Again, a gesture of goodwill might pay dividends, and one suitable move might be a self-denying ordinance on the matter of enticing into the school those staff of the LEA schools who would be most difficult to replace.

The task of management in relation to the DES

Of all the unknown factors which will affect the grant-maintained schools, the extent of the direct involvement of the DES in their management is the most significant. One aspect of it - the ability of a future Secretary of State to close down a GM school for political reasons - has already been mentioned. Also, of course, the DES has a major part to play during the transition process, as described in Chapter 8. But there is much more to the role of the DES than that.

From the point when the new instrument and articles of government come into force, six months after the date of incorporation, the Secretary of State loses the right to give immediate directions to the governors. He has a duty to pay the maintenance grant, and the power to intervene when things go wrong (or even if they do not). He may also call for reports from the governors or from the head teacher. The governing body, for its part, has to seek authorisation for certain changes: in the instrument or articles, in the nature of the school, and in the requirements of the national curriculum relating to the school. But on paper that is all, unless the Secretary of State determines otherwise, in his role as the one who decides the contents of the instrument and articles.

In addition, of course, the GM school is subject to visits by HM

Inspectorate. But HMI will be fully occupied, as their normal tasks will be increased by the effects of other parts of the Act. Except perhaps in relation to the first few GM schools, they are not likely to be routinely involved to a great extent.

What, then, may happen in practice? Communication between the DES and the GM schools will be of several kinds, and it is worth looking at this as a start. For its own benefit, the school will need to ensure that the DES has all the information which will enable it to fix the maintenance grant at the highest possible level, and will want to request special purpose grants and capital grants, whenever it can think of a reason which might justify them. The evaluation of such requests will not be easy, since the DES will not have anyone on the spot to examine the accuracy of the information or the merits of the request. If the number of GM schools nationally is small, no doubt some system will be devised, but if it grows into hundreds or thousands a whole network of regional DES staff will be needed.

Further, the DES will use to the full its right to require reports. It will, of course, need full financial statements for audit purposes. Judging by experience related to other central government initiatives, the specification of reports not limited to routine financial matters will be lengthy and detailed, and may in some respects be quite unrelated to the way in which the school is actually run. The GM schools will be expensive, and the resulting Treasury pressure to ensure that the money is being spent wisely will take the form of enquiries of this kind. The easier approach, through seeking to establish beforehand that the GM schools would be a wise investment, was unfortunately not used.

But all this is related simply to the passing to and fro of information. The next stage is to consider the extent to which the DES is likely to seek to influence policies and management within the school. No such intention has been made known, but it is easy enough to see the possibility ahead. The whole thrust of the Act reflects the frustrations of a major government department which has for a long time been able to exert very little influence, either directly in the state schools for which it had a measure of responsibility, or indirectly through the LEAs who held all the ground between it and the schools. The development of TVEI, in which the Manpower Services Commission was used as the instrument of central government in imposing a significant degree of direct control, showed what could happen when conditional funding was used on a large scale. The GM school presents the DES with an ideal instrument by which it can show the educational world that it can run schools as well as the best Local Authorities. It would be surprising indeed if, with the help of a set of grant regulations which gave it a wide and flexible power, the DES was able to resist such a temptation. The manner in which the DES has intervened in the past, for example in relation to the operation of the Microelectronics Education Programme, shows what can happen. Those who still feel, in spite of all the risks, that a change to GM status would on balance be beneficial, would do well to be aware of this.

Chapter 11 Miscellaneous provisions of the Act

City Technology Colleges

The part of the Act which allows for the creation of grant-maintained schools has 53 sections; that which does the same for city technology colleges has just one. It allows the Secretary of State to enter into an agreement with one or more persons, in order to establish and maintain an independent school which is so described, of which the cost is to be met in part (most probably the greater part) from public funds. The school must cater for the full ability range and the 11-19 age range, must be in an urban area, and must follow a broad curriculum with an emphasis on science and technology. One or more such schools may have an arts bias, and will be known as City Colleges for the Technology of the Arts.

The Secretary of State may impose conditions for the payment of grants, relating to both capital and running expenditure, and must give at least seven years' notice before discontinuing the maintenance grant. Apart from a statement prohibiting any charge for the admission of a pupil, a brief mention of permissible charges for school activities, and a few details about the winding-up arrangements, that is all.

Indeed, matters had already progressed so far, through the use of regulations made by the Secretary of State in 1987 before the Act was passed, that it is not clear why even that one section was necessary. No doubt the CTCs will be a roaring success (as individual institutions at least), and will show to the world what the LEA schools have so dismally failed to do - for at least as long as they enjoy powerful political support.

But there are just a few small differences, when comparisons are being made with LEA schools. The CTCs will have new or remodelled buildings, much new equipment, a greater amount to spend per pupil on running expenses, staff paid at premium rates, fewer curricular constraints, and the facility to select the most highly motivated pupils from the most supportive families across a wide and densely populated area. It is to be hoped that at least part of that admiring world will see how the trick was performed.

Charges for activities in maintained schools

The 1944 Act established the general principle of free education: 'No fees shall be charged... in respect of the education provided... in maintained schools'. That remains true. But in the years since 1944 the boundary line between the content of the free curriculum and what are generally described as extras has become rather blurred. In particular, charges for school visits have for long been accepted practice, as have charges for the residential costs associated with activities such as field trips, whose educational aspects were themselves part of the free curriculum. The new Act therefore includes a section which makes clearer, if not yet completely clear, where the boundary lies. It also confirms that no charge may be made in respect of admission to a maintained school.

There is still no explicit requirement to make charges - it merely becomes permissible to do so if the LEA, or the school (if the costs are otherwise met by the governors), so chooses.

The new provisions apply to all maintained schools, including grant-maintained schools (but excluding city technology colleges, for which the rules must be laid down under the agreement governing the establishment of the school). Charges may now be made for individual tuition in playing any musical instrument, and for board and lodging provided for pupils on a residential trip arranged by the LEA or the school. No change is made to the established practice whereby a charge may be made for the materials required for practical work, if the pupil wishes to take a particular piece of work home.

Charges may also be made in respect of optional extras. The charges may cover both the educational activities themselves and the associated transport arrangements, in all cases where the costs are incurred with the agreement of the parent of the pupil concerned. The same holds for the fees for public examinations, if the pupil is not being wholly or partly prepared by the school for that examination, and if the pupil is entered with the agreement of the parent. If the examination is prescribed by the school, and if the pupil fails to take the examination without good reason (in the opinion of the LEA if it is liable for the fee, or of the governors if the charge falls to them), the amount of the fee may (in principle at least) be recovered from the pupil's parent.

Otherwise, the general rule is that no charge may be made in respect of the education provided at the school during school hours, or the same out of school hours if it is required as part of any syllabus of a public examination for which the pupil is being prepared (wholly or partly) at the school. Specifically, no charge may be levied for materials, books, instruments, or other equipment related to such education, or for any associated transport or examination costs. Where no charge may be made, a pupil may not be required to provide materials which are needed for the educational activity.

No alteration is made in respect of the provision of food for day trips: pupils may thus be asked to bring a packed lunch, except for those qualifying for a free meal, for whom the school must provide a free packed lunch.

This is clear enough up to a point, but leaves many areas of uncertainty, which ought in due course to be resolved through regulations issued by the Secretary of State. Special clothing for PE, science or craft work, is not mentioned (except to the extent that the term 'equipment' is not to include clothing). Writing equipment has been generally accepted as a parental responsiblity, while being provided by the school where appropriate, but the extension of this convention to include calculators has not developed uniformly. There is a separate section in the Act, referred to below, which defines the obligations of the governing body of a school in respect of entries for public examinations, but this does not clarify the various issues involved.

No general charge may be required of parents which is in the nature of a contribution towards any activities taking place at the school. But requests or invitations for voluntary contributions are allowed, provided that the contributions are clearly stated to be voluntary, and that no distinction is made in the expenditure of such funds between pupils on whose behalf a contribution has been made and those for whom it has not.

This leaves three kinds of activity for which the rules about charges need to be made clear: those which take place other than at the school, those which take place wholly or partly out of school hours, and those which qualify on both counts. If the activity is outside the school but wholly within school hours, no charge may be made. If it is inside the school but wholly or partly outside school hours, it cannot (unless it is part of an examination course as mentioned above) be declared compulsory and thus comes under the provision for optional extras, as also described above.

The only complicated case, therefore, is the question of the charges allowed for those educational activities (not being required as part of an examination course) which are held outside the school but at least partly outside school time. The first set of rules for these cover visits taking place within a single day.

If at least half of the time allowed for such a visit, counting the activity time plus that part of the travelling time which is within school hours, falls within school hours, no charge may be made. But if less than half falls inside school hours, the whole time must be counted as if it were outside, and a charge for the whole trip (not just the part outside school hours) may be made. (The clause in the Act which states this rule is very badly worded, but this is what it means.)

To do the calculation, therefore, first find the activity and travelling time which falls within school hours, and then the activity time outside school hours. The midday break counts as outside school hours, and travelling time out of school hours should be ignored. If the second time is less than or equal to the first, the whole trip counts as inside school hours; if greater, the trip counts as outside, and a charge may be levied.

This is best illustrated by an example. Suppose the afternoon session is from 1315 to 1530, and the timetable for a trip is: leave school 1330; arrive destination 1400; leave 1630; arrive back at school 1700. The activity and travelling time inside school hours is 2 hours, and there is a further 1 hour of activity time outside, which is a shorter time. The whole trip thus counts as if it were in school time, and no charge may be made. If, however, the end of the activity is at 1830, the activity and travelling time inside school hours is still 2 hours, but the activity time outside is now 3 hours which is longer, and so the whole time counts as if it were outside. A charge may therefore be made.

In order to keep the activity time at 4 hours 30 minutes as in the previous example, while avoiding the need to consider charging, the trip could start at 1100, with arrival at 1130 and with 30 minutes allowed at a suitable time for a packed lunch. The total activity time now includes the extra 30 minutes, making 5 hours, and the return journey is from 1630 to 1700. If the end of the normal morning session was 1200, this would increase the total activity and travelling time in school hours to 3 hours 15 minutes (1100-1200 and 1315-1530), and reduce the activity time out of school hours to 2 hours 15 minutes (1200-1315 and 1530-1630). The second is now the smaller, and no charge may be levied.

The scheduled timings may thus be adjusted either to allow a charge or to avoid it, if the activity and one-way travelling time is anything up to about 10 hours. Note also that the calculations are based on times allowed, not times actually taken, and so no school could attempt to levy charges retrospectively if a coach was late.

The second set of rules, covering trips which include an overnight stay, is similar. Charges may be made for board and lodging (other than to certain parents, as noted below), whatever the timing or purpose of the trip. The figures used to determine whether a cost may be charged for the education provided are the number of school sessions taken up by the trip, and the number of half days likewise. A session is of course a morning or an afternoon of a school day, and a part of a session equal to at least half the full length counts as a full session. A half day is defined for this purpose as any period of 12 hours ending at noon or midnight, and a period of 6 hours or more within such a half day is counted as a half day. If the number of sessions thus taken up is equal to or greater than 50% of the number of half days taken up, any education provided on the trip counts as if it were in school hours. If it is less, it all counts as outside, and a charge may be made.

Thus a trip starting at 1600 on a Thursday, continuing over a normal weekend and ending at noon on the following Tuesday, would take up 5 school sessions and 10 half days. The number of sessions is just equal to 50% of the number of half days, and the trip must be counted as in school time, so that charges may be made only for board and lodging. If the departure time was 1600 on Friday instead, the counts would be 3 sessions and 8 half days, and charges would be allowed for education costs also. The longest course possible to count as outside school time, if spread over a normal weekend, would be one starting around 1430 (after the mid-session point, that is) on a Friday and ending late the following Tuesday, making 4 missed sessions and 9 half days.

Charging for the cost of transport broadly follows the rule for the educational activities related to it: if an educational activity outside the school has to be free, so does the transport needed to take the pupils to it. Transport required between the parts of a school site, or from the school site to another place where part of the pupils' normal education is provided, must be free; the latter covers sixth form courses shared between institutions. Also, free transport must be provided for the purpose of enabling pupils to take any prescribed public examination for which they have been prepared at the school.

All pupils who take part in activities for which charges may be made do so only with the agreement of their parents, and having so agreed the parents are then liable for the charges.

No charges may exceed the appropriate share of the actual cost. This cost may include staff costs, to the extent that these are increased above the level they would have been before allowing for the duties connected with the activity or trip: thus any overtime payments incurred as a result of the trip could be included, but not salary costs which would have been unaffected by the trip. This holds true even for the permanent staff of outdoor centres, all of whose work concerns such trips. No charge may be made in respect of the administrative time required, either by the LEA or on behalf of the governors.

Where charges are permitted, decisions about whether they are to be levied, and if so at what rate, are the responsibility of either the governing body or the LEA, depending on which provides the funds. If in the latter case the LEA decides to make a charge, it is open to the governing body to reduce or cancel the charge. If it does so the extra costs, which have as a result to be met otherwise than by the parents, are met from funds at the disposal of the governing body.

Every governing body of a maintained school, and every LEA, must determine and keep under review a policy for all matters related to charges for activities within its area of responsibility. The policy must include a statement of the circumstances in which the governing body (or the LEA) will remit, in whole or in part, any charges which it is empowered to make. For LEA schools, the governing body must also make a similar statement about remissions relating to charges which the LEA is empowered to make. A policy on remission, whether determined by a school or by an LEA, must provide for the complete remission of charges otherwise payable in respect of board and lodging for a pupil on a residential trip, if the educational activities of the trip are required to be free and if the pupil's parents are in receipt of income support or family credit for all or part of the relevant period.

The Secretary of State may issue regulations about such policies, both for charges and for the remission of charges. The regulations will state any requirements about the publication of these policies, and also about the publication of details of the times of school sessions, since these have to be known in order to interpret the policies.

A further section of the Act makes provision for charges to be made in respect of pupils at boarding schools, including residential education for pupils with special educational needs. To summarise, in the latter case the LEA must, and in the other cases it may, remit part or all of the charges. The full text should be consulted if more detail is required.

Entry of pupils for public examinations

A section of the Act, separated for some reason from those related to the curriculum and assessment, defines the extent to which governors of a maintained school must secure that a pupil being prepared at the school for a prescribed public examination is duly entered for it, at a time of their choice. Alternatively, they may arrange that he be entered for another examination in a corresponding syllabus, defined as one for which the same course of study is provided. Governors need not arrange for entry in a particular case, if they consider that there are educational reasons for such a decision. When they have determined whether or not to secure that a particular pupil is to be entered for a particular syllabus and examination, the governors must notify the parent of the details in writing. There is a further provision to the effect that, if a parent requests in writing that the pupil should not be entered, the governors are not obliged to do so.

This is a very curious piece of legislation, for several reasons. First, it requires governors to take direct responsibility for detailed decisions on matters about which they can have no direct knowledge, and for informing parents of those decisions. Second, it requires them to make educational judgements, on matters not of policy but of detail. Third, the decisions specified have for long been taken as part of the routine responsibilities of the teaching staff of schools, and there is no evident need to support or to vary this. Fourth, there is no attempt to clarify either of two contentious issues, one which routinely arises and another which looks set to do so.

The familiar problem is what happens when the responsible teacher considers that there are sound reasons for not entering the pupil for an examination, while the parents take the opposite view. Since the pupil in such circumstances will have been prepared for the examination, no charge may be made to the parent under the rules outlined in the section above, and hence the traditional compromise allowing entry at the parent's expense is no longer available. Hence the choice lies between entering the pupil at the school's expense and refusing entry through the governors. How the latter process will operate in practice remains to be seen.

The other question, which seems likely to become just as familiar, is whether a pupil preparing (often on an ad hoc basis) to retake an examination he has previously failed is to be defined as 'being prepared' for that examination. When examination fees were a charge on the LEA, such pupils were often allowed to retake the examination even when the chances of making a significant improvement were low. Under local management the cost is now met by the school, and the decision is not so easy. From the pupil's point of view, therefore, it would be advantageous to ensure that he attends a course of lessons, so that he is being formally prepared for the examination and can claim the right of entry.

This section is clearly of no positive value, and is both professionally objectionable and administratively unworkable in the terms set down. It creates confusion where little need exist, and points only to a missed opportunity. It is also an indicator - not the only one, but perhaps the most glaring - of how little those who drafted the text of the Act knew about what really happens in schools.

Employment of speech therapists in schools

The Act permits LEAs to employ non-teachers such as speech therapists in schools, in order to meet any requirements of a statement made under the 1981 Act. This is a useful idea, but the facility may not be widely used, partly because of the cost as such, partly because of the difficulties created by disparities between salary scales.

Grants for the education of travellers' children

The Act allows the Secretary of State to make regulations by which he may pay grants to LEAs, in order to offset costs incurred in providing for the education of travellers' children (and also, incidentally, of the travellers themselves). The terms of the clause are quite wide, and allow also for grants in respect of others of no fixed abode such as displaced persons.

Extra grants to aided schools

If the governing body of an aided or special agreement school wishes to make alterations to the premises of the school or move to new premises, the Secretary of State is allowed under the Act to pay a grant for the purpose of carrying out any preliminary work needed. This term covers the preparation of plans, specifications and estimates, but not the work itself. The level of grant may be up to 85%. Similar grants may be paid to a group of persons proposing to establish an aided school. No conditions attach to these grants about any later work on the actual project for which the preliminary work has been done or its implementation. The detailed provisions should be consulted if required.

Endowments in voluntary or grant-maintained schools

Where a voluntary or GM school has been closed (in the former case even if before 1988), and where the school has had an endowment which has wholly or partly been used for denominational religious education, the Secretary of State may by statutory instrument make provision for the endowment to be used in an alternative way. This modifies a provision of the 1973 Act.

There is an additional provision of a technical nature, referring to schemes under the various Endowed Schools Acts, which is designed to correct an anomaly that had become apparent.

Dates of school terms and times of school sessions

The general principle on the dates of school terms remains as it has been for some years, and as the 1986 Act confirmed: the dates are decided by the governors of aided (and now also grant-maintained) schools, and by the LEA otherwise. The LEA may allow some degree of flexibility, for example in respect of occasional holidays or the days set aside for in-service training.

The matter of the timing of sessions in non-aided schools is now more complex. The responsibility under the new Act lies with the governors, though they must start from the timings laid down (or deemed to have been laid down, if the LEA has allowed governors some freedom) by the LEA. If they wish to make a change, they must first consult with the LEA and with the head teacher (the latter being a formality if he has made the suggestion himself), and then make a formal proposal through the medium of the governors' annual report to parents; this must include the LEA's comments if the LEA so requests. After considering any comments made or resolutions passed at the annual meeting, the governors may decide to implement the proposals, perhaps with modifications. The changes may only take place at the start of a school year, with at least three months' notice given to the LEA, and after full information has been sent to parents.

All in all, it is a cumbersome system for dealing with a matter which is not normally difficult, at least as far as the LEA is concerned. In one respect, however, it may be contentious: if schools served by linked LEA transport arrangements decide on timings which upset such arrangements, extra expense will be caused, and perhaps also inconvenience to parents with children at more than one school. It is to be hoped that a high level of local co-operation will avoid such problems.

One point is of interest: the Act allows for the possibility of the one-session day (as did the 1986 Act). This would clearly be a contentious issue, because of the problems it would cause to families in which both parents had daytime jobs.

For aided schools, the times of sessions are also decided by governors, but there are no rules about procedures for changes.

Another minor provision of this section is that pupils may be required to attend places outside the school for parts of the normal work of the school, other than religious education.

Extensions to the 'Section 11' arrangements

Section 11 of the 1966 Local Government Act provides for funds to be made available, via the Home Office and the LEA, to schools with significant numbers of pupils who were in 1966 described as immigrants (or their children) of New Commonwealth and Pakistan origin. Though the terminology is much in need of a change, the grant system remains, and the Act provides for its extension to grant-maintained schools and city technology colleges.

Regulations concerning schools and teachers

The Act allows the Secretary of State to make regulations on a wide variety of matters relating to schools and those who teach and otherwise work in them. They may cover the qualifications of teachers (including exemption from those qualifications), probationary periods, staffing levels, rules about teachers and others employed by LEAs but not at schools, health and safety rules, educational records, the duration of the school day and the school year, and the granting of leave of absence to pupils. They may allow the Secretary of State to restrict the employment of teachers and others on various grounds, and to regulate and inspect premises used by boarding schools which receive fees from LEAs. The need for such regulations is unquestionable, but the same may not be true of the regulations themselves. There is no requirement that the Secretary of State must consult with interested parties before making regulations under this section.

Power of the Secretary of State to intervene

The 1944 Act allows the Secretary of State to intervene if in his opinion the governing body of a county or voluntary school is acting (or is proposing to act) unreasonably. The new Act extends this power to cover grant-maintained schools, and also rectifies an anomaly in the 1944 Act by extending it likewise to LEA special schools. A further power given to the Secretary of State in the 1944 Act, to intervene when either an LEA or a governing body is in default of its duties, is also extended to grant-maintained schools.

Contracts specifying no redundancy

The Act specifies that no contract made after 20th November 1987 relating to employment in a school may give protection against, or allow excessive compensation for, redundancy, and that any clause in a contract purporting to do so shall have no effect.

Modifications to employment legislation

It will be remembered that the local management scheme gives governors of non-aided schools with delegated powers the rights of an employer but leaves the responsibilities mainly with the LEA. This creates havoc with the normal processes of legal decision-making on employment matters, which are complex enough already - both for those working in this field and for those whose employment status comes under question. The Act makes an attempt to deal with the resulting problems in a very general and fundamental way, by allowing the Secretary of State to 'make such modifications in any enactment relating to employment as he considers necessary or expedient' for the purpose. Such a power, allowing a minister in effect to rewrite sections of an Act of Parliament on his own authority, appears to be unique.

Before using this power, the Secretary of State must consult with the LEA associations, any organisation representing the interests of the governors of voluntary schools, and any professional associations concerned. If operated in a commonsense manner, this provision may be of some help in resolving some of the more routine problems. But it is likely to prove highly contentious when the fundamental question is tackled: when the issue is dismissal, who is really responsible?

Schools in the European Community

The Act allows the Secretary of State to support in various ways schools for the children of British nationals working in countries of the European Community. He must provide such schools with appropriate information, and may provide inspection services, by request and on payment of appropriate costs.

Miscellaneous amendments to other Acts

Many of these are simple insertions which allow for the new category of grant-maintained school, for example to ensure that such schools come within the provisions of the 1960 Charities Act in the same way as other maintained schools. Three of these are perhaps worthy of mention:

1   When a GM school is specified in a school attendance order as a result of a direction by the Secretary of State, the governors have a duty to admit the pupil concerned.

2   The provisions of the 1986 Act related to sex education are extended to GM schools.

3   The 1987 Teachers' Pay and Conditions Act is extended likewise, with the governing body taking over the responsibilities given in that Act to the LEA.

The provisions of the 1944 Act about the registration of pupils are extended to allow the Secretary of State to prescribe by regulations that parents may have access to relevant extracts from the registration records. This is presumably intended to allow parents to check whether their children have been away from school without their knowledge; it is not likely to have much impact on a school's truancy level.

Implementation dates for sections of the Act

The Act itself specifies when some sections come into effect, and the remaining sections do so at times determined by the Secretary of State. The sections related to the following came into force on the passing of the Act:

a The powers of the Secretary of State relating to the establishment of the national curriculum, and to the Curriculum Councils;

b The publication of information about the curriculum, and the arrangements for dealing with complaints about the curriculum made from September 1989 onwards;

c Most of the provisions concerning the local management scheme;

d The provisions for grant-maintained schools and for city technology colleges;

e The power of the Secretary of State to vary enactments concerning employment legislation.

Some minor provisions concerning the local management scheme, and the new rules about the act of collective worship, come into force two months after the passing of the Act.

Of the remaining provisions, which come into effect when the Secretary of State so determines, the main ones concern:

a The provisions about those qualifications which require the consent of the Secretary of State;

b The requirements about the implementation of the national curriculum, including the rules to be observed before its full implementation;

c The provisions for development work related to the national curriculum, and for the modifications and exceptions to it;

d The rules governing admissions;

e   The provision for schools with delegated powers which are community schools;

f   The rules about charges for school activities;

g   The rules about grants for travellers' children.

The above is a summary covering the main points, and the detail should be consulted where required. It is the normal practice of the DES to issue circulars to LEAs when particular provisions of any relevant Acts come into force, and most LEAs will no doubt keep their schools fully informed.

Chapter 12 The Act as a whole

Curriculum, enrolment, and local management

From the point of view of the head teacher and governors of an LEA school, the three aspects of the Act which will most affect their school are (in all but a few cases) the introduction of the national curriculum, the new rules about enrolment of pupils, and the change to local management. These three are also, again with exceptions due to local conditions such as the proximity of a CTC, the changes which interact the most with each other. The first section of this concluding chapter considers the possible effects of the three together, and the marginal influence of the various other changes on the impact of the whole Act.

Much of the book thus far has been concerned with mapping out a future whose working rules - the ubiquitous 'regulations issued by the Secretary of State' - are unknown in much of their practical detail. When the interactive effects of changes are being considered, and in the absence of strong indications that the various sections of the Act have been planned as separate parts of a coherent whole, any attempt to look into the future becomes even more uncertain. In what follows, therefore, the speculative element is rather greater than in the earlier chapters; some of it will no doubt prove to be wrong, even before it becomes possible for a new government to cause a major change of direction. The addition of a few phrases such as 'it is possible that...' might have reduced the opportunities for hindsight critics to score a few points, but on balance it seems best to be more forthright.

The grant-maintained school is linked with the three changes mentioned above as one of the major innovations of the whole Act, and in the minds of some perhaps the biggest of all. The rules for its establishment and operation take up the longest section of the Act, and, if all eligible schools used the opportunity offered (and if the Secretary of State agreed to all the proposals), the functions of the LEA relating to education for the statutory age range would become marginal. Even the threat of opting out appears to give governors the right of veto over an LEA's attempts to use its legitimate planning function.

But the GM school can safely be dismissed as a distractor, the subject of much argument but the cause of little actual change. Indeed, it may be that this was what a Secretary of State of unrivalled tactical skills intended all along. The arguments over the rules for the ballot vote were lengthy but essentially trivial. If the attention given to them had been directed instead to the probable consequences of open admission and the national curriculum, the shape of the whole Act might have been different.

Be that as it may, the balance of reasons for and against GM status is so unequal that only very unusual local conditions are likely to make the change practicable as a considered act of policy. The complexity of the administrative task of running the school (particularly in respect of salaries, PAYE and superannuation), and the very real possibility of major financial difficulties, will be sufficient to discourage most governing bodies, and to create many doubts in the minds of individual governors; the power of a future Secretary of State to close the school should be enough to clinch the argument. The generous terms for grants offer little by way of comparable advantage, and the only other substantial reason for seeking GM status - to avoid closure - is unlikely to be matched by conditions enabling the school to survive in financial terms.

The city technology college may, for different reasons, be dismissed even more quickly. The principal reason is the small number of them, but the fact that their unit costs are clearly going to be well above those of comparable maintained schools will come under such continuous criticism that even the survival of the first few must be open to doubt. In terms of local politics each one will be divisive, and the only achievement of each will be to demonstrate that outstanding success can be achieved with a level of support and resourcing far above that enjoyed by the maintained sector. The CTC will be a local irritant, but no more.

Of the other provisions of the Act, little more needs to be said. If the changes in the rules for RE and the act of collective worship had taken place in isolation, they would have been regarded as quite important, and the same is true of the new rules about charges for school activities. But in relation to the larger changes their significance is small. There is little interaction with others, except that the income from chargeable activities may have a significant effect on a school's budget, particularly in the more affluent areas. None of the remaining changes has much impact on the whole picture.

But the potential for interaction between the three major changes is very great indeed. To explore this in detail, in relation to a given local situation, needs a close study of all three sets of rules to work out where the main pressure points will be. Only some very general ideas can usefully be mentioned here.

Any planning in this context must start with the admission numbers, and from that point on the central principles of the interaction process can be stated quite simply. For some schools, admission numbers will fall, rapidly and unpredictably. As a result, the school's income, calculated largely on the basis of pupil numbers, will fall, but costs will not fall correspondingly. To balance the books, economies will have to be made, mainly in running expenses because nothing else is effective in the short term. The items which will suffer will be those such as books and paper whose absence is felt most directly by teachers and pupils, and perceived most quickly by parents. The changes made necessary by the introduction of the national curriculum will thus become more difficult, because of an inability to meet the direct costs and because of the lack of flexibility in staffing. This last point is critical: one of the lessons of the falling rolls period was (or ought to have been) that the process of reducing staffing levels, in order to match the needs of the reduced number of pupils, is far more difficult than managing the school as a smaller unit but under stable conditions.

Meanwhile the neighbouring schools, with admissions healthy and income growing, will be letting the whole area know about their up-to-date computer suites and technology facilities, and their newly appointed specialist staff. Success will lead to further success, and those who miss out at the start - whether by mismanagement or just bad luck - will find it difficult, perhaps impossible, to recover.

In each of the sections of this book dealing respectively with the national curriculum, open admissions, and local management, the point has been made that thorough preparation is vital. In each case, there is time available before the new rules are fully implemented, which can be used for this purpose. When the three are considered together, the importance of thorough preparation becomes greater still.

The key issues of the Act as a whole

The three sections of the Act mentioned above will have, separately and together, a major impact on the work of schools and, if that were all, the changes to the system as a whole would still be immense. But these only account for a proportion of the total impact of the Act on schools in the public sector. Running alongside the management and operational aspects, which have been the main focus of attention thus far, are several wider issues. Some of them are important enough to merit full analysis, and no doubt will be so analysed as the education service settles down under the new rules. Even at this early stage, however, a brief mention of some of these wider issues seems an appropriate way to end a book which is designed only as a working introduction.

In addition to those mentioned in detail below, two others are certainly worth detailed analysis, but not in a book which is mainly non-technical. The first is the technical side of assessment, leading to the whole question of whether comparisons between estimates of standards, related to schools or wider areas, or changes over time, are theoretically possible. The second is the problem of constructing a workable formula for the operation of local management across an LEA. The technical difficulties associated with both of these have been seriously underestimated in the drafting of the Act, and the consequences will be far-reaching.

There is no simple way to classify the various other issues, because of the complex way in which so many of them are interrelated. But, taking partnership once again as the overriding theme, a possible approach is to consider the new place in the system as a whole of the various separate partners, starting with a newly powerful Secretary of State and ending with the person whose interests ought to lie at the centre, the pupil.

Issues involving the Secretary of State

The power of the Secretary of State in every aspect of the working of the public education service under the Act hardly needs underlining. From the establishment of the national curriculum to the settlement of the most trivial local disputes, he is in charge. He may well choose to limit the way in which he uses the various powers, and to the extent that this does happen the issue may not come to public attention to any great extent. The Secretary of State said himself, early in 1988, that the nature of the change concerned the devolution of authority and responsibility, not the enhancement of central control.

But it is not necessary to question the sincerity of this to express two kinds of doubt. First, there must be a long-term concern that a different Secretary of State, possessed of radical views of one kind or another, might start to use his powers to their fullest extent. One fairly obvious possibility was mentioned earlier in the book, in which a Secretary of State who was opposed on principle to grant-maintained schools closed them down within a short period of taking office. But this would be a minor change compared with what might happen to the curriculum, about which the powers of the Secretary of State are almost unrestricted. Perhaps these powers will never be used, but that is not the point: good government should not depend on ministers choosing not to use the full powers open to them.

The second and more immediate danger is of a quite different kind. The powers of the Secretary of State under previous legislation were small by comparison, but still large enough to be a significant administrative burden. Decisions on major matters, such as reorganisation plans involving many schools, have often taken over a year to reach, and even a decision to close a small school against no more than token opposition has frequently taken many months to gain the Secretary of State's approval. A small team of ministers, whose responsibilities also cover further and higher education and government-funded science work, could not possibly have taken personal responsibility for all these decisions, and therefore many have been taken by officials in the Secretary of State's name. When most of the decisions were the kind in which policy was involved, the procedure could be defended on the grounds that officials were implementing policy decisions made by ministers.

Now that the range of powers has grown so much, and has extended into areas of detail far below matters of policy interest at ministerial level, this is no longer so. An example may suffice.

The provisions relating to the national curriculum allow a request to be made, on behalf of a single school, that modifications be authorised in order to permit development work to take place. The formal provisions of the Act are that the Secretary of State, on receiving such a request, may grant it (with or without modification), may impose conditions, may require reports, and may revoke the permission. There is no conceivable way in which a minister can give personal attention to these matters, and no practical way in which policy decisions made by ministers can be used to guide officials in operating the system. The inevitable result will be an increase in power. not to the Secretary of State, but to civil servants who will take executive decisions unrelated to ministerial policy.

Of course, it happens already, and in practical terms is a necessary aspect of government. But it is by no means obvious that a movement of power from (in some cases) elected local government bodies to unelected and distant officials is desirable or beneficial. Nor is it consistent with the stated intention of devolving authority and responsibility downwards. Further, it is not likely to be possible at all, without a considerable increase in the number of officials appointed to do this work - an increase which the Secretary of State has frequently and formally stated to be unnecessary. There are major tensions here, and the best that can be said at the outset is that either the tasks given in the Act to the Secretary of State will go by default, or the cost of the extra manpower needed will have to be found. Neither offers any advantage to the service as a whole, and the losses (not least through frustration, when legitimate requests for decisions go unanswered) may be considerable. Further, decisions by the DES have in the past tended to require a response within a time scale quite unrealistically short, in contrast to the response time it achieves itself; this is likely to bring increasing frustration as the volume of work grows.

Of all the specific questions raised by the issue of central government policy-making and administration in the first few years of operation of the Act, the issue of the control of the curriculum is likely to be chief. The substantial devolution of control through LEAs and governing bodies to schools, from the earliest days of the nationally funded education service until 1988, had both good and bad effects, which do not require discussion here. But the process of changing this policy, radically and very quickly, will have far wider consequences than most of those who have spoken and written about it have acknowledged. The Secretary of State has taken on to himself and his successors a heavy burden - constitutionally, professionally, and administratively. It may prove greater than those who took the decision expected it to be.

Issues involving local government

The Act affects many aspects of the management of the education service at local government level, and it would be of little value to try to list and analyse them all here. But the central principle can be stated quite easily. Local government of the public education service involves deciding the overall level of resources, determining policies for the expenditure of the resources, and controlling in detail some aspects of that expenditure (particularly growth items). The new Act influences, to some degree, each of these three kinds of involvement. The total effect, once the system has settled down in its new form, is hard to predict; what is certain is that the effect will be considerable.

The level of resources is not, of course, a single figure which is decided annually without reference to constraints, and any summary is therefore bound to be misleading. It may, all the same, help to focus attention on the central issue concerning the link between local government and the Act. The main Council decision on resources is reached through a process of compromise: too low a level, and the quality of housing, drains, and education in the Local Authority area will suffer; too high, and those who pay the bills will object and, at the next elections, vote for a change.

In this process, and under pre-Act arrangements, the individual councillor has played a significant part. He was concerned both to keep his seat and (for example) to ensure that the primary school of which he was a governor was kept well staffed and resourced. (Of course, his personal and special interest might have been housing, roads or parks, but the analysis here is not intended to be complete.) The coucillor had, in the course of discussions in Committee, an opportunity to influence the allocation of resources to salary costs, running costs, maintenance and so on, both in broad outline and in some detail. He thus helped to ensure, if the right balance was achieved, that his school's needs were adequately met and that those who elected him were broadly satisfied. In doing so, he gained a measure of personal satisfaction and achievement, without which he would probably not have felt that the job was worth doing.

But, under the new arrangements, this is not how it works at all. The local management system requires the LEA to fix the general schools budget, and the rest is done by formula; the scope for a single councillor to feel that he is able to influence the detailed allocation of resources is greatly reduced. Further, the open tendering arrangements affect his ability to make decisions in other aspects of LEA responsibilities. Also, some schools may be taken wholly out of his influence by becoming grant-maintained (and, to rub it in, still being a charge on the LEA budget). A nearby CTC would have a similar effect. The new admission arrangements will make long-term planning (never easy within the local government system) very difficult indeed.

At the same time, the demands on the management of the service at LEA level will in some respects be growing. Governing bodies will be granting early retirement, off-loading surplus staff, and firing a few weak teachers, leaving the LEA to pick up the bill in each case. The admission system will be creating extra costs, at least in the short term, relating both to salaries and to buildings. The CEO will be asking for extra staff, in order to meet the demands of the assessment arangements and the new complaints system, and to give help to schools unable to cope with local management. The Authority's curricular policy will need to be changed to take account of the requirements of the national curriculum, and there will be constant demands for extra resources for the same reason - even if the LEA's own policy, had it been allowed to have one, would have been different.

In short, the work of a councillor is likely to become more confused, more restricted, less productive in terms of influence on specific projects, and less satisfying. Local government is, in most areas, a delicate balance - and some well-publicised stories of what can go wrong when the balance is upset for internal reasons serve to confirm this. A major external change, which not only risks upsetting that balance but is in some respects expressly designed to do so, may be expected to have far-reaching and adverse results.

Issues related to governors

The success of the changes affecting LEA schools depends (among other things) on there being a sufficient number of suitable and committed people to be governors of schools. To some extent, the need is not new, but the differences brought about by the Act are important enough to affect the willingness of potential governors to serve. The new responsibilities also raise doubts about the expertise needed within a governing body, in order that it may carry out effectively the task of management at that level. (There are still greater differences in the job of governor of a grant-maintained school, but these are ignored for the present purpose.)

The extent of the changes will be by no means uniform, since they depend on the degree of delegation by governors to the head teacher. Some delegation will be essential, but (at least in a secondary school) too much will make the head's job almost impossible; between these extremes, there is a wide range of possible arrangements, even among schools of a similar size.

The major responsibilities fall into several general areas. The familiar one of making senior appointments continues, and for headship and deputy headship interviews involves a more extensive procedure than before. General employment matters, such as requests for regrading, will become commonplace. Occasionally, a really difficult staffing matter will arise, which when it does will cause strains all round. The general management responsibilities will grow considerably as a result of the introduction of the local management scheme, and the number of meetings (including those of sub-committees) will increase likewise. Governors will have new responsibilities related to admissions, charges for school activities, and some minor matters.

A further area of major growth is that the governors now have a general responsibility for securing that the school follows the national curriculum (and, in advance of its full implementation, that the foundation subjects are taught for a reasonable time); the implications of this will probably not become clear for some while. But it is open to any interested party to make a complaint, either to the governors or to the LEA, that the governors have failed in this aspect of their duties. When this happens governors will clearly have to respond, and the only confident prediction which can be made about the result is that it will be time-consuming for all concerned. Much will depend on the relationship between the governors and the head teacher. It is even possible that either the head or the governors could complain about a failure on the part of each other to meet the requirements, and that would be even more complex.

However, there is a further new responsibility, for dealing with complaints, appeals and other matters affecting individuals. In principle of course this is not new, but in practice it has been limited in extent. Governors who have been involved in such matters will know how time-consuming they can be, and the Act now allows much greater scope for them. Some of these matters will involve disciplinary hearings concerning either staff or pupils. But most will arise out of the rules for the national curriculum - not just in general terms, but related to complaints by parents about variations to the requirements of the national curriculum for their child.

When the head teacher modifies some or all of the requirements for a pupil, for a period of six months or less, he has to give full information to the parent, who may if not satisfied appeal to the governing body. Further, any parent may request that the head teacher makes provision for modifications to the curriculum, and if not satisfied with the response may likewise appeal. These rules allow an awkward parent (or, worse still, a group of them) to cause disruption to the work of both the head teacher and the governors, to an extent out of all proportion to the importance of the issue itself. How the head teacher will cope with this when it happens is not clear, but at least it is (on paper) a part of the job he is paid to do.

However, for a governor who is trying to carry out an increasingly complex range of tasks in his own time and without pay, it may be a signal to bring his involvement in the role to an end. Not for the only time in the Act, the rules have clearly been written by someone who has no idea how they will work in practice. This can be seen most clearly in the rule which allows the governing body, after hearing a parent's appeal against a decision of the head teacher, to direct the head 'to take such action authorised by the regulations as they consider appropriate in the circumstances' - in other words, to overrule him. It is of course quite possible to claim that this is formally correct; but anyone who sees it as a procedure suitable to be enshrined in law betrays an alarming failure to understand how schools work. In relation to the task of school governors, it could prove to be the final and unacceptable burden.

Issues related to head teachers

It will be clear to the most casual reader of the Act or of the preceding chapters that the task of a head teacher, already difficult, will become very much more so as a result of the various provisions of the Act, separately and together. From the point of view of most head teachers during the passage of the Act, the main concern was that the change to local management would increase substantially the financial responsibilities, making him more an administrator than a head teacher, and this is fair. But it is only one aspect of the whole, and at the extreme the job of headship in a large secondary school with community facilities may become too great for anyone to be asked to undertake. A summary here would be inadequate, and the advice to anyone in the role (or thinking of taking it on) must be to look very closely at the implications of the whole Act.

Issues related to teachers

The central issue concerning the work of the class teacher was mentioned at the start of Chapter 1, and is the manner and extent of the direction by others of what he teaches and how he teaches it. The manner is as important as the extent: a high degree of direction, as for example in a team teaching arrangement, may, if given sensitively, bring more professional satisfaction than the relative freedom (often leading to isolation) of the teacher in a closed classroom.

The Act allows for a range of possible approaches, from something close to the best of previous practice to the worst that can be envisaged - a distant authority, giving directions written in unsuitable terminology ('programmes of study' for five-year-olds) which make unjustified assumptions about the pupils' starting points, about their real needs and capabilities, and about the resources available in the classroom. Clearly it could never in practice be as bad as that, for if directions of that kind were given the head teacher would have to intervene before the class teacher became involved. But the possibility of major clashes is undeniable.

The other issues related to the teacher in his classroom concern the balance between the actual teaching work and the new demands of assessment, record-keeping and report-writing. Beyond doubt the latter will be extensive; just how much is not as clear, nor can it be known how far teachers will be willing to do parts of the work outside the classroom in order to minimise the loss of teaching time.

But there are wider issues also. Effective manpower planning related to the supply and training of teachers, in the light of the expected demand for them, has been conspicuously absent since 1945, and in the early years of the Act there will be little spare teaching capacity anywhere to allow for the implementation of change. Most obviously, this will limit growth in technology, science, and foreign languages, but the strain will be evident generally, including the provision of supply staff to cover for teachers being given in-service training to meet the requirements of the Act.

At the same time, the falling rolls period is coming to an end, and the need for new teachers is therefore increasing after a period of very low demand. This change would be difficult to manage efficiently under stable conditions and with good planning; with rapidly changing needs and little planning at national level (and with many of the providers themselves undergoing major organisational changes), the outlook for the professional development of teachers looks unsettled. These questions of supply and demand are not just problems for management, but impinge directly on the work of the individual teacher: if specialists are not available, he may be asked to stand in, or even to retrain; if cover teachers cannot be recruited or are of poor calibre, he will have more work to do in helping the pupils to make up for what they have missed.

Bound up in all of this, and little understood in the places where it most needs to be, is the level of public esteem and recognition in which the teacher is held. It is perhaps the most fundamental issue of all, the most neglected, and the most glaringly absent from the text of the Act.

Issues related to parents

Those who turn from press reports about the Act to look instead at what the Act actually says will find much that has been summarised very fairly - the extensive powers of the Secretary of State, for example. But the claim has been frequently made that the Act gives power to parents (by implication, useful power, not merely the facility to disrupt), and this is simply not so. In addition to the immense powers of the Secretary of State, the Act gives considerable new powers to governors and, through delegation by them, to head teachers. But, as a glance at the index references will show, the additional powers given to parents are quite small.

The traditional level of influence of parents over the curriculum, before the introduction of the national curriculum, is difficult to estimate, because it depended not on rules but on local conditions. But when a strong body of parents was known to favour a certain kind of curricular emphasis, the effect was quite noticeable, particularly when there was active competition in the area concerning admissions. Parental preferences at the time of the third year option choices were also influential in encouraging schools to respond to market forces in establishing their curriculum. The change to a national curriculum may give head teachers a reason (or an excuse) to override such pressures, and so the influence of parents may actually decrease. Parents do have an additional right to object to (or to request) modifications to the curriculum for their own child, under the six-month rule, but this is not likely to exert much influence over the balance of the curriculum as a whole.

Parents have two specific new rights, and one existing power is strengthened. First, they have much greater influence over the admission of their child to the school of their choice. In itself, this is valuable. But the consequences for parents as a whole are by no means all beneficial. Suppose (to give a rather over-simplified example) that there are 300 pupils in a year group within a defined area, and that parents have a free choice between two schools which each have a standard admission number of 250. No longer can the LEA fix a limit of 150 or 175 for each; instead, free choice to parents between the two might produce (say) 250 opting for the more popular of the two, and 50 for the other. The result is overcrowding at the first, a variety of problems at the second, and dissatisfied parents at both. The notion that free choice is an unqualified benefit to parents and to their children is in practice not true.

Second, parents are given considerable powers to influence a move towards grant-maintained status. It was suggested earlier in the chapter that this is not a power that can be used in the expectation of bringing benefit to the school, and so it needs no further comment here.

Third, the power of parents to influence the policies of the governing body, through their appointment of parent governors, is greatly increased, because of the more extensive powers of the governing body under the local management scheme. This is doubtless a good thing for parents and, if the powers are used with both sensitivity and commitment, the advantage to the school as a whole may be considerable. But there is no justification for presenting this small change, together with a few illusory powers elsewhere, as a charter for parents. The real power, outside the school and its governing body, rests with the Secretary of State.

Issues related to pupils

The effects on pupils are implicit in every section above, and indeed throughout the whole Act. But the explicit provisions are few. Though there is no doubt that the central aim is a better education for all, the detail often gives a different message, most obviously in the failure to recognise that more time spent by teachers on assessing and by pupils on being assessed leaves less time for teaching and learning. Thus the total effect is difficult to judge.

For some pupils, however, the balance of gains and losses can be forecast all too easily. On the surface, the provision for special needs pupils appears adequate enough, and there were powerful voices in their support during the debate in both Houses. But the total effect is very different, particularly for those pupils not protected by a statement under the terms of the 1981 Act. This is a large group, and an assessment of their new situation seems an appropriate way to end.

Since 1981 the interests of these pupils have not been met in any consistent manner, at least to the extent that those of pupils with statements have been. Most are in ordinary schools, which may be allocated extra resources to meet their additional needs, but not in a manner which is linked to individual pupils. A school's resources (other than those earmarked for pupils with statements) are available for allocation within the school by head and governors, with no guarantees of fair shares anywhere; under the local management system even the extra staffing needed by, and usually allocated to, the special needs pupils is at risk.

But the pressures start further back than this. First, the statement procedure itself has become more complex, because of the additional section relating to modifications of the national curriculum. Since the administrative process has always been cumbersome and inadquately resourced, this new section will extend the delays, and also render it more difficult to give greater numbers of pupils the protection of a statement.

Second, giving schools their own budget will focus attention on the relative costs of providing for different kinds of pupil. The most attractive in cost-benefit terms will be the large band in the middle, who can be formed into homogeneous teaching groups of 30 or so. The most able will be equally valuable: their examination successes will be good for the school, their parents will be among the most supportive, and extra expenditure on their specialist needs (mainly minority courses) will probably be money well spent. But pupils with learning difficulties have no such advantages to bring with them. The formula which calculates the budget share will make some allowance, but probably not sufficient to cover the extra costs of small teaching groups.

This in turn will have an effect at the admissions stage. A pupil with a statement may bring enough extra resources with him to make him an economic asset, and if he is also bound to a wheelchair he may bring benefits of other kinds. But special needs pupils do not fit easily into a system which is strongly influenced (if not totally dominated) by market forces, either in LEA schools, in grant-maintained schools or in city technology colleges.

Having finally gained admission to a school, the pupil with learning difficulties then finds that the curriculum offered to him is based, not on what he needs, but on those parts of what other pupils are thought to need which he himself can cope with. In the 1981 Act, imperfect though it was, the pupil with learning difficulties was more highly regarded, and the new Act pushes him back towards the bottom of the pile. If he is left out of the assessment process, his limitations are made obvious both to him and to others; if he takes the tests, his failure will be more evident still.

It is perhaps not unreasonable to judge a society's priorities for its education service by the manner in which the service provides for pupils who come into their schools at a disadvantage, and who therefore need special help of one kind or another. By this test, the 1988 Act fails. But maybe the fault lies, not in society itself, but in a government which has paid little regard to what that society really needs in its public education service.

Index

A note on the Index
The entries in the index are of four kinds. The first is the conventional page reference to the book itself, which may be followed by *f* or *ff* to refer also to the following page or pages.

The second type of reference is to the Act. It consists of the section and sub-section numbers, printed in bold type. For the small number of sections not divided into sub-sections, sub-section 1 is imputed: thus **17.1** is a reference to section 17. A range of sub-sections may be indicated: thus **29.1-7** would indicate section 29, sub-sections 1 to 7.

Third, references to schedules of the Act are indicated by the abbreviation *sch*; thus **sch.12.83** would indicate a reference to schedule 12, paragraph 83. The abbreviations *f* and *ff* are not used in relation to references to the Act or to its schedules.

The fourth type of reference is indicated by a year number, and is a reference to the Education Act of the year specified.

Two points relating to the construction of the index may help the reader to find references quickly.

First, a complete list of references to some terms would be impracticable: these are *DES, head teacher, LEA, management, school, Secretary of State*, and of course the *Act* itself. A different key word should generally be used in these cases. Some key references to the *DES, head teacher* and the *Secretary of State* are, however, included, as are the main references to *LEAs*. A note under *school* explains the system used in this case.

Second, references linked to some key terms are grouped together. These terms are: *financial delegation; governing body; grant-maintained school; LEA;* and *national curriculum.* Thus, when seeking references to a term related to one of these, look within the relevant major section. For example, references to *programmes of study* appear in the section on the *national curriculum.* Cross-references are, however, included where appropriate.

Use of *above* and *below* in an entry indicates a cross-reference within the same major section. Thus 'Financial delegation, audit *see* audit' means look under the entry 'Audit', but 'Financial delegation, safety net *see above under* contingency funds' means look under 'Financial delegation, contingency funds'.